POLLINATING CHANGE

The Buzz Tour:
Change the Culture not the Climate

By Eve and The Bees

Eve Carnall, Steph Bradley, Miranda Shaw,
Sama Bakr and Paula Haddock

Published by The Green Woman Ltd

Joyfully published in England by
The Green Woman Ltd, in 2015 on FSC paper.
The Green Woman Ltd, Woking, Surrey, GU24 0HL
thegreenwoman.co.uk

buzztour.org

This book is dedicated to all those who supported the
Buzz Tour. Whether you gave a kind word, a story, a meal,
proofreading, a bed, or money, you made this.
It would not have been possible without you. Thank you.

To the reader:
You are going to read a lot about incredibly wonderful
people and impossible-seeming coincidences.
All we can tell you is, it happened.

CHAPTER 1 – An idea

"You have to do that... You HAVE to do that." Miranda stared at me intently and emphatically, the glazed smiles of a few minutes ago were gone. Squished together conspiratorially on the sofa, the New Years Eve party continued around us from the night before.

"Ummm.... er....." I shifted in last night's dress.

Miranda raised a stern eyebrow under an untamed balloon of wavy hair. The urge to obey my usually highly affectionate friend took hold.

"...er..OK.....I'll need a notebook."

On giant cushions under the stairs, out of the way of the dancing, I began to plan. I *love* planning. I love chocolate, dancing and singing more, but it's a close forth. It's like putting on an old favourite jumper (but one that I wouldn't wear out to the pub). A few years ago I decided to take a project management course but couldn't afford the £2000 course fee, so I bought the book for £15 and taught myself. When I passed the exam I felt I could do anything, learning anything I needed, all with just the swipe of a library card.

Frowning, I asked Miranda's opinion about the timing of the walk and she answered, "When we...."

"...You're going to walk with me?" I interrupted.

"Well after making you do it, I can't very well not, can I? For some of the time anyway," she said, smiling. I let out a sigh as I relaxed on a cushion. *I wouldn't be alone.*

A year earlier, I had read a book called 'Journey through Britain', about a man's walk from Land's End to John o' Groats. It was written in 1970 and I was shocked by how much had changed both culturally and environmentally. I wanted to understand my country, its history, its people and that issue always in my heart – how could we change in time to avert climate chaos? It had stayed as a nagging idea slowly evolving and growing, until I had told it to Miranda.

"Let's get out for a walk," I said. "I need to see the sun."

At quarter to four there were only a few minutes of sun left, just visible through the row of blue glasses and vases on the windowsill. There was a lot of hazy joyful agreement, but getting a tipsy group of a dozen people out the door was classic cat herding.

We strolled in a smudge along the bank of the Thames and I found myself walking alongside Paula. I knew her only as a beautiful smiley woman who'd seemed unduly impressed with the exuberance (not skill) of my alcohol-free dancing.

"Well I work in international development training but I'm studying a Masters in teaching Mindfulness. Have you heard of Mindfulness?" Paula asked me enthusiastically.

"Ooo, yes!" I answered. "I've got a friend who it's really helped with a long term illness, the NHS prescribed it. It's like meditation isn't it?"

"Yes meditation is part of the practice," said Paula. "Mindfulness is about being in the present, and paying attention to our experience, without necessarily judging it. So for example, you can cultivate an awareness that allows you to observe your pain, but not *be* your pain."

As we walked back in the twilight, I felt strongly that Paula would be a force of good. I wanted to be her friend, to help her and learn from her. I knew her work was part of making the world I wanted to live in.

One of the first stages of project management is to learn from previous projects, so I set about finding other people I could learn from. I mentioned to someone that I wanted to start from Totnes, as the home of Transition Towns and they said I should contact Steph Bradley who had walked from Totnes in flip flops, visiting Transition Towns.

I wrote down Steph Bradley and looked her up when I got home. 'Home' at the time was a spare bed at Miranda's house and the month before, it had been elsewhere for pet-sitting. According to Steph Bradley's website she had awoken from a dream with full knowledge of the places to visit. Steph had walked an amazing 2000 miles, hearing the stories of hundreds of people.

Steph's reply called me a fellow pilgrim and was full of kindness, advice and contacts.

I read SAS survival books, and made notes. I read a book on navigation for walkers, and made notes. Blogs on walking, fundraising, and speaking in schools (notes). I was in research geek heaven. Time spent reviewing educational material on climate change was not so fruitful; it only seemed to enrage me. It seemed to tell children that the world as we know it is coming to an end without telling them anything realistic the adults were planning to do about it. My notebooks became filled with page after page of earnest rants.

"We are no longer ignorant of the consequences of our actions and collective behaviour. The suffering caused may now take place thousands of miles and decades away from us, but to the persons or creatures who suffer, that suffering is no less real. Our culture, our economy and our government are failing our children and all those who come after."

"Hmmm, doesn't read like an advert for speaking in schools," I thought when re-reading. I had hoped to do school workshops on tackling climate change as a citizen not a consumer. But no one likes a politically controversial ghost at the feast. Yet since quitting my job a year and a half earlier, I increasingly lacked the desire to sacrifice honesty. Contacting schools saved me the dilemma. Despite my carefully worded emails and phone calls there was no interest in a workshop on climate change. I could see that this was an opportunity to get away from telling, and walk towards listening.

The route had to be roughly decided before I could approach groups, but at the start I really only knew two things: I would zigzag across as much of England as I could, and I would not be going through London. Growing up in the 'Home' Counties, you live in the gravity of an ever-expanding London. People all seem to get slowly sucked into it, physically and mentally. Your 'local' news, travel and entertainment are all about London. I felt that London had no need of my services to tell a story, but other places might.

One of the big decisions was whether to go all the way east to Norwich and back. I started to mention the idea and people would answer with derision, "Why would you want to go *there*?" although they had never been.

I began to answer, "*That's* why."

To understand, I would have to commit to really observing.

I had previously studied climate change, but in January I began an eight week distance learning course on climate change that Miranda put me on to. It began well, explaining the science very clearly. But as the weeks went by, it began to worry me. And then it began to alarm and anger me.

"Have you done this week's course yet?!" I asked Miranda as I waited for the kettle to boil.

"No, haven't got to that. It was starting to annoy me."

"So far they've proposed geo-engineering as a solution, and this week? Genetic modification and new pesticides."

Miranda stoically shook her head. "I put some comments on there about permaculture," she said.

"Yeah, me too, but it looks like the only solutions they're going to mention are from their own research."

"...That's funded by the biotech industry."

"There's hundreds of people reading this stuff, it's so messed up."

We never did finish the last week of that course. I wanted to get away from the feelings of impotent anger and *do something*. If I was going to get other people involved, the walk needed a name. I liked the idea of picking up ideas from one place and pollinating them with the next. There is an old traditional English custom that if something significant happens, a beekeeper must tell it to their bees. It was believed that if they did not, the bees might leave, stop producing honey or even die. My home that month was with my brother, and one Saturday I sat in the lounge, musing over ideas.

"Change pollination, inspiration migration, pollen nation."

"Swarm, indoctri-Nation," said my brother with a mocking grin as he came in and out, watering houseplants. I snorted slightly with laughter and continued.

"OK, steps of change, reconnecting, emergent, tell the bees, flowers of change, bee the change..."

"...sting in the tale, fear the truth..."

"...learning buzz, buzz words, buzz tour...oo, Buzz Tour."

"...Na," said my brother shaking his head. "Killer bees."

So I would be a bee. I would dress like one and I would pollinate ideas from town to town. I put together a website for the now-named 'Buzz Tour' and started to invite people to get involved. I didn't have to wait long.

At an anti-fracking gathering in Oxford, Miranda and I were volunteering to make the (vegan) food. It's not entirely altruistic on my part; I do like to be near the food. The best place to be at a party? The buffet table. Well, beside it. The pig in the sausage rolls probably doesn't think it's in the best place.

In between sorting out curries and soup we were in the meetings. Fracking involves injecting water and chemicals deep underground to fracture the ground and release methane gas. The many objections to it come under either pollution or climate change. Discussions were being had about a 'climate caravan', to travel around the country. I raised my hand.

"I'm planning something similar for this summer. Anyone's welcome to come along. It's going to be a walk, called The Buzz Tour." Five people came to chat about the tour at lunchtime, all with fantastic ideas. An energised Sama suggested visiting some of the anti-fracking protection camps, she'd recently spent time living at one. A dreadlocked Kara came and told me she would love to walk the majority of the walk. "But I'm trying to be realistic about what I can do, so let's see." Mel, a lawyer from London, also wanted to be involved.

In order to apply for funding we needed a bank account and for that, we needed a constitution. Writing the constitution turned out to be a wonderful exercise. What did we believe in and how did we want to operate?

The main purposes of the tour were:
- To support and publicise people working for a better society and environment
- To share skills and information to facilitate positive change
- For participants to be inspired and to inspire others

As I thought more deeply, principles of working began to emerge: respect, flexibility, resilience, sharing, personal transformation, people and process before outcomes. I planned the walk so that anything someone contributed was a gift, without commitment.

The following month there was another anti-fracking gathering, this time in Lewes, with Sama doing the food. Wearing a purple bowler hat with a big fabric flower, she leaned on the counter munching something. She could have been in her own kitchen baking a cake, rather than cooking a meal for fifty in an unheated art centre. She came confidently into the meeting to let people know lunch would be twenty minutes late. Utterly calm and unapologetic, she seemed to be enjoying herself. The food? Delicious of course.

CHAPTER 2 – Practise makes perfect

Of the people we'd met at the anti-fracking gathering, Sama, Mel and Kara were the most keen. Chatting with Kara about the walk she raised a lot of great questions, some I had answers for, some I didn't.

"Could we do a practice walk?" she asked me.

"...Sure!" I said. "That's a great idea!"

Scrabbling around trying to get free equipment for the first practice walk highlighted what we didn't have. It was only a couple of days before that I managed to borrow a backpack, which I stuffed with everything I thought I needed. The day before the practice Kara said she couldn't come, so it was just Mel and I that met at Banbury station. Banbury has been famous for cakes since the 1500's. These days Banbury is dominated by the smell of coffee and muffins because of the Kraft food factory. It has several industrial estates around the edges but the old town centre is an historic market town.

"I just need to decompress from London for a bit," said Mel when we met, sounding rather harried. We sat on a park bench near the river Cherwell and ate our lunch.

"I've been trying to put on weight," I said, "before the walk, but I just can't seem to eat any more than normal."

"I'm sure when you need to, your appetite will increase."

A man in a dirty sweatshirt with a bag of cider cans approached us and asked if I had a light. I fished out my lighter and he stayed to chat. He told us he was unemployed, and that it was nice to have a normal conversation with people. His friend came over and they wished us well on the walk. Normally I would avoid men carrying alcohol, so already I felt we were doing things we wouldn't normally feel brave enough to do.

Banbury canal was built in the 1700's and brought coal from Warwickshire. The railway followed in the mid 1800's and from the 1930's on, the town had a spike in housing development, which you can see as you walk across it;

Walking alongside the tree-lined canal out of Banbury we passed a long line of houseboats. Not yet used to our protruding backpacks we narrowly avoided knocking each other and passersby into the canal a couple of times. I was tied into my pack (because one of the straps was broken) and we realised if I fell into the river I wouldn't be able to get the pack off. *"Note to self,"* I thought, *"replace strap."*

We relished the opportunity as we walked, to talk about radical social change. Mel's frustration at the societal causes of climate change resonated with my own. We smiled with relief at each other, from having someone who understood, to share our thoughts with. We stopped for a rest break every hour, and each time I really needed it. Walking down into the valley of Ratley village there were old stone and timber buildings. We hadn't passed anywhere hidden to camp but there was the graveyard and a field next to the church.

Feeling nervous and trying not to look it, I rang the reverend's number on the church board.

"Well...I don't think it would work to use the graveyard," said the reverend, "it's Sunday tomorrow you see and people might arrive at graves and not be expecting a tent. There is a field out the back of the church though. I'm not in the village, I cover several churches you see, but there is a church warden. It would be best to speak with them, see what they advise."

"Wonderful, thank you, I will," I said with my best big smile.

"They live just next door to the church actually, just knock on the door and tell them you've spoken to me."

After a few minutes of conversation with the church warden and his wife they said, "You could put your tent up in the garden if you like?"

We most definitely would like, it sounded fantastic. Looking at the manicured lawn I had a sudden bit of a panic - I have to pee in the night, every night, and the image of me squatting by the dahlias didn't look a pretty picture. Shortly afterwards they seemed to have the same image and suggested that we use their annex loo, they would give us a key. So incredibly, on our first night 'roughing it' we were actually to have access to a toilet, shower, dry space to change and a soft flat lawn.

We walked a little further the next morning before turning back for Banbury, so that we could visit the site of the Battle of Edgehill, the first pitched battle of the civil war in 1642. Looking out from the escarpment now, all you can see are beautiful trees and fields below. It seems the men in both King Charles's and Parliament's armies were not very keen to die so a lot of them ran away or went off looting.

Each hill back to Banbury I fell further and further behind, and Mel had to wait for me at the top. My right shoulder hurt with a sharp pain that gradually got worse. It was clear that the pack I had borrowed would not do, and that I needed to carry a lot less weight. I'd been told that you should aim to not carry more than ten percent of your body weight on long distance walks. That would have been about 6kg, but the pack was somewhere around 13kg, all pulling on my shoulders. And that was without much food and water. After my repeated complaining about my pack and shoulder, when we parted Mel offered to swap packs with me for the next practice walk, to see if it was any better.

Back at home, I took everything out of the new pack and stared at my enemies. The binoculars, they would go. The book on plants, go. The survival tin, go. The stove, go. I lifted the pack again. Still heavy, but better. We'd see.

CHAPTER 3 – Healthy nettles

For the second practice walk it was to be me, Miranda, Sama and her friend Tom, walking from Oxford. One of the places I had applied to for funding was Lush, a toiletries company that fund grassroots environmental projects. Although we weren't able to get a grant, the Lush shop in Oxford offered to throw us a 'Charity Pot Party'. I had visions of us crouched inside a giant pot like a stripagram with people throwing money at us. It turned out to be a weekend where the store donated profits from sales of its 'Charity Pot' moisturiser to us and we had a stall to tell people about the tour.

Proud of (and simultaneously embarrassed by) our official-looking Buzz Tour canvas bags and business cards, Miranda and I laid out our stall with leaflets and draped ourselves in yellow and black fake fur. To top it all off we wore wobbly black and yellow sequined antenna. I'd hastily had the business cards printed two days earlier after being scolded by a woman for not having a business card to give her. We had gotten chatting as we sheltered from the rain together.

"It all used to be black," the woman had said gesturing at the sand-coloured Oxford stonework. "I read it was because of the soot from the old coal fires. Then they banned them and cleaned all the buildings."

"Nowadays we can't see the pollution," I said. "There's not the same incentive to do something about it."

I find it's good to look up in Oxford; there are so many amazing different gargoyles and lots of carved stonework. Unless of course it's late after a student night, then it's best to look down, and watch where you step. People say Oxford's streets are 'paved with gold', and they don't mean money.

Sama and Tom joined us on the stall with lots of hugs.

"So how do you know each other?" Miranda asked Tom.

"We met in Copenhagen, trying to disrupt the undemocratic summit," said Tom grabbing Sama's shoulders.

"Yeah, we got arrested together and unfortunately have been friends ever since," she said.

A steady stream of passersby came, many taking cards. One woman in her early twenties bought a Buzz Tour bag and stayed to chat to all of us. Sara, we found out, was doing a Masters in Sustainability but hadn't heard of Transition Towns or permaculture.

"Fantastic!" I said. "There's lots out there for you to discover. That's what we want to do, show people some of the amazing range of things that are happening." Sara had a wide-eyed smile and lots of questions. She took a card and said she might even join us on the walk.

We packed up the stall in the early afternoon and prepared to head off through Oxford. One of the obvious things about a visit to Oxford is the thousands of bikes, chained to everything. Signs are on railings warning that your bike will be removed if chained there; signs next to a chained up bike. It's common to see women in skirts and smartly dressed people cycling to work, as well as the thousands of students.

Our first stop was Broken Spoke where we met Ellie, who co-founded the bike co-op several years earlier.

"The museum owned the building and they were slowly converting it." Surrounded by tools, with a blue work apron and a flowery scarf in her hair she hunched slightly in embarrassment at our interest. "And then some us were like - 'how 'bout you give us some space as a bike workshop in the back, you know, while you're building it up?'"

"So how does the co-operative work?" I asked.

"Well at the easiest level you can just come here with a broken bike and we can help you fix it. People can also become a volunteer and help other people fix their bikes, and help us to refurbish abandoned bikes. It's an employee and volunteer owned organisation, so the people doing the work make the decisions."

A young bearded man in the bike workshop turned out to be preparing to cycle to Australia.

"It gives the ultimate sense of freedom," said Owen, whilst munching on a cookie.

"The fuel I use is...this," he said taking another bite and breaking into a hamster-cheeked smile. "I'm from Australia originally and I'd like to cycle back, and explore the planet we live on along the way."

I nodded, awe struck. "When are you leaving?"

"Hopefully Thursday but my wheel's not finished, we'll see." He showed us the bike frame. "I'm going up to Iceland, through Norway then down through Russia."

"Wow," said Sama, "You're taking a shortcut to Australia then," laughing gently.

Back outside, I gave Miranda, Sama and Tom a brief health and safety talk about countryside hazards. I'd emailed around a document that I'd cheerfully entitled 'Safety, happiness and health' but it seemed unlikely that anyone would have read it.

"...Cows. Cows are mostly just curious, but they can spook and charge, or step on your foot. They can sneak up on you. They have poor eyesight, so if you hold something out, they will think you are big and move away. Make firm, loud noises, but calmly. NEVER go near any animal with its baby or get in between them. Don't go near bulls, they're grumpy."

A quick lesson in how to use the map and compass, then I handed them over. It felt really wonderful to see people learning to use maps. When I first started working out in the field, my navigation was awful, but with help from colleagues and months of practice, it became one of my favourite skills. I hoped the others might come to feel that freedom too.

Walking out of Oxford to the North West, we joined the River Thames and strolled along past Port Meadow common. It often floods in the winter and some parts of it still had mini lakes. Much of the land and buildings around Oxford are owned by Oxford University, but Port Meadow has been common land for hundreds of years. We hadn't gone far along the river before we came to a tree that Sama declared good for climbing, and promptly shot up.

A little further on, we saw signs to a pub. Following a

winding pathway of leafy archways we arrived at a seventeenth century thatched pub with a weeping willow in the garden.

"Eve?!" called Miranda on her way through the pub garden. "Did you want a drink?"

My first solo expedition was by bike, aged nineteen. I'd only gone a mile down the road when I needed the toilet, so I stopped in a pub. I felt too guilty to use their loo without buying something, so I bought a pint. Another two miles and I needed to go again. An hour or two later I was so drunk I couldn't go any further! Sitting in a fuzz on the station bench, I was somewhat confused to see a much-loved ginger-haired second cousin get off the train. I'd completely forgotten he lived there.

"Alright Eve! What you doin' 'ere?" he said loudly.

"Well I was on my way to Wendover, but I've had too much to drink," I said smiling up at him. He cheerfully sat down next to me and we began to catch up on the intervening couple of years. He told me about his recent solo adventure hiking in the wilds of Scotland when he'd nearly died falling off a cliff and been saved by his walking stick.

"Always have a walking stick with you," he told me sagely.

"Eve?!" called Miranda. "Did you want a drink?"

"Um, a lemonade would be lovely, thank you," I said slowly.

I turned to ask Sama if she wanted some food and let out a bark of laughter as I discovered she was already up the willow tree. Her one, long, yellow and orange braid was swinging free amongst the rest of her hair.

When Miranda returned with the drinks, the four of us sat under the tree and Sama took up the video camera that had been donated to us. Across from me, Tom's face was dominated by an unruly ginger beard. His gaze kept sliding to anywhere away from the camera as he smilingly told us about his new hobby of archery.

"This is what we do," he said gesturing with two fingers whilst smiling at Sama who grew up in France, "to our French friends, to remind them that we still have our fingers to use bows and arrows, which kill French people. I'm pretty sure there are still laws somewhere that allow us to kill the French."

Tom took the camera from Sama and turned it on Miranda.

"So...how is the practice walk going? How have you enjoyed map reading?" he asked.

Around a mouthful of peanuts, Miranda nodded. "Mmmm, it's actually one of my most feared things to do, in life, is read maps, so this has been a really interesting exercise."

"Are you overcoming that fear?" he asked.

"Yeah, gradually. It's really interesting thinking about it in a different way," she said.

"What about the walking?" Tom asked.

"Good. Quite enjoying this half pint; hair of the dog. Note for the future, don't get drunk before walking," she said.

"Yeah, that helps," chipped in Sama.

"Sama thinks it helps. Maybe not...who knows?" said Miranda philosophically as she finished the peanuts.

Further up the Thames we passed the ruins of Godstow Nunnery. Inside the walls out of the strong wind, we dumped our packs. Miranda grew up in Oxford and proudly told us about St. Frideswide and the magic healing spring nearby. Then about the professor who told a girl named Alice and her friend the story that would become 'Alice in Wonderland' near the very same well.

"How much food do you think you'll carry?" Sama asked me as we looked around the ruins.

"About three day's worth? I want to save up a fair bit more money for all the expenses."

"If you run out of food, just fast that day. It's good to fast sometimes, you see it's nothing to be afraid of. I try to do a fast one day a month. It gives your body a rest. I've just read Satish Kumar's biography. He did an 8,000 miles peace walk, and one of his most precious weapons was to be penniless. We need to trust others and trust what nature will provide for us. We are not isolated individuals but elements of an interdependent community. If he could do it across the world, you can surely be safe on this small island."

I lay in the sun considering, while she skipped away to do cartwheels and handstands.

During the day, Miranda told us all repeatedly of the health benefits of nettles. "They have a full range of B vitamins and there's protein too. Nettle tea is really good for you. I'll pick some for dinner." She looked around at all the different plants with enthusiasm and the look of a woman on an adventure.

"This feels perfect," said Miranda happily.

"I'd love a cider though," said Sama.

"Oh yes please, can we have a cider?" said Miranda.

"And me!" said Tom. Miranda asked with her eyebrows if I wanted one. I smiled shaking my head. I stopped drinking when I quit my job. At first it was just because I had no money but after a few months I didn't fancy it anymore.

About three minutes later, Sama found a can lying in the middle of the path by the river.

"Is that?!" she said picking it up. "It is. Cider. It's full. Thank you!" she said to the air.

Another minute later and another can, just to the side of the path. Then another. Then another, both full.

"There's even one for you Eve," said Miranda, pointing.

"I'm all right thanks," I said smiling, and when she went to pick up the fourth can, we found that it was empty.

Walking through a field we found an information board about a farm's conservation work and we saw bee homes they had put around the fields - little bundles of wooden tubes. We walked on, debating and putting the world to rights until we found a patch of woods to settle in for the night.

"I've got all sorts for dinner. I'll pick some nettles to go with it," Miranda said moving towards a clump of nettles.

"Have you got gloves?" I asked.

"You don't need gloves, you just have to pick them in the right way, and avoiding contact with the edges of the leaves."

A short while later Miranda had a bundle of nettles and a red, blotchy hand.

"I've got antihistamine in my first aid kit if you want some?"

"That's ok, I just need...some dock leaves..." she said going off to search the surrounding vegetation.

We carefully removed all the sticks from the area for the tents. I set up Miranda's and my tent as she got out her stove, while Tom and Sama did their tent. By the time I finished laying out our beds, Miranda had already got the food on and gone for a short walk. A short while later Miranda came back from the undergrowth looking uncomfortable. I gave her a questioning look.

"I just stung my bum on some nettles," she confessed as we all burst into laughter.

"Look before you squat!" I called out.

Miranda cooked the nettles with the couscous and vegetables then sprinkled it with various nuts. It looked wonderful, but the nettles looked rather green still. Being of a cautious disposition I watched the others...and waited.

"Um, Miranda?" said Sama. Her eyebrows came together and she was slowly opening and closing her mouth with discomfort. "These nettles...? Um, they're a bit, um...*stingy*."

The following morning the dawn chorus was amazing; so many surreal different calls. We stood in silence together for a time and listened.

Miranda made porridge. Not the gruel that children dread, but a porridge that other porridge wants to be when it grows up. Seeds, raw cacao, sliced apple, cinnamon. Last night's nettles were almost forgotten as we chewed. Almost.

"That was a bit of a night," said Tom as we ate.

"Why's that?" asked Miranda.

"There was all this snuffling..."

"...Sam-aa..." I said with a smirk.

"...and I think a bloody badger came along and dug up the tent pegs. In the morning I couldn't find the exit; the whole thing had completely collapsed on us," said Tom.

"Did it?" asked Sama with mild curiosity.

"...." Tom turned slowly towards Sama in disbelief.

After we'd walked for an hour Miranda's looked pained by her knees. My complaining about my pack had begun the day before. Tired of my endless moaning, Miranda said "Come here!" and began to brusquely grab at my pack straps.

"I've already *adjusted* it, it *just* doesn't fit," I said petulantly.

"Hmmmm." Miranda doubtfully looked me up and down. "Stand still," she said sternly. Bracing against me, she pulled on the hip straps hard and was able to tighten them several inches and pull my pack up to my waist.

"OooOOOoooo," I said. It was immediately clear that this was a lot better. "Ooo, thank you. Sorry. Did I mention I love you and you're awesome?" My shoulder was still shootingly painful and making nasty crunching noises but the weight was now far better and I endeavoured not to keep mentioning it.

Further on, another horizontally curving willow tree provided seats for us all. I lay down along the lowest curve feeling my back click and aches all over. Sama was already smiling down from the high branches over the river.

"Come on up!" she said to me.

My eyes moved very slightly to look at her. "I'm fine here. The smiler monkey and the tree sloth," I said, covering my eyes with my arm.

When we arrived back at Miranda's house her housemates Rupert and Hannah were in. Rupert owns the house and has made it a hub; sooner or later all environmentalists seem to pass through it. We took off our boots and packs and plopped unmoving into chairs in front of the Aga.

When we had drunk our tea we started idly discussing showers. Rupert and Hannah nodded encouragement eagerly, saying they thought it was a great idea. Immediately in fact. They had been able to smell us as soon as we walked into the kitchen.

CHAPTER 4 — Meditation and bees

The date for departure was set for the first full moon after the equinox. It's good luck apparently to start new ventures at that time. The Christian celebration Easter comes from the Pagan celebrations of the Goddess Eostre or Ostara from the ancient word for spring 'eastre'. The Eostre festival was timed for the full moon after the equinox which is why Easter takes place on the first Sunday after that.

I had done my first online crowdfunding appeal and raised several hundred pounds, but not been able to get any grants. I used some of the money to buy a pack that fit me, but with only a few days to go there were still several items of equipment I had yet to get, or even to decide about.

Quite a few people I spoke to suggested I ought to take some form of weapon with me; mace, a heavy metal key ring, even a knife. It didn't seem like the right attitude, bad vibe. Yet I *was* quite frightened about rough camping on my own.

Sat on the floor, I noticed a book on a lower shelf of my brother's bookcase - the fortune book. It was written in the 1700's and was a book of thousands of fortunes, with about twenty to a page. There were lengthy instructions in the front but I simply asked, "Should I take a weapon," and flicked through with my eyes closed. I put my finger on to a spot on the page and opened my eyes.

"When you travel, providence will protect you," it said.

"Ah. No weapons then. That's pretty clear. Thanks." Afterwards it seemed obvious, it would be setting the wrong intention, the wrong approach.

Having wrapped up my personal affairs I stayed a night at my parents before boarding the train to Totnes. I looked down at my boots which my mum had polished that morning, returned to their original dark blue. Mum had bought them for me when I was sixteen, now sixteen years later they were still in use (but the leather was starting to crack - I should have polished them more). Dad drove me to the station. With support like this, I thought, I have to be able to do this.

I set myself the intention to observe during the walk. Not just to look, but to see things I wouldn't normally. So I began on the train. I count four spacious first class carriages as I walk through, all empty but for a couple of people in each. Entering the standard class the small luggage racks are overflowing, every seat has either a person or a bag in it. Elderly women have big suitcases on the seats next to them. I get frowns and glares at my backpack as I squeeze down the aisle, brushing people's arms or heads.

My mum used to travel on the train down to Barry to see her grandma and they would pack all the family's belongings into a trunk. The trunk would get collected a few days before and put on a train. By the time they arrived at my great grandma's it was waiting in the hall. "It obviously wasn't prohibitively expensive, that's what everybody did," Mum told me.

The hills become small and covered in trees while the fields also become smaller. Staring at the back of the seat in front of me I realise I'm frowning intensely. Every seat now has an entertainment screen on the back, like on an airplane, all using electricity. I rise up in my seat to look around but I can't see anyone at all using them. Mine won't switch off. I'd rather have a cheaper ticket, and somewhere to put my bag. Fares seem so high since the railways were privatised.

There are lots of little streams, drainage ditches and waterlogged ground around Taunton. In Taunton itself new, brutal blocks of flats are visible. We pass a picturesque abandoned factory then more construction sites. There's a shiny field of lines near Tiverton and with a shock I realise it is full of solar panels. I've never seen that before.

I overhear talk of things washed away by the flooding earlier in the year. A lone wetland field has been left wild, then order resumes, with partial flooding. Past the low-tide estuary with lots of small stranded boats, a sterile holiday trailer park then...the sea.

Sparkling and wave topped, most people in the train turned to look at it and the tone of conversations changes.

I haven't seen the sea for months and I missed it, though I didn't realise till now. Dark orange low cliffs with dark geological lines are close-by on the other side of the train. The railway line is so close to the sea, just a meter or so above the surface and right next to the edge. It seems so vulnerable. There are signs of a landslide near Teignmouth. The water near the shore is red with sediment like old blood. Then I realise that this is the line that got washed away by the flooding in the winter. It was on the news that people in Devon had been cut off, and the line was closed for months, it must only just have reopened.

In Totnes I catch the bus towards Steph's village, then it's a fifteen minute walk in sunshine. The lane to Rattery is incredibly quiet, some insects are buzzing but there's no car noise. There are bees and flowers and edible plants along the steep banks which line the road like walls. The cottage is like I imagined: old, with white walls, plants, a little wooden gate, and an open front door.

"Hello?" I call. I get my first view of Steph – wavy hair, shy smile and a long skirt. She tells me to feel at home and help myself to tea or anything at any time. She makes us a pot and we sit in the lounge. The house has art and coloured fabric in every direction. A black cat and two two-week old kittens are on the sofa.

"It changed my life. I'd never done art before or written a book. It will change your life too you know, this walk. You should write a book," she says.

"Great idea! I'll have to work out how to do that though," I said, mentally redoubling my commitment to note-taking.

It is so quiet at the cottage. I sit next to the squeaking kittens as they are batted about, being cleaned by their mum. Before laptops, fridges and cars, it must have been so quiet.

"There are some days where no cars go past at all. It's been the perfect place to write the book," Steph tells me. "I want to change the cultural story that people have for their lives, to give them a vision that they have a choice."

Totnes is the town that defeated Costa coffee, and the town that started Transition Towns. It would not be possible to shake a stick at all the environmental initiatives which happen there, your arm would go dead. Full of independent shops, a gurgling river, a castle, rare breeds farm and a steam train, it also attracts its fair share of tourists. Transition is a process for a community to work together to transition away from fossil fuels, and you can now find Transition Towns all around the world.

Steph arranged for us to have a stall at the library to discuss her book, 'Tales of Our Times', and the Buzz Tour with people. For the duration of the walk I was to wear only yellow and black and so for the first time, I donned my yellow and black stripped tank top. My orange and black fur was draped around the stall. The yellow and black stripes drew people to ask what we were doing.

It was amazing how quickly Steph elicited the stories of people we met. Then a lady who stopped to chat suggested that she tell her partner, who was a beekeeper. A short while later, a man with grey hair and a tweed waistcoat bounded up the library stairs and waited to speak to us.

"Hello! Do you keep bees?" I asked him excitedly. He smiled and nodded. "Are you the Barefoot Beekeeper?"

"I am. Phil Chandler," he said shaking hands.

Phil is passionate about natural beekeeping and has written several books about it. He agreed to do an interview with me later and he asked me about the walk. "How would you persuade someone to change the way they live?" he asked.

"Well, that's the thing, I wouldn't," I said slowly, smiling. "I can't come in from the outside and pretend I have the answers. I do want to change the system though and the system of choices. It's not helpful to blame people for the choices this system makes appealing." I start to feel like I'm being assessed and I'm not sure whether I'm doing well or not. After a few more questions Phil asks "What's your full name?" I tell him, and he nods with a slight frown whilst writing something down.

"Hello gorgeous girl!" I said as I spotted Eve in the pub.

"Paula! It's so good to see you! Sorry I'm late! I met a really interesting beekeeper in the library...then he just handed me a cheque for £100! That'll keep me going for a month!"

The timing had been uncanny. Eve's walk was starting in Totnes on the 18th of April, the same weekend as I was going on a meditation retreat in Totnes. It occurred to me that the resident Dharma teacher at Gaia house, Rob Burbea, had co-founded the Dharma Action Network for Climate Engagement (DANCE), and I should arrange for us all to meet.

The three of us sat by the river as seagulls squawked overhead. It was quite comical to watch Rob and Eve try to get started. "Would you like to start?"..."Shall I..."... "Is this okay? Would you like...?"

Listening to the conversation, I was inspired; inspired by the drive they shared, inspired by their compulsion to do something. For me, it was a turning point. I had been held back by a feeling of inadequacy in the face of the change needed. Watching them speak, I was reminded that each person can make a difference, both in terms of what they do and how they inspire and support others.

"...There are seeds beginning to sprout here and there that *look* as if they're not connected," Rob was saying, "but we'd like to draw them into connection. One element in that, one little sprout, is meditative culture. One thing that developing a meditative practice might do, is give us skill with our emotional life. A lot of what's happening to our planet and civilization is so painful, I wonder if a lot of people just disconnect from that.

"The second piece that is possible through meditative training is to develop enough resource, so I don't 'need' in a destructive way, because I have enough inside me.

"The third is a sense of the sacred. I mean that in the broadest term, there are many kinds of sacred. What's behind the current environmental crisis, driving climate change? You could point to a lot of things, but underneath all of them is this sense that Earth is just a commodity, that people are just cogs in an economic machine. So there's something that any kind of spiritual practice might offer, a deepening into the sense of the sacred. Once that's there it becomes hard to violate the Earth, to violate other people. That somehow in this modernist world we find a way back into the sacred is absolutely crucial."

Eve nodded. "How did DANCE come about?" she asked.

"Well," said Rob, "sometimes what I saw was the opposite of what we just talked about. Sometimes when a person meditates there's an image of a meditator as perhaps someone who's removed, or not bothered by what's going on in the world. But does it always have to look that way or is there space for lots of different personalities and expressions? I realised a lot of people wanted avenues for alternative responses, so really DANCE was set up as a forum and a platform for people to offer and create whatever they felt moved to. What made you want to do these interviews?"

"There are so many people that have a piece of this puzzle, and it's *respecting* other people's approaches. To say 'You are on my side'. You want our planet to survive. You want *life*. And I'm going to support you in that." Eve said gesturing emphatically. "It's about respecting that everyone has different methods and tactics...and I'm completely distracted, because there's a seal right in front of me!" Eve said, laughing with her mouth wide.

Behind me in the water I turned just in time to see a curious whiskered face looking at us. Then a dark back arched above the water, and was gone, leaving us all standing, smiling at the water's edge, the ripples slowly expanding.

After saying goodbye to Paula and Rob the day before, I hitchhiked from Steph's house and walked the Dartington-

Totnes path into Totnes. The woodland path runs near a stream but also partly near the noisy main road. Mosses were everywhere and there was a cascade of bluebells. I decided it was time to begin my 'smile tests'. In different situations across the country I would smile at everyone and note the proportion of people that smiled back and try to look for patterns.

Of course, one smile is not like another. You could smile with your lips closed or open, you could make eye contact or not. Your heart might not be in it. What if the other person was facing into bright sunlight? Despite all this I decided I would try to be as consistent as possible and work out where people smiled. The two-dozen relaxed walkers on the Dartington-Totnes path all returned my smile without much effort.

A couple of focused runners with headphones did not. Near a garage on a main road the five people I passed all had great difficulty returning the smile, only one managed it; several had headphones on and some were rushing, wearing office clothes. Through the one-lane high street heading to the Barefoot Beekeeper's house, the vast majority of people were already smiling at *me*. I estimated an incredible ninety percent return rate here.

"So Phil, why should we care about bees?" I began.

We were sat in Phil's busy lounge, full of dark colours, interesting artefacts and books. Below outside, was a courtyard with three of his beehives and just outside, a ledge where a seagull would sit and stare at him (because sometimes he would give in and feed it).

"Not everyone is going to get interested in bees but everyone should at least be aware of how important they are," said Phil. "Bees have farmed the land a lot longer than we have; shaping what exists by selecting the plants that produce their food, which reproduce themselves to become the food of herbivores, which are then eaten by the carnivores. They are an absolutely key species. The oldest fully formed bee fossil is believed to be around 100 million years old."

"Wow, so absolutely crucial to the ecosystem. How are we doing with saving the bees?" I asked.

"When you see media stories they're mostly actually talking about one species, honeybees. They are a wild species too but their population in the UK is mostly in beehives held by beekeepers. Their habitat of hollow trees isn't around because of the woodland management, development, and planting fir trees rather than deciduous. There are also around 25 species of bumble bees and around 250 species of wild bees in the UK overall. Certainly there are a number of species that are endangered because of our agricultural system and its reliance on the artificial pesticides and fertilizers.

"Honeybees have been having a lot of problems recently in the US and Canada because they have large areas of land down to genetically modified crops which then have massive amounts of pesticides. Also the way commercial beekeepers treat bees over there...is not something we do in this country at all. People will have heard about the almond pollination in California. Bees are raised in the southern states then transported two or three thousand miles in the back of big trucks, meanwhile being fed on high fructose corn syrup, which is derived from genetically modified maize. They are put on to this enormous monoculture of almonds. California produces 80% of the world's almonds in this huge expanse around the size of Wales. The trees are sprayed off with all kinds of stuff during the year and during the pollination season the ground underneath is then sprayed off so the bees don't pollinate anything else. The bees are taken there, because of the enormous number of them - around one a half million hives..."

"That's insane!" I interrupt.

"Yeah it's something like half the population of US bees are taken there every February. They're all mixed up together, so any diseases or parasites are going to get mixed in together. Oh by the way, bees don't actually like almonds very much, they will only pollinate them all because there's nothing else there. And also by the way the honey from almonds is also rather toxic and tastes vile. So those bees having been pretty much run into the ground are then taken to big holding sites and fed again on corn syrup to keep them alive." Disgust and anger were slowly building in his voice as it sped up.

"Then very often they are converted into what's called packages," he said, "divided into boxes, given an artificially inseminated queen, which isn't related to any of them, and then sold to amateur beekeepers to start their colonies.

"So when you talk about what's going on in the USA, it's actually a miracle they've got bees at all frankly. Beekeeping in the USA is a very different beast to beekeeping in the UK, at the moment, thank goodness. Most of the beekeeping in this country is small scale, amateurs with one or two hives at the bottom of their garden. At the moment we don't have the GM problem here, with their associated pesticides though the environment minister Owen Patterson wants to change that. At the moment, our biggest problem is agricultural chemicals, in particular the neo-nicotinoids (like Imidacloprid) produced by Bayer and Syngenta. They are systemic insecticides which are deadly to bees down to *extraordinarily* low concentrations. They are usually coated on the seed and taken into the plant as it grows, and so becomes part of the plant. It seems the effect is to undermine the bee's immune system. The pesticide companies say it is the virus that's killing the bees and they'll sell you some pesticide strips to kill off the mites that carry the virus. But what they don't tell you is that those same chemicals will damage the bees, and not only that, but if you keep using them, the mites will become immune to them."

"Ha! It's a classic! Sell someone a problem to sell them a solution," I said, shaking my head at the all too familiar story.

"Exactly! Now they're soaking up taxpayer's money to do research in order to find another chemical solution."

"So you must have an alternative viewpoint here?" I said.

"In natural beekeeping we allow bees to live how they want to live and all we do is provide them with nice warm dry accommodation. We don't get in their way too much, we can take a bit of honey if there's plenty but we don't have to control their lives. I've started to use the term Balanced Beekeeping. It's not putting the bees in a hollow tree and ignoring them (though that's perfectly defensible) but it's not commercial exploitation; the 'How can I get the maximum out of them and put the least in? I've become beeified, so it's probably a pretty permanent feature of my personality now.

"Anybody could create a bee-friendly zone, with plants and by not using toxic chemicals. Avoid buying bottles of stuff. Right now bees are having a better time of it in towns than the countryside. In the countryside there's more monocrop and they're sprayed with chemicals. Encourage your council to leave road verges uncut, not use chemicals and to plant flowers. Devon county council has got a fairly enlightened stance and leaves them pretty much alone."

Walking back to Steph's from Dartington I don't find any verges to admire on the narrow, winding A-road. Things are getting risky as I flatten myself against the hedges and stone walls every minute or so to avoid being flattened involuntarily. I decide today is not my day to die. Climbing up the bank when a slight gap appears, I awkwardly jump the overgrown spiky ditch. With years of experience of crossing barbed wire fences, I put my clothes on the top and swing over into the field. A few fields on, I try my best to sheepishly walk past the sheep to a tall metal gate. Despite my best efforts, the farmer does not take me for one of his flock and comes quickly out to investigate.

"Sorry to disturb you...or your sheep. I was walking the road but it got too dangerous, I'm trying to get out to Rattery. Is this the best way?" I ask.

"Yeah...you're best off going through here," he helped me by pulling back the overgrown gate, enough for me to squeeze through. He watched (*was that a little shake of his head?*) as I left the premises.

CHAPTER 5 — Quest for Arthur

Eve contacted me to ask about walking around England - I've done it you see - and she's about to. I walked to hear and share stories of people and communities who were starting to do things differently, to make a difference; people learning how to waste less resources, how to grow and share food and live more sustainably. I walked for 2000 miles in an old pair of red flip-flops, taking the tales I collected from place to place, retelling them as the folk tales of today's heroes.

I am inspired by the collaborative vision Eve has for her walk, and intrigued to follow her progress as she makes use of the things I have shared with her. I begin to wish I had had her to project manage me when I set out to walk.

On the morning of the walk in the market square in Totnes we are joined by my friend Matthew, another stalwart walker of pilgrimages that we'd met in the library. The Barefoot Beekeeper waves us off and gives us a cuddly bee to carry as a mascot. Eve clutches it under her arm.

We stride off down the High Street towards the river Dart; it's market day and the town is buzzing and we three in our yellow and black garb are barely noticed as, in high spirits, we claim the middle of the road and make our way to Bourton Lane, the old drovers road that leads east out of Totnes.

We trudge up and out of the town past the travellers who live in vans and caravans and the vibrant flowers that catch our attention in the hedgerows. We eat primroses, delighting in Eve's enthusiasm at her first experience, and learn hedge lore from Matthew. He points out the bent-over branches of a laid hedge. "How is it that hedges are laid?" "What's the name of that plant there?" Our questions keep coming and Matthew shares what he knows. We each of us feel keenly the lack of the knowledge our forbears would have had.

Just over a little stream, a goat comes out onto the rough track to meet us and I scratch between her horns. When she feels quite done she hops it back over the fence to the field from whence she had escaped, seemingly especially to have a little head massage. The sun beams down on us, and it isn't long before we have stripped off all the clothes we can, tying them about our waists and hanging them from our rucksacks. Eve, unused to her gear, would take several minutes each time to put things back on.

It hasn't been hot and sunny all spring though and it isn't long before we hit the quintessential enemy of the humble flip-flop. Eve and Matthew are in their walking boots, but I walk flip-flop clad as always and so the patch of thick sticky black mud holds up only my progress.

"Oh Steph!" exclaims Eve as we laugh at the sods of wet earth that continue to cling to my feet. I smile, shrugging.

We eat our packed lunches on the grass next to a winding stream. Bullocks in the field gradually begin to gather above us, and when they reach critical mass, we move on.

At mid-afternoon it's time for Matthew to catch a bus back home. Eve and I bid him farewell and head off to find the legendary Arthur. Ninety three and a half, my friend Arthur French is now sadly in an old folk's home. Arthur was part of Transition Town Totnes until he could no longer get to the meetings. We find him in Denbury, just a mile or so from our destination for the night, to present him with his half-year birthday present: a limited edition copy of my book.

When we arrive in the dining room Arthur is talking with a middle aged man with a coat and bag and an elderly lady is sat opposite him.

"Ah, well I will leave you to your new visitors!" says the man smiling as he collects his coat and bag. "See you soon."

We are quite humbled by this kindly elderly gentleman, who bids us sit down for tea and biscuits and introduces his friend, a retired headmistress who can no longer speak, but whom he includes in all of our conversations. It feels very significant to be weaving our two walks together in this way.

Arthur grew up in Stonehouse near Stroud. They used to catch elvers (young eels) to eat and a man used to come around and collect snails to eat. He learned to swim in the canal but then gradually the canal grew too dirty and they had to build a swimming pool.

Revived by our afternoon tea break, Eve and I make our way down the lane to Oakwood Denbury: the very special land education centre run by my good friends Steve and Sharona, who live there with their two children. I am delighted at the coincidence that Eve has chosen them as her first stop.

There were quite a few cars parked outside the wooden cabin when we arrived, but no sign of anyone. We went around to the back and there were lots of vegetable plots and some greenhouses, across the field towards a small wood we discovered to our surprise, a party! On the long wooden table under the woods Steve and Sharona had laid out couscous, cabbage and carrot salad, bean salad, cheese and fruit juice.

"Steph! What have you done to yourself?!" exclaims Sharona, "You look ten years younger!"

"I hope it was the walking," says Eve winking.

The other guests have already eaten and we sink gratefully onto the wooden stools and set about the food. Afterwards we we're eagerly interviewed by Jason Liosatos for his online show Global Peace Radio.

We bed down in a cosy little empty classroom in our sleeping bags. The next morning we wander around the woodland, polytunnel, and the many vegetable patches.

Steve sits us in the herb circle. The eight-sided array of raised beds is more than a growing area, it's also a teaching tool; here children learn the seasons and the growing cycle, about astronomy and about themselves.

Over lunch, Sharona and Steve told us how the school had come into being, despite months of planning difficulties.

"We're all on a great walk, a journey as humans," Sharona said. "We had over a hundred letters of support for our planning application. I really felt *alone* before, but now there's this feeling that we're in this mass community."

"There's loads of us" I said, "and there'll be even more."

Sharona nodded. "We're putting our heads above the parapet, just by being here. People have been frightened by it. We had support from Satish Kumar and the Schumacher College which really helped."

It's hard to leave after lunch. Eve and four-year-old Will are playing pirates, and the captain is reluctant to lose his deckhand.

"You will come back, won't you?" Steve asks Eve sternly.

"Yes, that would be lovely. It'll be quite a while though…"

"I think it would close the circle. Within a year?"

"That sounds doable!" nods Eve.

When we set off again, Sharona and Will accompany us. We walk slowly so that our youngest companion's little plump legs can keep up. Once they have turned back, we go on, following the lanes that will take us to Newton Abbot.

I have carried another copy of my book with me; it's a gift for the proprietors of Samson's farm, who hosted me on the first night of my walk, as a thank you. It's getting late though, and I need to be able to get back home for work the next morning. At Newton Abbot I pass the book to Eve to carry onwards.

Amongst youngsters on benches and shoppers to-ing and fro-ing between the nearby supermarket and the town centre, we sit and eat a snack. Eve gets up and chalks a message on the pavement - Change the culture, not the Climate - with a picture of a smiling bee.

Eve and I take each other's leave. It feels strange. She is the one to be walking on now; I am catching a bus back home. She lingers a moment; aware suddenly perhaps of the enormity of her undertaking, alone on the walk for the first time. I feel her aloneness yet know it is how it must be at this stage. I stand firm and wave, clutching the cuddly bee that is to go home to his owner, as Eve walks away, turning once or twice to wave. I watch as she crosses the road and disappears round the corner.

It is Easter Sunday 2014 and the Buzz Tour has begun.

CHAPTER 6 — A Devonshire accent

It was surprisingly hard not to cry. Steph had been such a good friend over the past few days. The second copy of her book was too big to fit in my pack so I carried it awkwardly in my arms, conscious that I must protect it until it reached its recipient. The owners of the B&B didn't know I was coming and it had been a few years since Steph's journey, but it was a lead. Ahead of me was just lots of map I didn't know, but this was a possible oasis.

I followed the River Teign north and crossed a footbridge in search of Sampson's Farm hotel and Nigel and Sarah Bell. Deep banked, fast flowing and tree lined, the River Teign had a great presence. Standing on the footbridge there was only the sound of layers of jostling water, air and leaves. The banks looked unaltered and curved where they wanted. I couldn't linger though as I was anxious to find my destination.

"Hello! I'm a friend of Steph Bradley. She sent me to give you this book she wrote," I said to the slim man in an apron. Nigel looked at me blankly with a little confusion. He was friendly, despite seeming very tired. "It was a couple of years ago, she was walking and she stayed here." Mild panic rose in me that I was not explaining things very well at all.

"Oh...ye-ehs, she was warking?" Nigel's accent was the first I'd heard in Devon as he smiled trying to remember.

"Finally!" I thought joyfully, *"Someone who was born here."*

"Oy rememberr, she ad er skirrt and flip-flops on."

"Yes," I confirmed. "She wrote a book about her journey you see, and the hotel is in it. This one's for you." I passed him the large blue book.

"What a luvely thing! Sarah!"

Sarah blossomed around a corner. Her dress and lipstick were an exuberant scarlet and her head scarf was floral and neat over her tucked-up hair. The blue floral apron looked like it had found its ideal home. There would be no shameful hiding in a draw for *this* apron. Despite my sudden appearance, Nigel and Sarah not only let me camp in their garden but gave me a wonderful dinner and breakfast too.

After they had finished serving breakfast, we sat in the parlour where its dark wood pews and large fireplace were made colourful with cushions. Sarah is an artist and her beautiful paintings decorated the room around us.

"People are obsessed about getting a bargain," said Sarah as we talked about what had changed, "but they're not really seeing the true value of things anymore. The whole thing about advertising concerns me. How extreme it is, how influenced we are by it, to want more *things* all the time. I'm reading a book at the moment called Affluenza. Have you read it?"

"No, I've heard of the term, but I haven't read it," I said.

"It really struck a chord with me." Sarah stirred her tea with a delicate teaspoon and leaned back in the chair. As she spoke her smile was always there, framing the words. "It's by a psychologist, Oliver James. He's writing about the fact that it seems to be the more affluent who are becoming more unhappy and more stressed." She paused and laughed gently.

"I wrote on my blackboard: 'It is more important to be, than to have.' and my friend came over and she said 'Ah well that's typical of someone with no money!'" The three of us laughed as Sarah and Nigel exchanged a look. "If you know you haven't got much money, you either change your circumstances or you change the way you think about it."

"It would be nice to get rid of the pressure of the borrowings, to do more charitable work," said Nigel. Near his head I could see a collection pot and in the toilets I'd seen a poster for a charity event. A customer arrived and Nigel left to see to them.

"I think as well," continued Sarah "something that's affected us, a few years ago we had some very, very life changing things happen to us. It reinforced things that we already thought. Three and a half years ago we were held up in the middle of the night, in our beds by masked gunmen..."

"Oh my goodness!" I whispered.

"...who threatened to shoot us, and wanted money and..." Sarah blinked her eyes slowly and shook her head as she held her teacup. "...different kinds of things." Her mouth widened in a grimace as she continued to shake her head.

"And our daughter. We were all bound in our beds and threatened." Sarah rubbed her forehead and eyes. "My daughter was twelve then. I think we recovered from it better than we would have expected.

"Then five months later, our daughter had respiratory arrest at Christmas and she..." Sarah began to rub her forehead and eyes again, blinking. "...So I probably spent about three months in hospital staying with her," she exhaled slowly.

"Then my mother died suddenly whilst my daughter was in hospital. And to keep on doing business, cause it doesn't stop. On the morning that we got held up, heh ha! We were held up at about four o'clock in the morning and at nine o'clock Nigel was serving breakfast for thirty five guests. And all of them had to be questioned later by the police!" she finished, laughing. "It really makes you appreciate what you've got, when...when those things have been almost taken away from you. So, the NHS, you know, I just think it's absolutely wonderful..."

We could hear Nigel saying goodbye to a customer.

"This is only my second time in Devon," I said, "and I noticed I haven't heard any Devon accents, Nigel is the first..."

"Well it's not quite, 'cause he's originally from Cornwall!" she said laughing.

"Oohhhh!" I cried with disappointment.

As I left the hotel with a wave, the wind was picking up and it was clear that rain was coming. As I turned into a footpath I saw a long stick in the ivy. I remembered my second cousin's words: "Always have a stick with you." Tugging it out, I discovered that it was longer than I needed, but after I broke the end off, it was just about perfect. The crooked nobble at the top fit my hand nicely.

Splishing past a clay quarry, I could use the stick to balance around the white puddles, although the traffic of fast cars meant I had to time my passing. The day stayed grey with gently persistent rain so I took a satisfyingly long respite in Chudleigh, making the most of my £1.50 pot of tea.

I was trying to track down a place called Embercombe, somewhere amongst the woods and fields. After a few wrong turns I arrived at the tall but welcoming gate. The long drive at Embercombe goes past yurts, wood sculptures, wood buildings and large outdoor wooden tables. With my staff and giant green poncho I arrived at the wooden office building and slowly removed and hung my many layers. The day had been a busy one for the staff of Embercombe. That evening they were starting a course, as well as taking in new volunteers. But my timing was excellent, dinner would shortly be served.

My loyal-blue boots were soaked. In the centre of the giant dinner-yurt was a big wood-burning stove where I propped them up. A wiser soul kindly saved my soles later, by moving them back from melting range.

The new arrivals for the Catalyst course were excitedly finding places on the wooden benches inside the yurt and getting to know each other. The eighteen to twenty-five year-olds had been asked to prepare a drawing of their life as a river and as we polished off our hearty vegan meal, many were making a last minute creation. Tomorrow they would introduce themselves and talk through the drawings. Chatting with the group at my table I joined them in drawing. The variety of styles really surprised me (then I was surprised at my surprise), some with lots of colour, others with waterfalls, whirlpools, some were abstract, some a map.

Existing volunteers had a meeting to try to explain what Embercombe was, to the new volunteers, and they let me listen. "It's really good at opening your eyes to what you do and who you are...a place where you can really be, with genuine people who can reflect you back. The founder, Mac, used to do leadership training, and one of the businessmen he worked with, David Mann funded Mac to start this place."

The following morning I climbed out of my tent and looked across the beautiful valley. Warming up in the drying room I collected my clothes. The evening before, I'd washed them in the sink and hung them in the purpose-built drying room. My final act before leaving was to interview the man himself.

"So what is Embercombe?" I asked Mac.

"Well its fifty acres of some of the most beautiful country in Devon," said Mac. "We've been here since 1999. Our mission is 'to inspire people to deepen as human beings and take courageous action for change in our world'. But basically its trying to say, at this time in our history, now, we can't stand on the sidelines and assume that everything's going to be ok. That each one of us in our particular circumstances is called to stand forward and, in our own way, according to our gifts and the things we love, to take action and participate."

"What sort of people come here?" I asked.

"We like to think anyone can benefit from coming here. The oldest person has been in their eighties. It's saying: 'What's my choice? What is it that I deeply and profoundly love? What are my deepest and most profound gifts?' Which are questions many people do not know the answers to. 'What are my deepest and most profound responsibilities?' When you answer those questions, of course you want to live that way.

"We have corporate groups that explore how business could be a force for transformation. Our current economy - the global economy - it's really clear to me that it doesn't work, to serve the needs of everybody, or our Earth. There are people all over the world I think that are trying to bring these things forward."

As I left Embercombe the wooden bench tables outside the dining-yurt were covered in vegetables as a large group of people chopped. I kept pausing to look at the steep green hills. Devon seemed so full of stunning landscapes and tiny valleys. The trees didn't have leaves properly yet, more of a vaguely greenish haze on their skeletons, but the birds' song was excitedly thrilled; I didn't know what they are saying to each other but they were very pleased about it.

Approaching a patch of woods I suddenly came upon a large work horse in a harness; Russet brown with a long straight blonde mane and tail, and a blonde nose.

There was a man adjusting the chain hanging from the rear of the harness.

"He's lovely! What are you using him for?" I asked.

"We're removing trees, he does less damage than a digger."

"Wow... can I watch?" I asked.

John was removing Sitka Spruce from the woodland to increase its biodiversity and then he was going to use it in his new biomass boiler. "We'll have to use a lot more of these horses, as fossil fuels decline with peak oil," John said.

Peak oil is the concept that with limited oil on the planet, at some point we will pass the peak of extraction. Some researchers believe we have already passed this point.

One helpful measure is energy out for energy in (EROI - energy returned on energy invested). In the early 1900's oil extraction was from 'gushers' where you could use one barrel of oil energy and get a hundred out. A 100:1 return rate. By the 1970's the best finds were exploited and the average energy out for energy in became 30:1. The Canadian tar sands energy ratio for usable oil is 3:1. But a capitalist economic system hides all of this, all we see is petrol at the pump. There is still lots of oil, it won't 'run out' but it's becoming a worse and worse deal energetically. None of this takes into account the environmental and social costs of course.

John led the horse down a steep slope across a tiny stream, with the harness bar and chain trailing afterwards. Then the pulling harness chain was wrapped around a log. The horse stamped quickly back across the stream and pulled uphill with big lunging strides; it's head nodded forward with each step and it's mane swung round its face. John walked (or leapt) along behind, next to the log, using long reins.

Heading on north, I passed through a railway yard, at its edge I noticed some information signs next to the footpath, something about the history of the railway. A footbridge over the river was just ahead of me and I was keen to move on. Then I saw something that made me stop. It was a crushed car.

Written, in neat type on an official looking museum sign, was the label:

THE ONLY TYPE OF GREEN CAR

"*Hang on a minute,*" I thought, "*what is this place?*" I turned around to head back into the railway yard.

CHAPTER 7 — Tadpole

The railway man looked at me with doubt and shared a knowing look with his friend. My large hat, walking trousers tucked into my socks and large backpack may have spoken before I did.

"I saw the crushed car and I wanted to ask you about this place. I'm doing a walk visiting environmental places," I said.

The doubt remained, but he paused what he was doing.

Slowly over the next half an hour it became clear that not only was Colin deeply committed to public railway for the good of society and the environment but he was deeply hurt by the way it was rotting away.

"They closed down 400 miles and 200 stations!" Colin exclaimed in pain. "And not because they weren't profitable, because of a government choice. Some lines are still eighty or ninety percent intact."

The Exeter and Teign Valley Railway is in fact, neither a museum nor a live railway yard. It is currently a railway reconstruction, the life's work of Colin Burges.

When Colin was seventeen, he began to restore a railway line. Cajoling and badgering the owners of the sections of land to allow him to extend it. But when he could go no further he abandoned the project and in 1984, he began instead, the restoration of the station at Christow, turning it from a plant-covered area with a couple of bits of concrete to a station with track, carriages and platforms. A small carriage also provides rides for children around the track.

The information room at the station includes maps of the old rail system, and a bewildering range of equipment and artefacts in every nook. Outside, a black barrel has been labelled with information about peak oil.

"The railway is not a thing of the past, it's our future. We have to get the cars off the road. This is what the state should be doing. We have a highly-engineered transport infrastructure and we need it for the times ahead. Instead they worship the god Oil and generally mess up the future," his hands were tense with frustration and every now and then his head would give a little shake of disbelief.

"I never thought it would be this long. We can restore them. We still have the knowhow; it would be fun even! I just want to get started."

The original line was a fifteen and three quarter mile stretch from Exeter to Heathfield, that took two railway companies, forty three years, and eighteen acts of parliament to get finished. Before it was then closed down. The restored section around Christow station sits like an island in the middle, waiting, to find the rest of the line.

In the yard were two carriages that Colin made as accommodation; Toad, the larger carriage, with a double bed and kitchen area, and Tadpole with two small bunks. Both were lovingly full of detail. Tadpole was originally made for children, with only the bottom bunk being big enough for an adult. The walls were richly coloured shiny wooden slats and a picture hung on them. Dark green bunks were next to a little table with a lamp and mini kettle. An old signal lamp and canteen of 'whale oil' sat on the outside shelf. He must have spent so many hours on it, on all of it. He had poured himself into this site, yet a lot of people didn't get it.

"The local people think I'm a crank," he confessed.

Chatting with Colin about the environment, society, climate change and transport I felt a thrill of discovery at finding such a person by accident. After a couple of hours we were still leaning against a carriage chatting and he offered me a bunk for the night in Tadpole. I'd walked hardly any distance that day, but the railway was such a special place and Tadpole looked so inviting!

Colin took the brakes off the tiny carriage and pulled it by hand so it was next to the river and showed me the outdoor loo made from a signalman's box. As I settled in and watched the river, my neighbours from Toad came and invited me round for dinner. Eating pasta on their carriage veranda, watching the sun go down I marvelled at the journey, at the wonderful space, at the kindness of the unexpected railwayman.

I snuggled into my bunk and discovered a bedtime story on the bedside table that Colin had written about Tadpole. Tadpole was made to mimic the old brake cars. Years ago the trains had the brake in a special carriage at the end of the train and a brake man was employed to operate it as the train went up and down the hills. In the bedtime story about Tadpole, the brakeman's night shift is described as he heats his coffee on the little wood stove, leans out of the train and signals the engine carriage, and dreams of one day making the little carriage into a sleeping car.

There was a long way to go to get to Bow the next day but I was confident I would make it before sundown. I hadn't passed any shops and as I walked the quiet lane I thought how great it would be to have a chocolate bar. "*Could I have a chocolate bar please?*" About twenty minutes later I passed a chocolate wrapper at the edge of the road, I pressed it with my stick to be sure, but it was empty. I sighed. Another couple of meters, and another wrapper, also empty. Then another, and another. These ones were full. I picked them to inspect them. The first was split. "*Forth time lucky?*" The other, although slightly misshapen, was intact.

"Ha! Thank you!" I said smiling to the air as I unwrapped and munched my prize.

I made it to Bow at eight thirty just as it was getting too dark to walk. I felt it had been absolutely as far as I could manage and decided to treat myself to egg and chips in the pub. Sitting back in the chair and taking off my boots had to be done very slowly, with exhaustion. I told myself it was the first week and it was OK to pay for food in a pub as a one off. My body needed the rest and I ate by the fire. Afterward I sewed little bee badges out of felt to give people as gifts. I'd been told that pubs were usually fine with you pitching a tent in the back garden, but this turned out not to be the case.

"If you'd asked when you first came in we could have

asked around in the village but it's too late now. We'd get in trouble with the council if we let someone camp," they told me with concern and admonishment.

Earlier I'd noted a school with an unlocked gate and a tree-filled garden as my back-up plan. Keeping an eye out for dog walkers I quickly slipped through the gate. Pitching my tent in the back corner, I hoped I would be concealed until daylight. My heart was beating hard whenever someone went past or a car's headlights swung near but nobody saw me and I climbed uneasily in and fell asleep, for a while.

Peering nervously out of the tent in the dim orange streetlight I checked if the coast was clear for a toilet dash. Contrary to horror films and my own imagination, there is not going to be someone waiting to pounce on you, nor will there be a giant snake/spider/dog in the bushes to rush at you. I woke several more times, my subconscious wishing to double check that we were still safe. Each time I reassured it that yes, we were absolutely fine. Thank you for your input, AGAIN, but I would like to sleep now. Finally, I woke to my alarm at five thirty, stiff and thick-headed to hear a few spots of rain on the tent.

I scrambled quickly out of my sleeping bag and threw all my things in my rucksack.

For weight distribution it's nice to have all your pack weight as close to your back as possible, but for convenience in the rain it's good to strap your tent on the outside of the pack.

I managed to get the tent down and my giant poncho on over the top of everything just before the main rain hit. I looked dodgy. There was no avoiding that. It was the early hours of the morning, I had my hood up, and a giant hump on my back like a turtle (but not the teenage ninja type, the thirty-something tramp type). I walked in a tired, dazed and painful haze. I should have walked less the day before, and slept more.

Through mid Devon the rivers seemed more polluted and there were more dairies. The hedgerows had less variety of plant life and I wasn't sure if that was natural variation or a change in the way they were managed. The rain kept coming and so did the hills; several villages and nowhere to sit. I began to wish out loud.

"It would be so nice, a covered bench, to sit and rest out of the rain. I think every village ought to have one," I said.

I paused on a yellow salt bin before tackling a big hill in Zeal Monochorum. When I reached the top of the hill I saw...a large covered bench, under an old tree. It was ornately carved all over and covered by a large wooden shelter.

"Thank you!" I said excitedly. Clearly the residents of Zeal Monochorum are a wise wondrous people. I ate my oat bar breakfast, legs swinging joyfully, called Miranda and my mum and marvelled at the beautiful carving on my heart's desire.

Near lunchtime I saw Lapford sat on the side of a hill. It had an unusually large number of solar panels on the roofs. Then the rain intensified and it disappeared like Brigadoon. My imagination began to fill in the marvels of exotic Lapford. It was much bigger on the map than all the other villages I had gone through. Clearly with so many solar panels, they would be an environmentally conscious village. The map showed a post office. There would be local shops, a little café where environmentalists would gather and work on changing society. Maybe I would meet an amazing person there who would offer me shelter. Heading up the hill and starting to pass buildings, a man leaned out of his car and asked me if I was lost.

"No, I'm just headed into town," I replied.

"Ha! *Town*," he said mocking the grandeur of the term.

"Oh, er village," I corrected.

The post office, I discovered, closed down a year ago. No, there were no shops in the village. Yes there was a pub, but it didn't open until the evening. I sheltered in the church briefly, but the rain showed no sign of stopping and it seemed rude to eat my oatcakes there. Don't judge a town by its solar panels.

The most direct way to Eggesford would be along the main road, but with no pavement and a heavy traffic of fast cars, it wasn't possible. The footpath I was forced to take, went a couple of miles out of the way, up a big hill and round. I glared down at the road jealously.

"In the future," I said darkly, "when there are fewer cars, we'll be able to reclaim the best routes. I look forward to that."

At a small farm I saw hens foraging under trees and a covered table with boxes of eggs for sale. I bought a box and hoped I would find someone willing to boil them for me. Hard boiled eggs make fantastic walking food. Filling and lightweight, they last for a week and a half as long as the shells are not cracked. Well, they may in fact last longer, but that was the longest I left them before 'chickening' out.

That night I camped in a campsite on top of a hill and they were kind enough to boil the eggs for me. I had my first shower since Embercombe, but I hadn't missed showers.

A few years ago I lived for two months with indigenous First Nations in Canada who were returning to their traditional territory and blockading against a proposed gas pipeline. We used to carry our water from the river and heat it on a wood burning range. Showering was done in tin bath with a jug. I decided to take the opportunity there to stop washing my hair with shampoo. I'd heard that if you stop shampooing your hair (but still rinse it) for six weeks, it will rebalance with natural oils and keep itself clean. I'd always wanted to try it, but been embarrassed about the transition stage. It turned out to take only five weeks. Five, greasy and itchy weeks, during which I kept it covered with a head scarf. At the end, removing the scarf was like coming out of a chrysalis to find shiny healthy hair. Several years later, the novelty of not needing to wash my hair still hasn't worn off.

Without an income I had had to get rid of all unnecessary spending like toiletries, but giving up makeup had been surprisingly more difficult for my ego. After a while of not wearing foundation, I stopped getting spots (and needing to buy spot cream). After a while of not wearing mascara, I stopped having itchy eyes with wrinkles and dark patches (and needing to buy eye cream). But, your eyes never look as striking. "*On the other hand*," I thought, "*our planet is dying, so get over it. Who really gives a shit if I wear makeup or not?"*

It was a clear sky that night at the campsite on the hill, so with no insulating cloud cover the temperature dropped to freezing and there was frost on the ground.

There are four ways you can lose heat. You can *radiate* it out as an energy wave like light (through your windows if you don't have curtains). Another object could *conduct* it away from you by direct contact (the ground when you're camping). A flowing substance like air or water, that you are in, could *convect* it away by the warm molecules moving away from you and being replaced by colder ones. You can also think that you are cold and your body will believe you. I once chatted to a night security patrol guard in Canada. He was from Poland. I was compulsively shivering in my many layers and I asked him how he kept from getting cold. "Tell yourself you're not cold," he said with a shrug.

At night, the main form of heat loss from the Earth is radiation, straight out into space. This means that if there is cloud cover, it intercepts the radiation and keeps in the heat. The reason that we get dew and frost is because if it is a clear night, the heat just keeps radiating out and the atmosphere above becomes so cold that the moisture in it condenses or freezes and falls to the ground. That's why the ground air temperature could be above freezing but frost still form, and if something is under cover, it doesn't have frost on it.

Well I tried telling myself I wasn't cold, but I didn't believe me. Despite my allegedly four-season sleeping bag I was really cold all night. That could have had quite a lot to do with two acts of false economy. The first was buying the aforementioned sleeping bag used, on eBay, despite the comment 'some stuffing missing, but can easily be repaired'. The second was taking only one half of a roll mat, to save on weight. Foam roll mats weigh next to nothing, and cold legs and feet will stop you sleeping. On the bright side, during my nightly toilet stroll, the stars and the Milky Way were vibrantly visible in the clear sky.

CHAPTER 8 — Entertaining angels

During the early days of the walk, my parents were somewhat concerned. Being daily readers of a tabloid, it appeared only a matter of days until I would be attacked. So they arranged to take a holiday in Devon and meet me along my route, so we could all stay in a B&B. The luxury of another pub meal and a real bed gave me a nine and a half hour sleep. In the morning I surprised myself, and them, by managing to eat a large full English breakfast.

"The thing that's amazed me is all these wonderful kind people you keep meeting – everywhere! It's not like you read in the papers is it?" my dad said.

"No Dad," I answered smiling, "it really isn't."

The farm B&B had pictures and ornaments of horses everywhere, filling the deep windowsills in the large breakfast room. The owner, Jonathan, kept work horses as well as training those of other people. In the yard we saw him lead two horses, clipped together, to a red two wheeled horse trap. The larger black and white shire horse was mentoring a russet brown one. The mentor stepped neatly over the central tow bar, pulling the newbie alongside.

The speed of my walking was becoming clear to me by now, and that speed was: slow. I had arranged to detour to North Devon to meet Hector Christie but I now realised it would add a couple of weeks on to the trip. I decided to see him anyway but not walk the detour. My parents wanted to see the village of Clovelly, which they'd last visited thirty years ago, and afterwards they would drop me off to meet Hector.

When we arrived at Clovelly on the coast, there was a sign requiring visitors to enter through a tourist visitors' centre. It also then required visitors to pay £6.75 to enter the cliff-side cobbled village.

"None of this was here before," Dad told me.

"There's a beautiful view, when we get there," said Mum.

The entire village is owned by one family and had previously had large numbers of visitors that were deemed to be excessive. The tiny village does indeed have beautiful views, as well as donkeys, a miniature museum and cafés. But the price is like the famous cobbled streets – very steep.

Hector arrived to meet me at the train station in a large five-door car that had seen better days. Resonating with enthusiasm and with an enormous smile, he was fresh from a football game. Tall and thin, his shoes were ripped and his t-shirt had a hole in it. He was full of energy for his new anti-GMO (Genetically Modified Organisms) campaign as we drove to meet his friend Karen and discuss plans for a national demonstration.

"Most of the GM crops are developed to be resistant to a pesticide and then farmers can use more of it. The GM crops do work for the first few years," he told me "then you're using the same herbicide, resistance builds up and Roundup stops working. You only have to look at what's happening in North America. At Rothampstead Research they inserted a synthetic cow gene into a wheat plant to repel aphids. If there had been long term independent testing to prove it was safe I wouldn't have a problem with the GMO itself. Now that's never been done. There are even heritage breeds of plants that exist that do many of the things they're developing GMOs for. But of course you can't patent heritage breeds."

Karen was managing the social media for the campaign and they discussed what towns already had someone organising a demonstration, and where they still needed to find someone. The demos were to be a few days before the international 'March Against Monsanto' day. After the previous year's March Against Monsanto, Monsanto's share price fell considerably.

"Protest is one thing they really listen to," said Hector. "Just standing outside, with a banner, these big corporations absolutely hate it. They like to promote a nice squeaky clean image. It's not difficult to show they're not. Anyone who wants to join in will be sent a poster like this," he said gesturing to a big picture of Snow White killed by a poisoned apple with the Monsanto logo. "They'll be given this biohazard tape to wrap around the area, and sheets with the chants."

"What has it taken to organise a national demo?" I asked.

"Sheer bloody-minded determination!" he said smiling grimly. "It's not the first one I've done and it won't be the last."

Arriving at Tapley Manor we crunched up the sweeping driveway and around the back of the stately home. The grand building had white stone pillars, red bricks, dozens of windows, carved stone and ornate black gates. Hector locked up the car in the garage. "To keep it from the bailiffs," he explained.

Hector's kitchen showed busy disarray and every wall was covered with photos, posters, newspaper headlines or letters. Most related to Hector and his friends but a third of one long wall was devoted to a beloved dog, Brian the bull terrier. Dinner was steamed greens and duck eggs from the garden, on toast - delicious! Hector is vigorously against supermarkets and the industrialisation of agriculture. He once undertook a campaign against a new Tesco in the area, with a sixteen year-old. The two of them ran door to door and delivered flyers to *fourteen thousand* homes and succeeded in fighting it off! Other activities involved lying in the road or hanging a banner and scampering (yes, despite being then in his forties, scampering *is* the right word) down in time to avoid multiple police cars.

Hector told me of the time he interrupted Tony Blair at a Labour conference to confront him about the Iraq war.

"I got in with a little help from the angels," he said, "because the Interpol records were in a muddle at the time. Rather than admit there was a problem, they let me in!" He beamed and hit his knee with delight, "You just have to go in with confidence." And Hector certainly can radiate that, but to sum up his manner more accurately, the word you need is charming.

"I had help again at the G8 with Gordon Brown. I booked late, claiming to be press and when I arrived they said 'oh yes we spoke to you on the phone' and I was the only one they didn't check the papers of!"

Shouting that the G8 were a criminal group interested in exploiting poorer countries, he received cheers of support as he was dragged away.

"The policeman told me 'I should arrest you, but I agree with everything you just said' and he let me go! Quite a number of times I've had the support of local police, but when you target a corporation, it's another game entirely. It's the corporations that rule the world."

In 2013 Hector Christie was arrested for damaging genetically modified crops being grown by Rothampstead Research. They sent twenty-five police cars to collect him.

"I naively asked at the time if there had been a burglary or something," he told me. "But they said 'no, they're all for you.' That's when I started to realise I was in trouble."

During his court case he was repeatedly threatened with a fine of over £50,000, which would then be dropped to £4,300, to shuttle him exhaustingly between hearings at the Crown and Magistrates courts. He was warned by friends that an attempt might be made on his life if he continued to attack the GMO corporations.

"It was incredible good fortune to get in," he said. "They had infrared cameras but with help from the angels I walked past the cameras and two guards four times, visualising an invisibility cloak." Because of its close weave, the fence could not be climbed. It was high, with razorwire and a deep ditch dug all the way around. The reason Hector had to walk past the cameras several times was he needed to walk back into the woods to get a log, which incredibly, he used to pole vault over the fence!

"I felt the angels literally lift me over," he said.

Listening to story after story of coincidence, I did start to wonder if perhaps the angels were indeed enjoying the show.

After dinner, we watched videos of protests at global summits that Hector had attended over the years. Violent clashes between citizens in bike helmets throwing stones and police in riot gear with guns. Violence for defence is a difficult issue for many. Most people would agree that if you are violently attacked you should be able to violently defend yourself. Ghandi's famous non-violent approach was not pacifism but rather a tactical choice against a more powerful enemy, which included destruction of property (for example weapons) to prevent violence. Some count destruction of property as violence, some do not. What about when your attackers are powerful corporations or investors? At what point is it justifiable to defend yourself, your children, the unborn, or your planet with violence? From my experiences everyone's line is different and it is unwise to judge.

"The key is to come at it from the side, take them off balance. At the G8 summit at Gleneagles I was with a group of friends all in kilts, with helmets and bushy bright orange beards. As the police charged, we sang them summer holiday and all lifted our kilts... showing pictures of prime ministers over our crotches. It just totally threw them!" he said laughing.

"We *can* initiate change," he said. "The radicalisation of a few people during foot-and-mouth *did* have a big impact on the government and hugely reduced the slaughter. It's so easy to get despondent but the little actions that people take have a far bigger impact than we realise."

Hector led me past protest banners leaning against the walls and classical portrait paintings hanging on them, to my room with a several hundred year-old four poster bed in it. I laid out my sleeping bag on the bare mattress.

In the morning, we toured the grounds and Hector picked a gift of vegetables for me. In the large Victorian style red-brick walled garden were rows of vegetables and a greenhouse. Elsewhere the permaculture garden had a 'Welcome to Permaculture' sign and was filled with different fruit and nut trees and multiple layers of food. Everywhere was busy, yet it all looked so...beautiful. It was the most beautifully arranged permaculture garden I'd ever seen.

"It's a jungle of beauty," said Hector emphatically. "Jenny is the gardener who's managed it the last ten years. There are four layers of food. The ground cover layer, your sort of perennial salads, through that you can plant your root vegetables. For example your onions next to your carrots (which keeps the carrot root fly away). Above that you have your shrubs like gooseberry. Then your trees above that. It doesn't *matter* if you don't pick everything; it just goes back into the ground as humus. This has been here for nearly twenty years," he said relaxing and smiling, affection coming into his voice. "As you can see, it's just... a jungle of food."

On the way back, Hector took me to see his cattle. Large long red hair and *big* horns (they were all bullocks). They had floppy fringes over their eyes that reminded me of the hairstyles boys had when I was a teenager.

"They have the highest rate of injuries to farmers, this breed..." he said cheerfully. After a couple of minutes Hector suggested that we move them to the other field as it would save him having to come out later with others.

"Err..." I said.

"It'll be fine, you just stand there by that fence then follow them slowly behind and I'll lead them." He opened the gate, then, hands in pockets, he started calling them by name and they stamped over. "Come on then. Come on, come on, come on!" he kept encouraging them.

I hurried up the slope after them and struggled with closing the gate. When I turned, they were already out of sight. The grassy garden slope alongside the lane had chunks out of it, in large fresh hoof-slide marks...

When I rounded the corner at a trot, I was relieved to see Hector getting the last bullock into the other field.

"It's a bit of a silly thing to do, to move them by yourself," he said looking a bit guilty, then laughing. "But I'm quite glad I got away with it. Don't want to have to go back and get a load of hippies out to get them, they sometimes stampede everywhere...but that's all part of the fun of them."

I wasn't certain if he meant the cattle or the hippies.

CHAPTER 9 — The Earl and Pilgrim

In Tiverton the rain was coming down heavily. Asking around, didn't give me any leads so I headed to the tea rooms at the edge of town, near the viaduct of the Grand Western Canal. Tea, cake and endless folding and unfolding of maps. Hopeful that the rain would let up, I studied my route.

In the days when a large number of goods were shipped between London and Bristol, ships were sometimes lost at sea as they navigated around Lands End. The Grand Western Canal was intended to connect the Bristol Channel and the English Channel. In 1796, an Act of Parliament granted permission for the canal, and the first section from Lowdells to Tiverton was finished in 1814. The canal is fed by a number of freshwater springs and is cut through deep embankments in places to keep it level. By the mid 1830's the full plan had to be abandoned because of the difficulties and cost, but the canal reached as far as Taunton, carrying coal and lime. The lime was used as an additive to soil.

Big lime kilns used to sit along the steep canal bank and lime would be loaded into the holes in the top, and after heating, the finished lime would be shovelled out of the arched chambers at the bottom onto the barges and pulled along the canal by horse.

I decided I could delay no more and set off. Pulling my giant poncho on and off over the backpack was a frustrating energetic struggle, of contortions, jumps, flicks and jiggles. After a while I realised the breaks in the rain weren't long enough to be worth it, so I just endured the sweating, in-between the downpours.

Flat, well-made paths and the quiet of the canal were a delight and although it wiggled around, it was much easier going than normal footpaths. I passed the ruins of some old lime kilns. Several beautiful villages passed by temptingly, and I took the opportunity to wash out some underwear in a pub sink and take some paper towel to stuff in my shoes at night.

During a break in the rain a cyclist passed me wearing a beautiful jumper and I called out a compliment. She stopped to chat for a while before continuing on. Occasionally I would pass underneath a bridge where a runner, dog walker or cyclist was sheltering, waiting out the showers. I greeted them cheerfully, and kept on. One bridge had both a walker and cyclist, already soaked, both sullenly checking their phones. The rain continued and water was squeezing out the toes of my shoes as I stepped.

"Eve!" I looked around in shock to find who was calling. Hanging out of her upstairs window which overlooked the canal, was the cyclist with the pretty jumper. "I've been watching out for you, come in for a cup of tea!" she called. Warmed and drier, when I set out an hour later the rain had stopped.

I came across an unexpectedly wide flat patch of grass by the canal side that looked like it should have been for a small bridge or a lock. It was perfect for my tent.

I sat outside for only a few minutes more after eating, because I began to be attacked.

"Bastards!" I shouted.

With the cloud cover it was nearly dark, and the mosquitoes were beginning to hunt. Mosquitoes are my enemies. They love me, I am their delicacy, their buffet, their delight. I used to regularly get four bites a night at home. Every few bites one would swell up to about the diameter of an eggcup. Every few dozen, one would swell up to the size of a dinner plate and I'd have to take anti-histamine. And once in a while, one would swell and keep swelling, until it encircled the whole limb and I'd have to go to the doctor for antibiotics. A bite on my feet would have paused the whole walk. Getting in to the tent was a vigilantly observed procedure, as close to an airlock as I could manage: outer zip, boots off, inner zip, bed socks on, legs in the sleeping bag, then breathe.

In the morning it is chill with a beautiful mist hovering over the canal as the sun rises. Crunchy oat bars have become my breakfast of choice, cheap and quick. I can be on my way in less than half an hour from waking.

After the canal ends I pass an old stone barn, and it looks like a war zone. The plaster has fallen off in chunks and the wall is largely made of a brown crumbly looking substance, elsewhere stonework is visible. There are deep rows of holes that look like bullet holes. As I get near I hear buzzing. Then I see the bees, masonry bees I'm guessing. There are dozens of them, flying in and out of the holes. The only other time I've seen something like that was a sandstone cliff on a beach.

A detour to Cotford St Luke near Taunton will let me stay with a university friend of Miranda's. The village is relatively new and the entire village does not exist on the map I have from the library, so I have the strange quest of heading to where I think it should be and then following the directions kindly given to me by Miranda's friend.

On the way to the village, walking up a gently sloping field, I pass lots of clumps of reeds. They are as tall as me with a meter or two between them and they sit in a natural looking arrangement that looks very pretty. I'm confused for a minute at the sight of something that does not appear to be a crop. Then I spot a raised blue-plastic barrel on the edge of the field.

The next morning I am walking through fields and along streams, and for ten minutes straight I hear gunshot almost every second. I wonder how many of the birds that were hiding in those reeds are left. I wonder if somewhere at the end of the day there will be a heap of carcasses, because they've shot more than they want to eat.

Miranda told me to go to the Lush shop in Taunton, she'd called them and told them about the walk. When I get there I am greeted with celebration. A tea and a seat quickly come and then I'm offered a foot massage! Soaking my feet in a fizzing blue bowl then having them rubbed with a scrub and oils is an amazing treat. I must be the luckiest person to be able to do this walk.

It's at this point that I had to say goodbye to a couple of pairs of socks. After all the rain I hadn't been able to dry things on the back of my pack, and a couple of pairs of socks had rotted. I put my last clean pair of socks on after the massage and hoped I'd get a dry spell.

I wandered with hazy curiosity around Taunton but it felt like I was dowsing where there was no water so I headed out west along the River Tone to camp.

The next day began in the Levels; kilometres of drained land in Somerset with canalised rivers and streams. I passed a couple of men with a large flexible pipe and a noisy bowser and motor. It was only afterwards that I realised it was a mobile pumping truck; they were pumping the water from one ditch to another to reduce the flooding. The last day of April, but the effects of the winter floods remained.

Passing a house, I stopped to ask for water.

"You're very lucky," the man told me. "A couple of weeks ago you wouldn't have been able to get through. All this was flooded...for months." He gestured to the road, fields and paths. The flooding had stopped just short of his house and had cut him off from the main road.

Thinking of all the life and biodiversity before the wetlands were drained and turned into crops put me in a sombre mood. Climbing up towards Stoke St. Gregory by chance I passed an environmental outdoor education space. Boards within it showed the expanse of Somerset that would flood naturally without flood defences. It was most of it.

With a changing climate, how long would make sense to hold the waters back? What would happen to these people? Would we collectively take responsibility for our climate refugees or just leave capitalism to deal with them once they could no longer get house insurance?

At the top of the hill I found the owners of the environmental centre. It turned out to be a willow farm. Also at the farm were a free Willow and Wetlands visitors centre, museum, workshops and café. Looking out at the Levels from the environment education space had filled me with sadness, but the people at the willow centre helped restore me.

Baskets and boxes of all shapes and sizes. Trays, fencing, garlands and hoops all woven out of willow. Stacks of willow for people to make their own items. I turned around in the shop, smiling at all the biodegradable products that could be bought instead of synthetic. My favourite by far though, were the coffins.

Woven by hand in different shades of willow, each coffin took about twelve hours to make. With no metal in them, the coffins were fastened with wooden toggles, while the edges were a line of nestled V shapes like a Celtic knot. Unsurprisingly the coffins are becoming one of their best selling products. In a large concrete room five craftspeople were each working in their own area in stern concentration.

Most of the willow grown on the farm doesn't actually end up woven at all though. Next time you look at a charcoal drawing you're probably looking at some of this willow. The majority of artist charcoal in Europe comes from this one farm.

They gave me a gift of some charcoal and I looked forward to finding someone artistic to give it to. About half the projects I visited gave me something, which I was able to pass on to someone else. It became quite a fun game for me, trying to guess the best person to give which thing to, waiting for a sign.

Down the other side of the ridge, the shapes of further hills ahead rose up out of the plains. I passed a village called Beer. You've got to love the way the English name villages. The sun was beaming hot and I ran out of water again. The day was filled with long, straight, flat roads. Dehydration began to feel uncomfortable and added to the aching pain in my hips. At the end of an imaginarily 'endless' road I reached a farm, but the gate had angry warning signs and barbed wire all over it. I'd started walking eleven hours earlier and by this point I was exhausted. My hips, shoulders and knees were very painful and I was desperate for some water.

I was aiming for a campsite, up on a hill and I couldn't see how I could make it the last bit up the hill. But I did, very slowly over the next three quarters of an hour. I shuffled painfully into the campsite, only to discover I didn't have enough cash.

Over another hour later I made it to the cash point. My hips were too painful to take more than narrow steps. Be very wary of a 'mile' – it is a generic term used by lots of people, which can mean anything from less than a kilometre, to more than four miles. By the time I got there I was moving like an old woman, bent and shuffling.

I gathered up the food I would need for the next couple of days, and cash, but as I left the shop I knew I couldn't face walking back. The sky was nearly fully dark. When I reached the main road, I forlornly stopped and stuck out my thumb. I shuffled on a bit more, before coming to a wretched stop.

"Hey, would you like a lift?" The driver was a bearded rocker in his twenties in a black gig t-shirt. My saviour.

"*Yes*. Yes please." I lowered myself into the seat, while my joints shouted at me for my disrespect.

"You looked like you were really struggling in Sainsbury's."

"Yeah, I overdid it today. Long walk. Thank you *so*, so much. It is *so* kind of you," I breathed.

Walking to the sink to brush my teeth at the campsite was a no-go. Unless I was imminently going to pee myself, I wasn't moving from my tent. I leaned out of the tent to spit and lay down as my hips reiterated just how displeased they were.

The following morning, although still very sore, I was able to move around at normal speed. It was incredible.

"*I am so grateful for my youth. Sleep is a wonderful amazing thing. Body, you are an amazing wonderful thing. Thank you so much, I am so sorry for yesterday.*"

The campsite owners took pity on me and gave me a lift into Glastonbury. They'd run the campsite together for more than four decades and lived there for longer.

"Has it changed much?" I asked.

"Glastonbury has. It used to be a market town...But now...It's full of shops...that you'll probably like."

Back through Street we passed the out-of-town large corporate warehouse stores and an outlet village that must support Glastonbury's shoppers.

Glastonbury was busy as the couple dropped me off by the ruined Abbey. Around me were old two-storey buildings and coaches of tourists. The red brick and light stone buildings certainly looked like a pretty market town. As I started to walk further into the town centre things immediately looked different.

Dishevelled people in colourful rag-edged natural cloths were wandering around. People with backpacks, dyed hair, dreadlocks, decorated wellies, others with cloaks. "*It's not even the Glastonbury Festival*," I thought. "*Is it always like this?*" Shops with the word 'Avalon' in, with fairies in the windows. In all I counted around two-dozen shops selling crystals, statues of fairies, colourful clothing, Pagan and magic books. Elsewhere were alternative medicines, African and Indian imported goods, and meditation and yoga. Often the shops were next door to each other, and all were apparently thriving.

I understood now what the couple had meant. How must this all seem to the old farmers? Although I have a number of Pagan practices and think crystals are wondrous, I didn't feel inclined to buy anything. Some things felt so raw in their commercial nature. How were those crystals mined? Is that statue plastic and made in China?

Seeking sanctuary I followed signs to the library but it was closed. Wandering around, I saw signs to another library. Opening the big oak door it turned out to be a library of mystical seeming books. The Library of Avalon describes its collection as esoteric. The books include religion, magic, legend, environment and psychology. The volunteer librarians were very kind and when I asked where to start hunting for environmentalists they told me I needed free cannabis.

I wondered what they thought I looked like.

Free Cannabis turned out to be a man, who legally

changed his name in support of the plant. The Hemp in Avalon shop is his business and his passion.

"It's a wonder plant," he said with love. "Food from the seeds, leaves and flowers. The seeds are a superfood, essential fatty acids, omega-3, omega-6 and rare omega-9. All eight essential amino acids as well as being mineral rich. It's a medicine too. You can make almost anything from the fibre of the stem or burn it as a fuel. It grows faster than wood. Chipboard, rope, clothes, paper, biodegradable plastics, hempcrete building blocks. Even back in the '30s Henry Ford made a hemp plastic car that ran on hemp ethanol. But the cotton and timber industries and the inventor of Nylon in the 30's were hugely successful at lobbying. A lot of politicians were in those industries too. So they got hemp made illegal."

Hemp is one of the earliest domesticated plants, we've been growing it for, a whopping... wait for it, over twelve... *thousand* years. Early Chinese paper was made from it, as were textiles across the East.

One of Free's suppliers, Sivargo, came in to drop off hemp t-shirts. "How long have you lived here?" I asked him.

"I came in 2004. It's the spiritual heart of England and people are drawn here." I raise a questioning eyebrow and nodded, inviting him to go on. "There are different chakra points around Earth. At the moment Glastonbury is the heart."

"So where do you two think I ought to go, while I'm in Glastonbury?" I asked them smiling.

"Tomorrow's Beltane so there'll be May Day celebrations."

"*Of course!*" I thought. "*That's why the visitors are in town.*" Sivargo handed me The Oracle.

Sadly I had not been bestowed with a cryptic all-knowing fortune teller. The Oracle was 'The unique free guide to holistic Glastonbury and local area'. My feet were feeling a bit raw from the previous day so I thanked them both and sought out a café to rest and consult The Oracle. In the café a lady in her late twenties told me she'd lived here all her life.

"There used to be shoe shops, and a Woolworths," she

said. "We get about a million tourists a year." I tried to imagine how many fairy statues that must add up to.

Flicking through The Oracle there were spiritual pilgrimages, family gatherings, oracle readings, hand-fasting services (a type of marriage), music, craft fairs, past-life regressions, feminine power, yoga and consciousness, lots of different therapies, earth walk – communing with the spirits of the land, and lots of dance lessons and events. I wondered though, once you had communed with the land spirits, where did you go to do something about protecting them?

There were some large Beltane celebrations the following day. Although I hadn't travelled far, it seemed I would be sticking around. Beltane is a Pagan festival celebrating spring and fertility, often using bonfires in the evening.

I rang up Miranda as my safety contact to let her know where I would be staying. She had instructions from me that if she did not hear from me for two days, she was to start a search. I might have been in rather a state after two days but because sometimes I might not have signal or battery I didn't want her to cry wolf.

"I'll find somewhere to pitch the tent, maybe near the Tor," I said with far more ease than I felt.

"I'm so jealous!" she said. "I can't believe you're in Glastonbury for Beltane." Miranda's own May Day celebrations in Oxford would involve listening to the 5am choir and jumping in the river, both Oxford traditions for the last five hundred years.

I felt compelled to recommence the search for environmentalists. Maybe they would be at the Tor. Dragging myself and my enormous pack slowly up the hill I started to scout out places where I might be able to pitch my tent later. Above me the Tor loomed. I was halfway up, just before a gate. I felt like I *should* go up, because it was Glastonbury after all, but I was so tired. Constantly trying to find people was mentally tiring and my body was still recovering from the day before. There was a feeling of guilt if I stopped.

"Other people get to have breaks. It's okay to sit and enjoy a moment," I persuaded myself. *"Do what you need. Stop*

searching and look after yourself." So I flumped my pack down and started to spread out my poncho to sit on. No sooner had I begun, than a woman coming down the Tor asked,

"Are you going to camp here?" The tone wasn't hostile.

I turned around. She looked friendly and was dressed in smart casual outdoor clothes. I decided on honesty.

"Well, not right here, but yes probably somewhere on the Tor. I thought I'd sit and rest for a bit," I answered smiling.

She returned the smile and came closer. "We camped near here for several weeks when we were in between houses a few years ago. Are you here for Beltane?"

"No, that's just good luck. I'm walking finding people doing things for the environment. Do you want to sit for bit?"

"I've got friends all over the world." Trinity told me a while later, "and all of them are reporting the weather doing strange things; monsoons coming too early and the like."

Trinity does conscious cooking for a living. She creates recipes to help people in their spiritual journeys.

Large grey clouds moved slowly in our direction as we chatted. We munched some dried apricots and dates and then I had my hard boiled eggs and oatcakes. Some conscious cooking sounded like a good idea for my spiritual journey.

"It's hard to change society, we just have to totally step out of our comfort zone, because it's not working at the moment," she said. "Going to protests and normalising dissent is part of it. Going to things, sharing food together and connecting."

"I'm surprised there isn't more obvious environmentalism in Glastonbury," I said.

"Yes...it can be difficult place to organise in, difficult characters," was all she said and I didn't want to pry.

The clouds looked like they would soon leak so we packed up, Trinity for home and me for a pub. As I walked back into town the rain began to fall in irregular splots.

"Where do you think I should go for shelter?" I asked a couple. "I'm on a long environmental walk."

"There's the George and Pilgrim on the high street. That would be appropriate," they offered.

"Pilgrim...that does sound right. Good plan, thanks!" I said.

As I got near the pub the rain was beginning in earnest so I hurriedly wobbled the last bit down the high street. Inside was the cosiness of an old English pub: nooks, wooden panelling, stone floors, arched windows, big fireplaces. Every table was full of people who looked like they intended to be there a while, except for one small empty table with three little stools. I dumped my bag at the table and my layers, approaching the bar in my bright yellow and black striped polar neck tank top that bulged unappealingly around my boobs.

Ordering my cup of tea I overheard the two men next to me. They had just met up and were saying they should go find a seat, but didn't think there were any. The thinner faced man saw me over his friend's shoulder.

"Do you *like* that top?" he asked, incredulous.

"I do," I answered cheerfully; "it makes people like you talk to me. I'm doing a walk around England about the environment, called The Buzz Tour, so I dress as a bee."

Both men had turned around with interest.

"Oh, well I'm the local Green Party member. My name is Earl," said the second man with a weary smile.

"Ha!" I said loudly, beaming. "I've been looking for you all day! Would you like to sit down and join me? I've got a table with three seats."

CHAPTER 10 – A well and Wells

There is a certain thrill when something happens serendipitously - a feeling that you're on the right path; that you are exactly where you are supposed to be, at exactly the right time.

"I've been a Green Party member for thirty years," Earl told me. "It started with an anti-road protest. Now the environment minister Owen Patterson wants a new wave of road building."

"I think I saw a leaflet about that, but it's not something I noticed on the media," I said.

"If you want to know what's going on," Earl told me, "read the news about the country from outside of it. The bias in our media is all the way through. For England I use Al Jazeera or Russia Today."

"What are you working on in Glastonbury?" I asked.

"Well three years ago I started the Avalon Community Energy Cooperative (ACE). Because basically we're all being ripped off by the big energy guys. With a co-op the dividends and money stay in the community."

"Fantastic! I'd love to find out more about that," I said.

"What do you do for shelter as you walk?" Earl asked me as he finished his drink.

"Sometimes the groups I visit put me up, or I have a tent."

"Well you're welcome to crash at mine tonight. We're going to go and do some jamming...you coming?"

"Thanks! Absolutely, sounds great," I said nodding. It might seem a little strange for me to go to stay with a man I'd just met fifteen minutes earlier but I was in no doubt that I was not only safe, but with exactly the person I was supposed to meet. Earl's manner was slightly world-weary, kind and utterly relaxed. It took me half a minute to gather all my layers and put my bag back on. Far quicker than the five minutes it used to take at the start of the walk. Now I knew the eccentricities of all my things and the exact order they had to be put on in.

We crossed the street to Earl's upstairs flat. It was full of his paintings; on the walls and in stacks against the furniture. The lounge had sofas, coloured cushions, a painting area and a day bed. There were also lots of healthy-looking houseplants.

Earl lives with chronic pain, which means he rarely leaves the house. Roy had been busking in the street below for the previous week. Having watched him for days from the window, Earl struggled downstairs and asked him if he wanted to go for a pint and do some jamming. Although the George and Pilgrim was just across the street from Earl's house, because of the pain of walking there, you wouldn't often find him in it.

We sat in the lounge as they played guitar and sang. One very large painting behind Earl was of a river, edged with white floating lilies. I joined in loudly with the songs I knew. Snuggling back into my chair, with music, paintings and interesting companions, I felt elated at my good fortune.

The next morning I rose at six thirty to go to The Chalice Well for the Beltane celebrations. The Chalice Well is one of the oldest holy wells in Britain. The Tor was surrounded in mist as light rain came down. I could see the hazy silhouettes of about a dozen hardy folk up on the Tor.

When I arrived at the well garden there was a group of about forty people milling around by a café shed. Some of the women were in long coloured skirts. Benches surrounded a small bonfire. The garden had a large flat lawn with a tiny curving stream through it, and carefully planted flowerbed slopes. It took me a little while to realise that the ceremony was taking place further into the gardens. Inside a walled garden, the water was channelled into two rectangular shallow stone pools where people could bath in the healing waters. The well cover was lifted - a beautiful dark wood circle with curving metal around the edge and decoration across it. The well itself was decorated with flowers and a couple of people sat in quiet contemplation around it.

I could hear drums and someone projecting their voice in a happy but serious way. Through a doorway in the brick wall, the view opened up into a clearing with steeply sloped sides. The effect was like an amphitheatre and there were a hundred or so people gathered, many wearing flowers or colourful clothing, covered by anoraks to protect them from the drizzle.

There were many different parts to the ceremony, which was already well underway by the time I arrived. Water, fire, earth and air were being honoured with different prayers. We all then held hands and an embrace of peace and love was passed around from one person to the next. There was clapping and singing, with a small band using traditional instruments, including various drums. The two women and one man conducting the ceremony were dressed in loose-fitting long clothes, dresses, tunics, cloaks, bright colours and flowers. There were fertility dances, and a symbolic passing of the maypole through a hoop, to fast clapping, cheers and suggestive laughter.

The maypole was then carried to where it would be used later in the day for the dances. During the maypole dances, colourful ribbons attached to the top of the pole are held by the dancers as they pass under and over each other, creating a woven pattern around the pole.

It was time to get out of the rain and get some breakfast, so I headed back to Earls to find out more about ACE.

"What we want to do is set up a combined energy park. So it's not just a field full of solar panels. And combine the different energy production with food production," Earl told me. A big poster board showed a drawing of what the energy cooperative hoped the park would look like, with crops, pools and sheds.

"For example," continued Earl, "there will be chickens in the sheds and solar panels on the roof. Then the chicken muck will be used in an anaerobic digester."

"Ooo, I love anaerobic digesters – using waste to generate bio-gas, lovely," I said. "What do you think of these solar panel farms? All that tech, and isn't it a waste of farmland?"

"You can plant the fields with wildflowers, and sheep can still graze them, underneath the panels," said Earl.

"Ahhhh. I'd assumed they would break them," I said.

"Cattle would, but sheep are fine," said Earl.

"That's sounding better. What about all these other parts?" I said gesturing to the drawing. "You'd grow hemp?"

"Yes, the waste digestate from the anaerobic digester gets spread on the land to feed the hemp. The hemp seed can be made into oil and the fibres into insulation and the plants can also be fed to fish in aquaponics," said Earl.

"I've heard of aquaponics, but don't know much. It's using fish isn't it, rather than hyrdoponics which is plants?" I asked.

"It combines the two because the waste from the fish is fed into your hydroponics to feed the plants. You use what energy works best in an area, but the principles of mixing energy technologies and food production is what's great. Here on the levels in Somerset we've got a lot of water and a lot of old peat diggings, and that's a great way of storing energy.

"A windmill would pump water up to store it in an ex-peat digging reservoir. Then, when we need electricity, the water will flow through a micro hydro-electric. It's like a battery. Solar thermal would heat the fish and chickens. The tubes are filled with a liquid that doesn't freeze and transfers the sun's heat to pipes in a hot water tank.

"I had some pretty serious health problems around fifteen years ago and I was basically housebound most of the time but I still wanted to engage with other locals to make things happen. It was difficult at first because you're starting something that no-one knows if it's possible. Then we got together a team of about six of us and we got it to go. We're going for government funding and we'll do a share offer.

"The Centre for Sustainable Energy in Bristol, they've been helping us a lot. The Cooperative movement and Greens have been helping us a lot too. As a company you do a share offer and the shareholders get paid a dividend. Well if they're all local people, it's very different from paying one of the big six energy companies.

"What we do today has a cost," said Earl, "but we're not gonna bear it. It's the future generations that pay, because there's always a time lag. Our carbon emissions are going into the ocean, building up energy like a dynamo that will be increasingly hard to stop."

I nodded sombrely and we stared at empty space.

"Have you been to The Green Gathering?" asked Earl.

"No, I've heard of it, but never been," I said.

"You really should go," he said. "You'll find lots of environmentalists all in the same place."

"I'll have to see if I can go there," I said.

On Earl's advice I was to head to Wells to find Maddy Milns, who was also involved with ACE as well as Transition Wells. I was relieved when she answered her phone. I explained about the walk and that I'd been talking to Earl about ACE.

"Would you have time to meet me and tell me about your work?" I asked. Her tone was busy but she agreed to a coffee.

As I walked to Wells, the rain became heavy and persistent; my waterproof wasn't up to it, and although the poncho kept my torso dry everything else was wet. When I got there I bought a new waterproof jacket (in bee yellow) and went to meet Maddy.

"I knew one of the other founders of ACE through the Green Party," she told me. "We appointed an energy consultant and that provided the group with lots of expertise and shortcuts. Leapfrog is an organisation that provides help to groups like ours. We're really fortunate to have a great range of skills in the team: organising, financial, local politicians and two people who work in renewable energy."

"What about Transition Wells?" I asked, "How long have you been involved with that?"

"It's been going for four or five years," said Maddy. "What Transition talks about is that we need to transition from a society that's predominantly reliant on fossil fuels, oil in particular, and prepare for a future where there isn't any oil.

We've reached peak oil, now it's the hard-to-get stuff. We need to find renewable resources. As a grandmother, the future is important to me. I think it's everybody's responsibility to do what they can to secure the future. How are you funding the journey?" asked Maddy.

"By donations," I said. "We did a crowdfunding appeal before I left which bought the backpack, jacket and will get some food, but it won't cover campsites."

"Where will you stay then?" she asked.

"People I visit have put me up or I've got my tent. People have let me camp in their gardens or I find a little spot."

"Where are you going to stay in Wells?" she asked.

"I don't know yet. Sometimes churches let you sleep in the churchyard," I said. Maddy said she would check with her husband but I might be able to stay with them. "Thank you! Well, see how he feels about it," I said.

A few minutes later she came back and confirmed that we could head to her place together for dinner.

Various outdoor and exercise shoes and clothing were hung or stacked near the door at Maddy's house. A friendly dog greeted us and we went through into the open-plan kitchen-lounge with full-length windows looking out onto the garden. While dinner was cooking, we chatted on the sofa.

"Tell me a bit more about Transition Wells," I said enthusiastically. "What sorts of things do you do?"

"At first we showed public films, and then a lot of people wanted action. The core group kept going and became more action-focused. We ran a swapping event a few times to reduce waste. Retired people were able to give their time, which was essential. We got a grant and were able to get a thermal imaging camera and offer free heat surveys of people's homes. We're going to run an energy day with exhibition space for companies, with speakers and free entry.

"I started attending the Transition Wells meetings in 2010 and it's been a very inspiring time; meeting lots of really interesting people from all parts of the community, all joining together, because they want a better future for their grandchildren. I'm very motivated by working for a *community* in that way. Wells is small enough that you feel you can have a big effect. In my view it's about bringing people with you. Transition is deliberately not political but it attracts people who care about the environment."

"How did you get support?" I asked.

"Contacting and influencing local leaders is important," said Maddy, "and them recognising their responsibility to lead."

After dinner there was more discussion, ranging from our experiences and feelings on family, love and society, to life purpose. I felt a great affinity with Maddy and that we were able to talk about things close to our hearts, although we had only met that day. Maddy shared a metaphor with me from a team day she had been on once.

"We were all in a big circle and given drums. We were told to keep drumming. Whatever happens, you must keep drumming...but of course you can't. Sooner or later your hand hurts and you have to stop. But what we found was, as long as even just one person kept tapping quietly, other people would come back in and it would crescendo again. But if everyone stopped nobody wanted to start again, we felt we had failed.

"If someone keeps it going even if it's really quiet, other people will eventually come back in. You have to rest. The important thing is not to give up. Sometimes you can make a suggestion and the time isn't right. It's about just keeping suggesting it and eventually the time will be right."

The following morning Maddy shared ideas of people to find, and then the conversation moved on to women's liberation.

"So much of it is overcoming learned behaviour and internalised oppression," she said.

"Yeah," I agreed, "it's all around us, reinforcing the behaviour. Do you know that rule to look for in films?"

"Two women who talk about anything that isn't men?"

I nodded. "Few films pass it, and if you then check if they speak positively, there's even less. So all the time films are telling us, other women are your enemy – evil stepmothers, bitchy colleagues, false friends. Your status and safety comes only from men. You must please men to succeed or live through your sons," I said.

"It's such an unhealthy message, that we have to see and to overcome. Strong communities will be so important to survive the future," said Maddy.

Maddy told me what she learned about disaster resilience from a friend at the Centre for Sustainable Energy (CSE).

"In an area near a city all the plans focus on the large population centres. There's limited resources so in times of disaster, Bristol would get all the emergency services and emergency aid. The smaller rural populations here would be left to fend for themselves."

"Wow. Yeah, I hadn't thought of that. In Canada they train up ordinary people so they are ready and in the right place, because they're more remote. We're less self-reliant here."

"Part of it is a lack of awareness. It's important to show the weaknesses of the system and make the corporate criminals visible," said Maddy.

I was left with a lot to think about as I waved Maddy goodbye.

North of Wells the land rises up into the Mendip hills. Spring is later here; the wild garlic isn't flowering yet. As I go up the hill there is a big drop in temperature, then cold air hits me in full at the top. Lots of the trees haven't got their leaves yet, which surprises me. Thankfully there is a large tree with buttressing roots and a me-sized nook, so I can eat my oat bar. The cold wind can drain your energy really quickly without you realising and when you've got a long way to go it's not a good idea to try and tough it out.

After I sat down, a couple of riders came past, training for the Golden Horseshoe race across Exmoor. It made me think of Surfers Against Sewage. Although surfers are not primarily environmentalists they mobilised effectively to campaign against pollution. Horse Riders against Climate Change? Climate change affects everything, yet it is harder for most people to react to than simple pollution.

The large lakes and open hilly vistas of the Mendips filled me with joy. I was enjoying the magnificent view when a bullock came over the brow of the hill...then another came over. I stopped admiring, and started walking firmly towards where I hoped the stile would be, over the hill. As I crested the rise I saw that it was a very large field indeed.

I was halfway across it and the other fifteen to twenty bullocks quickly mobilized in front of me.

My heart beat banged in my throat as I put my arms out either side of me and began to walk in a dead straight line to the stile. Generally cows don't seem to charge unless they are startled, you have a dog, or you get between them and their young. But bullocks, well, they can be a tad frisky.

The young cattle came from across the field to form a loose group facing me, blocking my way.

"Cuuuuuming throooo. Cuuuuuming throooo," I said loudly and calmly which made them stop, and some of them retreated. After a minute, a couple of them seemed to regain their courage, egged on by the others, and moved towards me with their heads down, legs jumping and stamping.

I was very relieved that Steph and Miranda were not there. "*They would not be enjoying this at all*," I thought.

Two of the bullocks were stamping their feet.

One large bullock broke away from the group, and with his head down, began to trot towards me.

CHAPTER 11 – Word pollution

I kept walking straight at the bullock, annoyed at how hard my heart was beating. "CuUUming throOO. CuUUming throOO," I said again.

The bullock continued towards me, but at the last second it jumped to the side and ran away, to the back of the group. Then the second one started to approach but lost its nerve before going very far and moved to the side. With their two champions defeated, the other bullocks moved out of the way as I came through and formed an escort either side of me. The first one was the only one to stay in front on me. It kept running in front of me then turning to try and face me down, each time moving to the side a little earlier and running away. By now it seemed more like a very large and playful puppy; one that would easily break my foot.

I made it to the stile, closely surrounded by the bullocks, and swung up on to it with relief, looking down at them. If I hadn't been so frightened it would have been quite fun (same goes for life really).

"Good luck boys," I said in parting, wondering what their fate would be. I imagined them patting each other on the side and congratulating themselves on their bravery. That persistent little bugger would certainly have won himself some kudos.

"And did you see what Barry did? Charging like that?! Wow. He's gonna be the BULL."

I had to get to Bristol that night, in order to catch a train to Global Power Shift in London the following day, so I pushed on past Chew Lakes (which I'd seen from the hill), but as the afternoon wore on, I knew I wouldn't make it before dark.

It was part of the message of the journey for me to walk, to experience the reality. To recognise that walking is a normal and viable way to travel long distances. That we needn't be frightened of a future with less fossil fuels. But I didn't want to hurt myself for that message. The idea was mine and the person I must answer to was my own conscience.

There are no buses, so I begin to hitch. I head away from the pleasant lanes and walk along the nerve-jarringly busy roads with my thumb out. After two hours I manage to get a lift, so I should be just in time to meet a friend at the pub.

Riding in the car is fast and disconcerting, but walking through the city is more unnerving. There is an assault of words and colours. Caution CCTV Exit keep clear Goods yard Push button No skateboarding Warning Your key to happy.

Letters and numbers are on all the lampposts and I can't seem to stop reading everything. I had never noticed before. I must normally filter it out. Adverts are everywhere, stopping me from thinking. I keep catching people's eyes, some look so grateful. *For what? Eye contact?*

To let Cyclists dismount Emergency vehicles only Have you paid? *I don't know, have I?* Fire assembly point Booking offices No Smoking *Word pollution, cognitive white noise, madness.* No vehicles beyond this point *I doubt I'll own a car again.* Keep left *I'm not likely to go to the right but politics means nothing without a planet.* I'm not sure where reading ends and thought begins.

With relief I find the pub and order a lemonade just as my friend arrives.

"Hello you. There you are," said Fai, suddenly appearing beside me.

"It is *good* to see you my friend," I said looking at his face. Chinese features and a big smile always made him look younger than his years. Fai is one of those musicians who can jam along, or launch into a solo, not only on the guitar, but the piano, and most spectacularly, on the violin too.

The way I'd found to live with little money for the previous two years involved moving around quite a lot, filling gaps of need where I could find them. I pet-sat or did other work in exchange for food and accommodation. All of which meant that regular practice with a band wouldn't work.

We chatted in the pub about the journey, our old band, Fai's work on climate change and inevitably, about the emotions which arise from any honest look at the global climate crisis. The restrictions on scientists to explain the horror of climate change without any emotion. Fai was lamenting the way people don't react to the severity of climate change.

"When you tell someone upsetting news but you don't sound upset, it doesn't reach them," I said. "Every day we watch the news and someone who is not emotionally reacting tells us about things we really ought to be reacting to."

"I've not considered that aspect," said Fai.

"If the emotions are not engaged, we don't change." I said.

"But you can't force it," he said.

"Yeah, if you feel forced, it won't connect," I agreed.

"What are you doing with music these days?" asked Fai.

"Not counting improv, I haven't written a song in a year."

"What?! Well sort it out!" said Fai. I nodded smiling.

"My lyrics never seem enough now. How do you write a song about Armageddon? All the phrases have been abused by adverts or movies, it's cliché."

"Well, tonight you will!" said Fai slapping me on the back.

Fai's housemate Matt joined us and we walked to their flat in central Bristol. "I like the bustle," said Fai, "at the heart of it."

While Fai cooked dinner, Matt and he started a bottle, and the jokes flowed even faster than the wine. The banter whipped back and forth like a married couple but with more of the presence of a stage comedy duo. Sat on the back of the sofa with my legs on the seat, I watched the match like a tennis fan, and laughed squinting down into my tea.

In the corner my tent was drying. With the frequent rain I had had to keep putting it away wet and it was beginning to smell of rot and have tell-tale little brown spots. Matt brought his keyboard and drums out. Fai turned with a flourish and asked, "Well how *do* you write a song about Armageddon?"

"No idea!" I said laughing. I started a sing-song voice to the notes of The Sound of Music's 'How do you solve a problem like Maria?' "How do you write a song about Armageddon?"

Matt and Fai struck up the music and we improvised a few verses, interspersed with laughter. It felt physically amazing to relax with friends and to laugh. The songs began to come but other than the mad dancing around the room, the only thing I remember was a rock number I called the Bee Sting.

The next morning I walk briskly to the station smiling to myself, but the assault of adverts and instructions has me feeling edgy by the time I get there.

At the train station the audio instructions start too. "DON'T LEAVE YOUR BAGGAGE UNATTENDED" *Stop telling me what to do, what to think, I'm trying to think something else.* No Smoking Way Out. *Is there one?* Please ensure brake is <u>on</u> when on the platform and please stand back from the edge at all times.

If you look up, there are CCTV cameras everywhere you go in English cities, up high and out of your normal gaze. There are two first class and seven standard carriages on the train bound for London. There is a platform and train alteration with six minutes to go. The rumbling deep noise of the train engine obliterates any announcement. Stressed faces are all around me as we all turn questioningly to each other. Did you hear it? No, did you? Someone caught it and we rush off. Old people carry their luggage up and down stairs. After the running platform change we are waiting, and some people are smiling and laughing in their groups with relief. The new train has five standard carriages and three first class. Standard is busy. We are told we had to change because we needed a different train to London. From the conversations around me, people wrongly assume it was to give us a bigger train.

In London I feel like a photo that's been overexposed. Letting in too much information, white washed. It's one thing to observe, but the extent to which you are able to avoid reacting is a skill and takes energy. London feels like a psychological battleground, the frontline.

Global Power Shift began with an international conference in Istanbul in 2013. Its aims are to strengthen and diversify the climate movement. People from all around the world were invited to put themselves forward as climate leaders and then return to their countries to stimulate more action.

The UK Global Power Shift Conference came about as a result. The conference took place in the lecture theatres of University College London and although there were probably less than a hundred people, they represented a wide range of climate groups, many of which I hadn't heard of before.

Lindsay was one of a small group of volunteer organisers for the conference and was to be my host when I returned to Bristol. She was flushed and a little stressed but full of a deep warmth when we met. You could tell she was really *present* when she spoke to you.

The workshops and seminars included strategy, movement building, alternative economics, communicating climate change, and the upcoming COP climate talks in Paris. There was also mention of a terrifying proposed trade agreement called TTIP that I didn't emotionally take in at the time. When you reach out and look at the bigger picture it can be a huge relief. It can also tell you more things that you need to come to terms with. To hear the size and strength of other groups working on the problem was wonderful. One discussion that gave me a thrill was that of joint future actions for 38 degrees, 350.org and Avaaz. Physical action involving these three groups sounded amazing.

Both 38 degrees and Avaaz had only campaigned online at this point. At the time of writing Avaaz has around forty million members. In the five years since its launch it has become the most powerful online activist network in the world. 38 degrees is a UK online campaigning group with over 2.5 million members.

350.org is a worldwide climate change movement that calls for people to stop investing in fossil fuels. It was started in the USA by environmentalist Bill McKibben and his students. When you reduce or remove your investments from something, it is known as 'divestment'.

There was a great deal of understanding that day, a shared desire to come together for a shared purpose. Many of us talked about making the movement visible to each other. Everywhere I had walked I had found kind people protecting the environment.

Just how many of us are there?! How many others like us want to act on climate change? We all wondered. Many discussions were about solidarity – how to support others and recognise that their purpose and struggle is also ours. In reading about political change I learnt that significant change is usually preceded by a coming together of diverse struggles which had previously seemed unrelated. It sounded good.

I met up with Sheila, an activist film-maker, my host that night in London. As Sheila says, she's often 'the only brown face in the room' when she goes to environmental meetings and wants that to change. The first time I saw Sheila she was interviewing Caroline Lucas, the Green MP, during an anti-fracking sit-in at Balcombe. I was stood behind them on a chair doing legal observing. During the course of my four hours of observation I don't think I've ever heard someone speak more sense than Caroline Lucas did, about women's rights, our society and environment. After the interview, Sheila decided to sit down with Caroline and the others who were protesting. Bright signs, banners, colourful outfits and political chanting were all around us. Some people were drumming and playing music.

Caroline Lucas' son, arrived from another protest against the fracking site and sat down next to his mother. He was the first one they took.

I watched the police gradually become more aggressive and determined to remove the group, although it wasn't obstructing the fracking itself. The protest happened at the same time as the 'Reclaim the Power' anti-fracking camp and the fracking company had already decided to suspend operations for the duration of the camp. The sit-in group was composed largely of Disabled People Against the Cuts, so some were elderly and some were locked onto one person's wheelchair. One elderly man had to leave when he no longer had the strength to lie on the concrete. He left in tears. "I'm sorry," he kept saying, as everyone applauded him.

As the police formed lines to corral the wider protest group, two or three people pushed back. From my vantage point on the chair I saw four large riot vans behind the gate. The police got into the vans and put the visors down on their helmets. Along the road earlier I had counted another twenty or so police cars and riot vans.

The police told the press to leave as they could not guarantee their safety. I remember a Guardian photographer saying, a little disparagingly, that he had covered wars and would take his chances. The police formed a wall around the group and moved to block the view of all legal observers and press. So I never saw what happened next.

Amazingly, that wonderful photographer managed to get between someone's legs on the other side and, with a zoom lens, caught the moment that the police used a torture technique on Caroline's son. Pressing a thumb deep into the nerve on his neck caused him to howl in pain and release his arm from those next to him. It was only on seeing the photo the following day that I understood what had happened.

Caroline turned in distress and more police came and took Sheila from the other side. One by one they were picked off and taken to the waiting police vans. I wrote down what I saw, the names of the arrested, the badge numbers of the police, and called the activist legal team. It was the first time I'd seen people get arrested, and the first time I'd heard of an MP getting arrested protecting the environment.

"*I may not be in her constituency,*" I thought, "*but she's definitely my MP.*" It made a lasting impression that would later compel me to volunteer for two months in support of her re-election campaign.

I knew they would get bailed, but it felt like those entering the police van were disappearing into a black hole. There were over thirty people arrested for anti-fracking actions that day, and over 130 over three months. That evening and the next, there was huge cheering and relief as our bailed friends returned to the Reclaim the Power camp.

The next time I saw Sheila was at a protest performance against oil sponsorship of the arts, then again on the day of her and Caroline's trial. I sat in the court seats with a dozen others, an observer again, to give my thanks. When most people go to court they have one family member with them and it can be big help to know that people support you.

Travelling to Sheila's house there is another movie poster on a bus of a warrior man. Another advert on a van; "Saving the world from mediocre coffee". It's almost physically painful.

"Why am I doing this to myself?" I think. But there is a truth to beware of. Once you start to see, it is hard to stop. The Museum of Zoology says. "Engage with rare and beautiful specimens." *Very dead specimens. The live specimens are becoming rarer by the day. What does it mean to engage?*

The next morning I find I can't face going in to the conference. As we sit on high stools at the kitchen table with our tea and toast, Sheila's cat bats its food-ball around. We chat about Sheila's work as an activist filmmaker, the walk, the future, and occasionally, I burst into tears. When I go to the loo I realise my period has started. *"Ah, at least that explains the crying,"* I think with relief.

I make it to the conference for the afternoon discussion groups and leave with a feeling that I've stuffed my brain full of new people and new ideas, like nuts in a chipmunk's pouches. I will have to carry them with me and take them out individually to eat later. The ideas, not the people. This is not a horror novel. Giant Killer Chipmunk.

CHAPTER 12 — Writing on the wall

There had been a mix-up for my first night back in Bristol, Lindsay wouldn't be back for another day or two and Fai was away. We called around people we knew and Miranda put things out on social media asking if anyone could put me up. I received a phone call from a woman I'd never met, mentioning a person I didn't know, offering to put me up for the night. I had no idea how she had found out about it, but I accepted with eager gratitude.

Walking to her street the houses and yards seem messy, but there is a box of vegetables being offered for free. "What do you need?" Jacqueline meets me with unselfconscious generosity at the door, as if it is the most usual thing in the world for her to offer her home to strangers. She chats with a couple of her neighbours. Another friend is helping her to fix her van. Jacqueline's housemate Grace is intensely working on some coursework but pauses while we all sit down to dinner.

Grace and Jacqueline had only moved to Bristol a year ago for a Practical Sustainability course, and decided to stay. Jacqueline was now going to study leather tanning and Grace makes willow baskets as a hobby. In the lounge I saw a stack of the same willow bundles from the willow farm in Somerset.

In 2015 Bristol is to be the European Green Capital, and funding and attention is flooding into the city in preparation. With our current mobile population, once a city gets a reputation for something, people, courses and organisations move there, and it reinforces the reputation. Many of my friends had moved there in the previous year and I was looking forward to seeing some of the things that were drawing them.

Walking through Easton in Bristol I see a lot of run-down looking properties and untended gardens, but then sometimes vegetables and plants are offered for free. It's a more racially diverse part of the city. Sofas and mattresses are outside a couple of houses. Some houses are painted in bright colours. Colourful graffiti pictures are in a number of back streets, dark and spiky, a bit aggressively masculine in style, but not overtly violent or sexually oppressive. There are women and mixed ages all around, but also a couple of men sat alone with alcohol.

Quite a lot of people stare at my breasts which look rather unseemly strapped into the rucksack. It makes me feel bad. I decide either not to wear the tank top or not to have the chest strap done up in public, even if it's painful. That's all it can take to enforce conformity, a stare. I aspire not to care.

The cycle path is teeming with people, walking and on bikes, with and without children. I realise its bank holiday Monday, May the 5th. The days have gotten a bit lost to me.

Despite the mix of politics in the area, it is the huge billboards of the well-financed UKIP that I keep seeing. Leading up to the European Parliamentary elections they are everywhere. One poster shows the four male party leaders, three with EU symbol gags over their mouths. In my mind's eye I see a fourth gag over UKIP, labelled prejudice. There is no picture of the female Green Party leader Natalie Bennett. In fact at this point I have never seen her on TV or in a newspaper, although the Green Party is polling level with the Liberal Democrats.

Many people I had met had conflicting views about whether to vote at all. With the European and the general elections approaching is was a passionate question. Many people, especially younger voters, want a 'no confidence' vote for the entire political system. Russell Brand famously expressed what many young people are feeling when he called for people to not vote, although he shows support for Caroline Lucas. If we do decide not to vote, it is assumed to be apathy or consent unless we take steps to be 'counted' as dissenting voters. Those considering a non-vote are those most likely to vote for radical reform, so without them the remaining vote moves towards the status quo.

I find the Eastside Roots Community Garden sitting around the edge of Stapleton Road train station, which used to be fearfully avoided by local residents. The community group was given the land temporarily until the station was developed. About half of the space of the project remains, as development has now begun. Tiers of flowers and vegetables go up the slope and a cat is sitting on the steps. It's been very successful in creating a community space where people feel safe enough to come, reducing drug dealing and crime. Soon the other half will be built over too, but however long a project like this lasts, it shows what can be achieved in those time gaps. How tenacious life, and people, are.

I wander around but when I see a sign to St Werburgs City Farm, it feels like an invitation to a treasure hunt. There are gardens with raised food beds that are part of the farm, but the farm itself is further on under the railway bridge.

The sign reads "Welcome to St. Werburgs City Farm! A green oasis in the heart of the city. Entrance is free, but as a small charity, donations are gratefully received." Dozens of families are all around the farm enjoying the sheep, goats, chickens, ducks and pigs. There are houses just opposite the field and a large area of allotments nearby. At a time when many people in cities have little understanding of agriculture, access to a city farm can have life changing consequences. I find Becky in the office and ask about her volunteering.

"I care for the animals and during the week we have clients in, adults with learning difficulties," she tells me.

"How did you find out about the farm?" I ask her.

"I always knew about the farm but as a child I'd never been, although I only live ten minutes away. It seems stupid that I'd never been. I started doing an animal management course and I needed work experience for that. So I came down here and started doing work experience when I was sixteen. That got me interested in farm animals and I went on to do agriculture at Harper College, and managed to pass that, somehow, with a distinction. Now I have a boyfriend who's a farmer weirdly enough, so I help out on his farm and work here still."

"Wow so quite a change," I say.

"Yeah, coming from a non-farming background to this," she says smiling with her hands in her pockets.

The farm has a large children's playground and a café that looks like it has been designed by either by Gaudi or a Hobbit. The curving wooden building with organically-shaped curving windows was indeed designed to copy the famous style of Gaudi's work in Barcelona. Don't be deceived, I know almost nothing about architecture, but when I visited Barcelona I fell in love with Gaudi's buildings, so he's the only famous architect I know. The shapes, the mosaics, the colours! No other buildings seem so *right*. His work seems to me to call up the best of what beauty could be in a building, to lift my heart up to the wonder of human creative love for a space.

The pillars inside the café are shaped like tree trunks with branches, and everywhere there are natural curves. Sitting inside with a hot chocolate, I smilingly film the building and a woman working on a laptop asks me what I'm doing. When I explain my quest she tells me that she runs a company helping people to build their own homes. Steffie has a warm smile and a very open look to her face so it's very easy to sit and chat as if we already know one another.

"I've got a business called Bright Green Futures, helping people with self-build houses," Steffie tells me. "I've always seen climate change as the most pressing issue to the world. I went to university to study renewable energy and I built a house in an eco-housing community. So I really wanted to help other people to live in a really beautiful space that is also caring for the planet and each other. But I was stuck in conventions, I was a single mum with children so I thought I had to keep my job, to keep a stable income. There were lots of things I didn't know and I was scared. My consultancy job was environmental but limited; it was only ever projects that the government would fund. Then I did training with an organisation called Balanced View about Open Intelligence. It is really about being natural and relaxed all the time and finding your own solutions to any problems. Once I started the training my world really opened up, all my relationships became completely harmonious. In terms of setting up Bright Green Futures as a business, I was scared but I was totally able just to do it anyway.

"Now three years down the line, we've got the most eco-friendly, the first A-rated housing development in Bristol. The people who worked on it, loads of them said they've never had so much fun working somewhere. We're living there with other people who are training with Balanced View, so we're all supporting each other. We're bringing our children up in that kind of space which is totally respectful and loving all the time. I know you probably don't believe that that's possible!" she says laughing. "I wouldn't have believed it until I actually saw it, and I wouldn't have believed I could do what I've actually achieved, and that it could come easily. It feels so nice to live a life where you take care of the planet, and of your friends, and of yourself. To people who don't, you can say 'we don't have to live like this, we can all get together and solve all the world's problems.' Bit by bit, we will do it."

I'd been constantly addressed by billboards in Bristol, but there's a different kind of public messaging famous in Bristol —graffiti. Passing back under the railway bridge I meet a man with a spray can adding to the already full graffiti mural along the long wall and I stop to chat. He is putting an outline on a large picture, then his tag (graffiti signature).

"I didn't do the picture. Bit cheeky really," he admits. I'm put in mind of my parents' neighbour's cat, spraying the bushes.

Some graffiti is simple 'tagging' where the writer marks an area or is leaving a message for a specific group. The tag is often repeated all over an area. Other graffiti may include more complex artwork or wider political messaging.

Bristol is the home of Banksy, the now world-known graffiti artist whose art challenges ideas and questions dominant culture. A masked man throwing a bunch of flowers, a girl with a red heart balloon, and two male police kissing passionately are a tiny fraction of the work of this prolific artist. Many of the images interact with the surroundings, for example appearing to come out of a window. The images sometimes have a space to allow the viewer to become part of it, for example by pretending to hold something.

The identity of Banksy is unknown, but it is almost certain that there is a support team involved and the works are accomplished through collaboration. Banksy has never been caught, which is amazing considering the scale of work including a month-long daily campaign in New York. Other street artists ensure that they keep quiet. The image of Banksy has been very carefully controlled and was portrayed as a single man for years, but recently it has been suspected to be a group of women and men. Whoever Banksy is, I'm very grateful for their work. Long may they evade the law.

Around Bristol I saw different types of graffiti, some direct messages, some abstract, some subtle, some blunt. Not for the first time I saw a swastika by a main road, and wished I had a spray can. A lot of graffiti contains sharp shapes, over-sexualised or violent images. The majority of graffiti (rather than specifically street art) is done by men and perhaps for men? It can leave me feeling that the images have as little relevance to me as the billboards. Some graffiti artists like Banksy go further though, cutting through the noise of images with a counter-message that makes you stop.

Opposite St. Werburgs along a wall are a series of large, well-painted bees. One of the bees is holding a giant red crayon and appears to have written the message 'Protect your bees'. When a message does reach me it's like seeing a smiling friendly face amongst a sea of angry strangers. Walking over an ugly road footbridge someone has sprayed "Live Free" on the ground. Outside an anarchist community centre are colourful images of people fixing bikes.

There are definitely a lot of things to be said and a lot of other voices to be heard, other than those who can pay for a billboard. Taking out a little pack of coloured chalk from my bumbag, I leave a few messages of my own.

I am to meet Lindsay and her friend Julia in a park. Like many English parks, the 'public' toilets are locked, presumably because of drug use. I was shocked when I found out that the reason some loos have blue lights is so that people can't see their veins. I remember visiting Tokyo, where all the toilets were open all night, with no vandalism. I guess its part of our culture in England to vandalise, but it's not something I understand.

Lindsay and Julia are both meditators and members of the Dharma Action Network for Climate Engagement (DANCE), that Rob Burbea helped start. Over dinner, pauses punctuate the conversation, as they contemplate what has been said. There is no rushing to express opinions, as everything will be heard. The thoughtful nods and compassionate conversation are punctuated with spontaneous laughter.

Later, sat together in my room, Lindsay tells me the story of how she got involved with DANCE.

"I had all of these different assumptions about what 'type' of person you had to be to be 'an activist'. They were forms of denial. I used to say that climate change 'wasn't my thing'. I think about that statement now and it's like saying air isn't my thing, or water isn't my thing, soil and food aren't my things. We don't sit separately from the environment, it's not 'somewhere else.'

"I'd been a practicing Buddhist for many years. One of the key aspirations with Buddhist practice is that of freedom from delusion. I realised that if I didn't turn towards the evidence coming from our scientists for the last forty years, then I would be in denial. If you choose to not know a truth you're living a lie and it's really hard.

"There was a statistic from 2013 — the RSA survey on stealth denial said that 67% of the British are in a state of denial when it comes to climate change. They intellectually understand what's going on but they don't emotionally feel it, because it's too much to feel. The fact that the government and the people that are supposed to be looking after us, aren't looking after us — that's a huge thing to face. So DANCE offered me two things: one was the ethics of what it means to be engaged with the suffering of the world, and secondly it meant that I could turn towards that which frightened me.

"DANCE has enabled us to support each other. To get *off* the cushion, after you've done your meditative practice, and bring that into service for your world. Last year I did a three month silent meditation retreat at Gaia House. During that time there was this deep yearning which arose, which had arisen many times before, to be of service to life, to work out what it was that was my particular purpose. On retreat I was guided by Rob Burbea to stop trying to find the answers, but instead plug into that great yearning. In doing so, the world opened in ways I couldn't possibly have imagined, the conversation of nature became apparent in a way that is difficult to put into words.

"I started educating myself, realising the extent of the denial which had kept me politically inactive. I wanted to get engaged and I wanted to wake up, and in doing so my heart has continued to crack open to the reality of the suffering of our planet. It has totally altered my path and there is now no other choice of the work to be done. The choices we make individually are no longer sufficient; the extent of what we are facing requires collaboration, mass participation, but more than anything — action, not words.

"I have no doubt that all the connections, all the amazing people that I've met since then, all the work that's flowed out like a giant wave of purpose, was from plugging into that deeper yearning which arose during retreat. We haven't chosen to be born into these times, and the reality of what we're facing is frightening and can feel overwhelming. But we have unimaginable reserves to draw upon, and connections that extend outwards in multiple directions. To not deny the reality is the invitation for each and every one of us. This is what we're facing. So let's get to work."

Hearing the purity of purpose in Lindsay's words I felt instantly bonded with her. I knew that her success was my success. It reminded me of when I met Miranda. Miranda's has become one of the most important friendships in my life, just because someone facilitating a protest meeting asked us to tell the person next to us why we were there.

Over the next day, I formed an impression of Bristol that seemed to revolve around growing food. Looking at the events I saw advertised, most were to do with food and local food production. I walked past a lot of large allotment areas which is unusual in a city, but is a big part of the feel of Bristol. Returning to Fai's place for a day was a surprising oasis of continuity. I felt restored, and eager to get going again.

It was national self-build week so I returned on Steffie's recommendation to St. Werburgs to find the Wild Goose Space. The building is used as a community and business space by the community. Every one of the fifty-odd chairs in the meeting room was full, with people wanting to build their own homes, or businesses wanting to be involved.

Wild Goose is a community of self-build homes. The forty dwellings were built by their owners as a group with aspects of shared ownership. Self-build homes are classified as 'custom build' and not all planning authorities are comfortable with custom build, but there are many organisations who can offer help, including The National Self-Build Association.

The community that surrounds the Wild Goose Space became aware that a developer had entered a planning permission for a standard housing development and decided to mobilise to object. Not only were they able to get the developers planning permission refused, but they submitted their own proposal for a mixed development with custom build and community-focused buildings, which was accepted instead. The majority of people who then got involved were first-time buyers. Some designed their own homes, some used architects and they all shared the services of a structural engineer. Large tasks like pouring concrete were done together. As you might expect, a quality of life survey for the area found that residents have more local friends, less fear of crime and more general joy in their area and community. They have collectively stopped thefts by chasing after people.

When listing what it takes to make a project like this happen the factors were: ownership, a range of skills and experiences, range of funding methods, teamwork, mix of voluntary and paid work, persistence, good legal support, self-belief and a *lot* of meetings. In the rain we toured the curving site. The individuality and love was so apparent in the buildings. A house is made of bricks and stone, but only love can make a home.

Walking out of Bristol I pushed on in the rain and didn't stop. This is a foolish thing to do. If you take a ten minute break every hour you will get further and not exhaust yourself. I knew this, but I am a foolish human being at times.

By 6pm I felt I didn't want to go any further and looking at the map, I thought that the field I was walking through was my best bet for a quiet camp for quite some way ahead. The tall grass looked comfortable so I folded it down. I felt that the occasional dog walker wouldn't mind my presence tucked out of the way and I was far enough from an urban area to reduce the risk of random attack. I was nervously in my sleeping bag at seven. When I nipped outside in the night, the sky was a bright orange. The clouds were reflecting all the light pollution from Bristol and I had no trouble seeing — it was like a giant streetlight overhead. Other than that obligatory toilet trip, one other thing woke me.

Rustling...somewhere behind my head. Heart pounding, I sat up. The rustling stopped. I stopped breathing to listen, and after a few seconds it started again. I tapped the bottom of the tent where it met the wall behind my head. The rustling stopped. I waited. More rustling. Then squeaking. I frantically tapped the bottom of the tent, then lay back down again to wait. After a long interval, a much-reduced rustling resumed. Content that I was in no imminent danger of mouse attack I pulled the toggles of my sleeping bag tight around my head to muffle the sound and went back to sleep.

I didn't wake up until seven the following morning! Twelve hours lying down might sound excessive, but my body definitely needed it. With relief I saw that the clouds had not deposited rain, and had prevented the formation of dew. For once I could put the tent away dry, but the earlier rain had left its mark. The geology had changed to clay and I slipped and slid over wet footpaths.

As I left the village of Frampton Cotterell I found a tea room in which to eat a hot breakfast, and drink magic elixir. The tea room was packed with men...men in beachwear...men in women's beachwear. It is difficult for men to fit everything into beachwear designed for women. Not being familiar with the local customs of Frampton Cotterell I did not want to be quick to pass judgement. I listened (one could not avoid it), until they struck up a conversation with me. My first silent guess of 'stag do' had been wrong, but my second of 'rugby players' was bang on. They were on their annual team tour day and, except for the minibus driver, the drinking was well underway. It was going to be a messy weekend.

I felt I was getting into my stride now, even if it was a slippery muddy one. The pack was still too heavy but I enjoyed walking, looking around and thinking. I saw people rushing to jobs and shopping. I felt so grateful not to be going to a job, not to be buying things and to be fit enough to walk.

Walking through Yate, a sterile shopping centre full of chain stores, describing itself as 'The heart of the community. 4 hrs free parking.' I wondered how the community felt about its 'heart' being described as such.

Nowadays shops mostly have little relevance to my life. Five years or so back I had to sell my flat when I divorced. I'd been saving money since I was sixteen and I'd put my savings into the mortgage. The thing is, you don't own a mortgaged house. The bank does. And houses can devalue. At the time I was still largely locked into a way of viewing life as secure or insecure, the concept of resilience had not yet taken root. My best friend told me 'It's freedom, and cheap at the price'. She was truly right. Removing the sword of the mortgage from over my head was a huge relief, and so was the clear out of possessions — with every bag I got rid of, I felt physically freer.

On the walk, the burden of possessions was very literal. Anything I bought, I would have to carry, which immediately put me off.

In Ridgewood community café next to a nursery, the chairs and sofas sit under large skylights, the stone walls are covered in pictures and the staff are immensely friendly. Sitting with my tea I look around with affection at the many mums and their babies. Another three mums with pushchairs come in. Well dressed, their huge smiles and body language show their relief at having time together out of the house. They are happily talking about the number of children they want. Two of them want four, and one wants five. "But my husband doesn't, he's one of three so he thinks we should stop at three."

The offhand tones make me sag in my seat. I'm thirty-one. I would like to have a child too. Just one. But even if I were blessed with a healthy child, it would be at odds with what the future seems to have in store for my life. I hear one of the ladies say her brother has four children too. I finish my tea quickly and leave.

It's harmful to compare one life journey with another. There is no script. I don't know for sure why I want to have a child; it could be ego, a need to love, long-term tactics, biology. Yet, I honestly feel like I want to meet them...out of hope.

The tower monument in the distance was on top of the hill and I felt a disappointment and realisation that my shoulders hurt, my legs hurt and that I wasn't going to make it. I looked at where it was on the map. On paper it was closer than I had intended to go that day, yet I could see I wasn't going to make it to Dursley that night. There was nothing else to do but keep walking anyway. It was not as if I had anything else to do.

A few hours later I was standing at the base of the monument buffeted by the wind, feeling rather humble that I had underestimated walking so much and given up hope so easily.

However things appear, if that is the direction you believe in, do not give up hope. Our achievements can and do outstrip our imagination.

The beauty of the Cotswolds really grabs you as you walk in from the west and being able to see where you are headed and how far you've come is quite a shock. Fields, hills, hedges, patches of trees.

I stood for a moment leaning into the wind and found that it was able to take a good portion of my weight, except when it suddenly changed and I tottered forward. As I walked along the hilltop my backpack was catching the wind and it became difficult to walk, the noise was tremendous and I found myself staggering to the side constantly with the gusts.

Suddenly my backpack cover was ripped off my pack and went flying off across the hill and car park. Desperately I waddled after it as fast as possible. About eighty meters further on I was rewarded when it became stuck in a hedge.

Coming down the other side of the hill through steep woodlands, I was out of the wind but the trees were not. They swayed and groaned most alarmingly. I felt I was not in a good situation.

I was about two thirds of the way down the hill when I suddenly heard a loud CRACK explosion, very nearby.

CHAPTER 13 — Singing Stroud

The large branch fell with a THUD and small snapping noises about ten meters behind me.

"Time to *GO!*" I called loudly. "Time-to-go-time-to-go!"

Around me, the wind whooshed and the trees swayed back and forth. I half jogged, half waddled down the slope as fast as I could with the pack, watching my footing intensely. The wind dropped as soon as I got down off the hill, looking back up at the wood I could still see the rows of trees moving alarmingly. The temperature rose by a good five degrees at the lower altitude, causing me to strip off layers.

It was late by the time I arrived in Dursley, nestled in its gentle slopes. Laura met me with an energetic smile and self-conscious excitement. She spoke with love and pride about Dursley. Her admiration flowed for projects in Stroud and Bristol, like Made in Stroud and the Bristol Pound.

She gestured to several chickens wandering around loose as we approached the back door of her house. "These are the girls," she said.

We went straight into the narrow but light and colourful kitchen for a cup of tea. The round knobs on the cupboard doors and draws didn't match; they were patterned and in different colours. A red woven heart shape hung near the window. I sat on a stool against a cupboard feeling very at home as a black cat came and went.

Listening to Laura's story of transformation, I heard the same process that was repeated by others.

"It's great to have positive ideas but in order to act, it's sometimes necessary to create a bit of space. I was a busy full time working single mum, so although I had great ideas it was difficult to put them into practice. I stopped full time work when my children went to different schools. First I had to create the space in my life, then the hope could come,"

Laura sees a future for Dursley that brings the community together and creates space; creating a better future together not just in terms of physical space, but in time as well.

Since Laura took her "leap of faith" she set up her own business, Field Fresh, making natural skin care. She spoke with passion about encouraging the production of native plants that could be used in skincare so that we could reduce our imports. I found myself nodding along emphatically. Starting my own eco-toiletries business, The Green Woman, with my sister we had encountered similar difficulties.

"I think many of us agree that the old economy is broken and not fit for the future," she said "and we're trying to find ways to create a new economy and feeling our way. But of course, we all experience it differently. I have some toes still in the old economy but I'm trying to gradually build new economy ways of earning so that I can make the shift from one to the other. The gift is that since creating space in my life, other things have emerged too."

Transition Dursley is starting a pop-up shop to sell local people's crafts and goods and being involved with the project is a great source of pride for Laura, as is the creation of a community permaculture garden. Laura attended a permaculture course a few years ago but now has the chance to use her skills and practice them in her community.

The next day I waited by the car for Laura. The chickens wandered loose, with no fence. "Don't they wander off?" I asked gesturing, as Laura locked up the house.

"No, they know where home is," she said with affection, "and it's a good way to get to know your neighbours, if they do venture there occasionally."

"Do you have difficulty getting them in at night?" I asked.

"No, they take themselves to bed. Sometimes they don't want to go to bed and it usually means there's something wrong with the coop. Usually red mites, they bite the chickens and it's very uncomfortable. It's really useful that they can tell me, they know what they're doing," she said smiling.

The irrepressibly positive Laura took me into town to show me the start of the permaculture garden. The garden sits at the rear of a community building and is currently derelict, awaiting the volunteers who will be working on 45 small projects to transform the design into reality over the next year.

"We're starting with consulting all different community groups. We'll have permaculture ideas flowing through it and the overall design will break down into lots of smaller sections so that people and groups can take ownership of sections. Dursley In Bloom is planting some of the flower beds. A local secondary school is helping to make the furniture. We want to use rain capture to channel the water through the garden. It's having a staged approach with a plan for each."

Afterwards Laura made us packed lunches and walked with me out of Dursley; along the back of the houses then along the edges of an orchard and elderflowers. "I'll have to come back with a bag for that," she said. Then into the hedge-edged fields. She pointed proudly at the flowering hawthorn.

"They used to call it bread and cheese," she said. "The children would eat the leaves with the flowers on their way to school, or the new rolled leaves." We made ourselves some 'sandwiches' and I was pleased to find that the hawthorn flowers took away most of the bitterness of the leaves. I still looked forward to my real cheese sandwiches from Laura.

Laura showed me that I could eat new beech leaves, when they are still very thin and a little fluffy on the edges. I found I liked the taste very much, like a tart green apple. For the next week they were to be a frequent snack. Rain began very heavily in a sudden squall so Laura headed home and I hoped she would not get too wet on the way back.

The sudden intense rainstorm passed quickly though and I was left with sunshine. I took a break in the bottom corner of a lush tall-grass meadow. As I lay out of the wind, I looked up at the clouds above; they were racing at an incredible speed.

Walking towards the Cotswolds, the steep hills formed a beautiful beckoning vista. It really made me feel I was *getting* somewhere; the geology was changing yet again. Walking up a steep field, there were hills which converged in beautiful curves, with a large still-bare tree halfway up. Loud birdsong and breeze through branches were all I could hear.

At the top of the hill I looked back and could see the monument from yesterday. The one I thought I couldn't reach, and there it was, impossibly far behind me already. The wind was phenomenal and I could barely stand so I didn't linger but headed on to Stroud.

The energy company Ecotricity began in Stroud, and water and hills are defining features of the town. It grew around the confluence of two rivers, as well as having a canal. Looking out from a vantage point on the hills surrounding Stroud there are very few buildings visible and instead a lot of trees and green meadows.

Walking through Stroud I see a lot of 'Vote Green' posters in people's windows. Exhausted after the sun, wind and hills I am greeted at Alison's house in Stroud by her friend Jane, all gentleness and caring. "What do you need?" the same question as Jacqueline. What a beautiful question to ask someone. I resolved to ask people that.

Jane and Alison tell me of many spiritual aspects and the connection with Mother Earth. When dinner is served the two ladies sing together a blessing, as a lovely lilting round, before we eat.

"For sun and rain, for grass and grain. For those who toil on sea and soil. That we may have our daily food, we give our thanks and love to God."

We talk late into the evening of concepts that I can't quite absorb. When we are all relaxed, Jane brings out her sounding bowl. Made from a rich coloured wood, it's larger than a fruit bowl with about nine strings across it. The sound is more resonating than a guitar, more like a harp. Grey hair tied back, with two broken fingers strapped up, Jane slowly plucks the strings. Her hand injuries were due to an unfortunate dog walking incident and combined with others, were the reason for her stay at Alison's while she recovered.

The instrument was beautiful in feel and sound. A few years ago there was a great storm and a giant branch fell from the great old sycamore tree at Hawkwood College in Stroud. Sections of the branch were taken to Devon where it was made into the only sounding bowl made from a tree that is still living. When Jane first played it she didn't even ask the price (which turned out to be considerable), she knew it was meant for her. Jane teaches singing and uses music in therapy to help people free themselves.

An interesting historical point which came up was that our western music as we hear it today is different in feel than it was before industrialisation. Historically musical instruments were tuned to a particular key, which was composed of the overtones within a note, but with modern instruments we compromise so that we don't have to retune for songs in different keys. As a result, some of the notes are a little 'out' and don't resonate nicely with each other. The other aspect which I had not realised, is that the note 'A' today is not the same as the 'A' from the 1800's. Originally our instruments were tuned based on an A resonating at 432 Hz, but as musical audiences became bigger the instruments needed to be louder and so they were retuned to a higher tension at 440 Hz. Humans are very subtly yet strongly affected by resonance and frequencies, which is part of our love of music. Instruments tuned to only one key (like the sounding bowl) can be fully in harmony. Improvisation with other people is easier with instruments in the pentatonic old tuning.

For a few months I've been searching for the shared experiences. The things that link us together, to reach one another, but Laura said something that stuck with me. She'd said "There is no true shared experience." Now Alison repeats this, "We all experience everything differently - there is no *true* shared experience." I don't really want to accept that, but the idea takes root and a few days later I will already have changed my mind. It is not perhaps to the shared experience that I must look, but to the shared purpose. In deciding who to share the road with, where they are going and how they are getting there is more important than where they started from.

Many different people on the journey so far had assumed things about me, as I connected with them: that I believed in 'the absolute truth' of an afterlife and the spirits, that I was an atheist/Christian/Pagan/Buddhist. It is very hard not to use labels, but I think we must try. Once we have given something a label we stop asking questions.

Upon leaving school, or a relationship or work I felt I knew things. Until I realised that many of the things I had been taught were not right. In fact quite a few of them were downright harmful. Beginning my own education was a shock; new people, new places and dozens of books: politics, history, emotional intelligence, environment, psychology, social sciences. When I left school, curiosity had been drained from me; learning was a stressful chore you did to get a bit of paper so that at some point you would get a job. Children are suffering education for a future that won't exist by the time they get there. Most people I know leave formal education determined never to learn again, so that they are robbed of one of the greatest treasures in life - self creation.

We all learn throughout our lives; the people and culture around us teach us constantly. We are a malleable species of phenomenal learning. We can direct that learning, or it will happen anyway. Then you have to ask yourself if the things you are being taught are what you want to learn. That behaviour that you do — was that what you wanted to learn?

I spend an hour in the afternoon the next day drinking tea with an alchemist. Jonathan has worked for many years at Ruskin Mill College helping people with disabilities to learn practical sustainability skills.

"But alchemy," Jonathan tells me, "is about the transformation of the human being. It is a different way of thinking and approaching problems. An alchemist does not just reduce things to the constituent parts, but sees a distinction in qualitative aspects and spiritual aspects. For example, the difference between dew and groundwater.

"Salt, sulfur and mercury are used in alchemy as principles in nature," continues Jonathan as I nod, frowning with concentration. "Alchemy relates natural transformations and processes back to human beings and what does it mean in relation to being human. How things *behave*, rather than what they *are*."

"Ahhh, ok." The last sentence clicks and I keep nodding. I can understand parts of what he's saying, but it would be a lot to expect me to grasp much with only an hour's tea-introduction. I can see how the different perspective of an alchemist gives some very interesting insights.

With pleasure, I think how far I've come in the last two years. A few years ago, for starters I wouldn't have deliberately spoken to Jonathan. It's very easy to believe in yourself when the industrial culture keeps telling you that you are right and other's wrong.

I love science. Yet for me science is a quest for understanding. The best science to me is 95% observation, 2% theories and testing and 3% luck. I am saddened that we (I am including myself) seem to lack the patience now in science to observe and to understand. I compare it to the young Charles Darwin on his ship, collecting dust at sea and asking questions, for years; questions that led to a global concept of the movement of nutrients in the atmosphere.

"People have assumed that consciousness in the past is the same as it is today, but it's not," says Jonathan. "Our experiences are very different and that affects our thought processes, so they can be very different." Some fast nodding from me, this ties in with my limited understanding of neuroscience and makes a lot of sense to me.

"Like with languages," I say. "You think differently if your language has different words available."

"Yes, and you can see the evidence of the changes in consciousness partly through the historic change in language," says Jonathan. "It can be very misleading to try to judge the actions of the past with today's thought processes. We need to shift our consciousness to deal with the future, and I believe that to be happening."

My next tea-talk is with a composer and choir mistress called Sheila, who has written an entire show of orchestral choir pieces about bees. The first concert of which, raised over £500 for the Natural Beekeeping Trust. Alison had played me some of the music earlier and I jumped at the chance to meet the composer. Sheila started a community choir and after taking courses on choirs it has become her work. I asked Sheila what it's like to live in Stroud.

"There is a lot of singing and dancing in Stroud. There are about fourteen community choirs (that don't audition) then there's the church choirs and the choirs that audition."

"Ha! That's amazing!" I exclaim delightedly.

"Stroud was in the early industrial revolution with wool mills because of the rivers, but then the mills moved north where the water pressure was higher. It feels like now we're at the beginning of this revolution. There's something tangibly positive for the future here," she says.

Initially ideas may seem strange here, yet they are all grounded in a practicality. These are people working hard to make the future better, and I find myself becoming very fond of Stroud, and its singing inhabitants.

"It's a healthy place to live too," says Sheila. "People live well, but there are higher rates of asthma and arthritis because of the damp. The word Stroud actually means damp."

Later I asked Alison what she thinks of health in Stroud - I hadn't seen many obese people.

"There're lots of hills that people have to walk up," she said. "The local doctors' surgery partly uses some Steiner methods and thinking. They don't accept payments from the drug companies when they recommend a drug, and so they're in financial difficulties. Doctors normally get payments for certain prescriptions they issue. There are bonuses and seminars and conferences all paid for by the drug companies." I'd heard this before from a friend who is a pharmacist, but it was interesting to hear that the surgery was in difficulties without the drug company money. Like a back-door privatization of the doctors.

I gather all my possessions together in the hallway and return to the kitchen for a final cup of tea, where Jane and

Alison teach me more songs: an African walking song, songs for morning, a song for night and several folk songs. As I learn them I record them on my iPod so I won't forget — seventeen songs in all. I look forward to having walking companions that I can sing them with (they are mostly rounds and are very pleasing when sung together).

"Morning has come, night is away. Rise with the sun and welcome the day..."

Jane and Alison see me off from the door, playing a couple of small drums. It feels great to get my pack back on and walk down the steep hill into the town centre. I've been on the journey for twenty four days now and it feels like this is my natural way of life.

After dropping off my backpack with the very friendly staff at a vegan café I make my way up the steep rolling green hill to Hawkwood College where they offer short courses and retreats. The courses include art, ecology, religion, therapies and personal development. I was there to see Bernard, the gardener of an unusual farm. I pass a marker stone alluringly carved with some sort of symbol and I feel very strongly that this is a place that people behave with respect and spirituality towards the land. There is also the great old tree that Jane's sounding bowl came from, and next to it, a natural spring. Underneath its canopy is a semi-circular wall built into the ground and from it flows a gurgling spring. In a walled tiered garden behind the manor house I find Bernard.

"Hawkwood College is a centre for adult education that's been going since 1946," Bernard tells me. "It runs all sorts of courses. It grew out of the Rudolf Steiner movement and was linked to other initiatives across the country. Further down there is a biodynamic farm with cows and sheep. It is run as a Community Supported Agriculture (CSA) farm with monthly paying members who are supporting the farmers. Then members can come and collect their vegetables every week. A biodynamic farm works from the premise that the whole farm is a living organism and that by working to improve the vitality of the soil, plants and animals, really good quality food can be produced. As far as possible we make sure that the things needed by the farm are produced on the farm."

Industrial agriculture focuses on yield and the appearance of food and so our food in England today is far less nutritious than in 1940. Government records reveal a steady decline in trace nutrients during that period. There is no way of telling the trace nutrients just by looking at a vegetable.

"So what do you do in biodynamic farming?" I asked.

"In order to enhance the vitality we try to work with the life processes. We continually bring living material in the form of compost to the soil, not artificial fertilizers. Biodynamic preparations are used to increase the vitality in the plants and soil. There are compost preparations which regulate and bring balance to the compost and guide humus formation in the soil. Other preparations guide the growth of plants."

"So what's in a preparation?" I asked.

"We work for example with cow horns, filling them with manure and burying them over winter. When they come out they are transformed and full of fungi. We take the substance out and stir it in water and spray it out in small droplets over the land. We've got some that are ready to dig up if you'd like to see?"

In the orchard Bernard clears an area of grass and digs a small hole. From underneath the soil he produces a cow horn, one of over a hundred that have been laid together in a tight-fitting circle. The material inside the horn is no longer recognisable as dung, it has a sweet soil smell and is full of little white balls and threads, which are the fungi.

Once the preparation is added to the bucket of water it will be stirred for an hour continuously. Bernard carefully demonstrates the motion to me; he stirs the water into a conical vortex and then reverses the flow, into another vortex.

"It is a process that dissolves the substance in water and brings its energy into rhythmic movement. It is this movement carried by the water and transferred to the soil which stimulates healthy growth," he tells me.

I was surprised to learn that biodynamic farming began ninety years ago with a series of lectures given by Rudolf

Steiner and was a precursor for our modern organic movement.

It's tempting to try to explain the results that Bernard describes in scientific language. But I think first I need to view it as a cultural story, a visible result of a different way of looking at the world. I don't think I'll really get it if I keep trying to translate it. The visible effects I can understand but Bernard has a truth which also includes energies and beings that I have no feeling of. Biodynamics feels in many ways like an approach to agriculture that is akin to magic. The traditions of spells and magic have been undermined and persecuted so much that it is hard for me to have a clear sense of them. We have a long history in England of suppressing traditional wisdom at home and abroad so it makes sense for me to think twice about things I think I 'know'.

I'm due to get walking again but when I get back to the café for my bag, I get a call from Bernard, inviting me to dinner and to stay. "My wife Karin is a long distance walker too and she would love to meet you," he says.

In the richly colourful house, with dark blue locally-made crockery, I look at the pictures Bernard has handed me whilst he's cooking. They are black and white images of a building in an architecture book. The building is the Goetheanum, and its construction is the most amazing building I've ever seen. From the outside it looks beautiful and reminiscent of Gaudi's style, while the complexity and love devoted to the inside are incredible. The reason I've never heard of it before is that it was burned down by arson over ninety years ago, just two years after it was built. The Goetheanum was built during the First World War in Switzerland using wood from all over the Europe and was a highly complex symbol of peace and humanity. Right through the war people from different countries travelled to bring materials and to work on the giant domed wooden building which was full of amazing carvings and painted inside. Every type of wood used in different parts had symbolism. After it was burnt down, Rudolf Steiner designed a different building made out of concrete, and that building, is now an important cultural and spiritual centre.

After a healthy dinner we retire to the cushion-filled lounge. "How long were you walking across Europe?" I ask Karin.

"It took 6 months, to Dover, then Ostend, across Belgium, through Luxemburg and Germany to Dresden, and through the Czech Republic to Prague. I wrote a book about the journey, 'Touching the Horizon'," she said.

Karin works as an art therapist and runs a support group for people with chronic conditions or who care for others. Both Bernard and Karin have a very caring manner. Karin took me to their office and showed me a bookcase full of maps.

She lent me the next maps for the journey and as with the one's I got from libraries, I would post them back when I was done. The problem I had encountered with libraries was that they never had the local maps in stock. I later learned to get into the habit of stocking up on the maps for further ahead and to use the smaller scale cycling maps.

Even though I'd come to like Stroud very much, I felt relief when I put my pack back on and got walking. Three nights in one place was the limit. I wanted to keep moving, to keep meeting, learning and discovering. It was beginning to feel addictive. Every time I 'captured' a wonderful interview or met a special person it was giving me a high. Even if sometimes I knew that I didn't fully understand what I'd heard.

Sometimes it is impossible for you to see or understand an event or concept, it is too far outside what you know, but with time and repeat exposure it may come. Take the concept of extinction. Men simply could not understand that they had killed, for all time, the infinite-seeming dodos or passenger pigeons. That they were gone. Forever. We create stories and concepts to help us make sense of our observations, but when new observations come along that do not fit the existing story we have great difficulty letting that story go.

Walking through Stroud for the last time I head to local shop 'Made in Stroud'. Looking around the bright shop there are candles, art, pottery, soaps, cordials, clothing, and toiletries.

"I've been working here for three years now," the young woman behind the counter tells me. "It started as a Saturday job when I was in school. We sell products that are made by people in Stroud. There's been a lot of local trade around here that was shut down by the recession, so it's been really important recently for artists and crafts people to have a consistent place. It's something I'm really proud of, working here. We've got over two hundred makers, yet it's a tiny town."

My final stop is the Stroud Valley Project shop. Pine shelves display biodynamic seeds, bee homes, bat boxes and posters.

"It was set up to support people working in the environment and also to provide educational opportunities for people to learn about the environment," Claire tells me. "The last couple of years with the economic situation it's been quite a struggle. We were fully dependent upon grant funding until a couple of years ago. Then we set up the shop and all sorts of things to try and make money. This weekend we've got a plant swap and sale. We do badger watching and take people up on the commons and look at orchids and butterflies. We're doing a course today about growing vegetables."

Claire introduces me to Fred who helped start GlosCAN a Climate Change Action Network. His clear thinking, organisation, dedication and drive are a wonder to behold. It's wonderful to hear the things he's working on - a declaration to be voted on at the council, a march to coincide with the International People's Climate March in September. I feel like this is someone who's really going to get things done and indeed, as I write this I know that's exactly what he does. The Stroud climate demonstration in September not only happened, but had a turnout of 500 people! For a town the size of Stroud that is the most incredible achievement!

Leaving Stroud I take the footpath along the dry canal, which has wire fencing and workmen around part of it. There are a dozen volunteers for the Cotswold Canals Trust in high viz jackets and gloves. Harry is volunteering and fills me in on what I can expect ahead of me that day.

"About six miles up, through the golden valley, it rises up onto the escarpment and you've got the Daneway and the Sapperton tunnel — two and quarter miles. When it was built it was the longest tunnel in the world," he tells me.

"What's the plan for the canal then?" I ask Harry.

"It's a two year project. There are volunteers working on the restoration six days a week, with larger groups on Tuesdays."

As I walk towards Cirencester the canal looks more forgotten and feels in places like a scene from Lord of the Rings, a ruined civilization with nature slowly covering it up and taking it back. Greenery extends right up to and over the edge of the canal wall, trees arch overhead and in places, are even growing out of the bottom of the canal. Parts of walls have fallen in.

The Golden Valley is full of dappled sunshine, trees, rare plants, and at a little distance, the steep, green valley sides. At the end of a steep forest valley I reach the entrance to the Sapperton Tunnel. The partially-ruined tunnel entrance has large stone blocks, decoratively protruding bricks and is flanked by two pillars built into the rock. The next morning Miranda is to meet me at a pub so I amble on, through a large wood with stern warnings to leave by 6pm. It's well past that but I'm not about to camp by a roadside.

Arriving at the pub I discover it would best be described as a gastro pub. Walkers are definitely not welcome and my backpack and muddy boots are viewed with alarm. The rest of the clientele are wearing shirts, pearls, polo shirts, heels and parking very expensive cars. They also all appear to be getting absolutely *wasted*. Ever the optimist, after ordering an orange juice I enquire how they would feel about my pitching a tent. The refusal is immediate (no need to check with the manager) so I return to the woods and tuck my tent in behind the wall.

When I return to the pub garden, I do my best to eat my oatcakes surreptitiously. As the sun goes down, a man comes out into a large pen at the rear of the pub to put away the chickens. His voice at first encouraging, quickly becomes aggressive and impatient when the chickens don't do what he wants. He shouts at them, calling them stupid and a few other things, moving aggressively at them. It's amazing how often men assume an animal is stupid when it doesn't do what they want it to. I wondered if their coop could have red mites, and how long it would take for anyone to notice.

I decided it was time for me to retire to the woods. It was difficult to fall asleep, but I kept telling myself that I was well-camouflaged and no one was likely to come past.

Sometime later I'm awoken suddenly by a loud snuffling next to the tent... *Badger, got to be... We don't have bears here, there's nothing here that would attack the tent... How big are badgers? Can they hurt you?* Too scared to go check, I assume it's a badger and clutch my sleeping bag until it goes away. Eventually I fall back to sleep.

And am sharply awoken by gunshots.

CHAPTER 14 — A river begins

Heart pounding, I'm already sitting up in the tent, before I quickly decide it's better to lie down.

"That's why it said to leave by 6pm, you plonker! The gunshots were definitely in the wood, but not very close... *No idea how to judge the distance, but surely that wasn't close enough to hit me?"* More shots, making me jump.

"Definitely not super near, but not that far either. What could they be hunting? Rabbits? Deer? Badgers? Not game birds? Would they be shooting horizontally?"

There's a long pause with no sound at all... Every other creature in the woods must be as scared as me. After a time my bladder wins over my fear and I sneak out, holding the tent zip carefully with both hands to open it as quietly as possible. I crouch by the wall to do the necessary. The fields beyond are bathed in light and it must be a full moon. I'm torn between going to look and staying hidden. Keeping low I hop over the wall and stand at the edge of the shadows, watching and listening. I cautiously lean out just enough to see the moon for a few seconds, my circulation functioning loudly.

I duck back to the wall, over it and into my tent. I'm annoyed, at myself, for being such a bloody coward. There's a beautiful wonder of nature out there and I'm cowering in my tent. *You're not in any peril. I wish my friend was here. What would she think if she saw you like this? Silly girl.*

The next morning is clear and sunny. Although I'm tired from the disturbed night, I pack my tent up early to avoid being spotted and go to lie in the field on my poncho in the sun. The weather has turned and it's going to be a hot one. I decide to go searching in the woods for clues and after half an hour I have seen two seats up ladders but no corpses. *Deer then perhaps?* A colleague once told me that deer don't look up. *That's good then, they would have been shooting down, not horizontally.* With hindsight though, this was during the government's unscientific badger cull for TB. Perhaps the badger that had disturbed me was on the run? But perhaps it is better that I did not think of that at the time.

As the time of Miranda's arrival approached, I found a seat watching the road, upright and alert like a puppy. Several people came round the corner, who were disappointingly, not Miranda. Through the foliage of the lane I caught a glimpse of a backpack and I got up and walked closer. By the time Miranda came around the corner I was jogging over with my arms high.

The excitement and the fear were mounting. I was so joyful at the thought of seeing Eve but terrified at the thought of what I was about to do. With a strange awareness I knew that it was definitely exactly where I was meant to be. I got in my dad's car (after the moral battle was won by logistics) and as we drew near to the village we found the road was closed, so I got out to walk the rest of the way to the Tunnel Inn. I was slightly worried that my dad would get lost on the way back since we had followed the sat-nav on my phone to get there.

As I waved goodbye to my dad and walked off, I took a deep breath, readjusted my bag, and put my designated walking hat over my plaited hair. It felt like I was beginning my adventure – I plait my hair whenever I travel to stop the curls getting out of hand. I glanced left over a stone wall and was rewarded with the most delightful view; wild flowers, and dandelions just going to seed, spheres glowing gloriously in the midday sun. Head high and arms swinging I walked up the hill and through the trees.

Despite our daily chats there was much to catch up on and Miranda and I spent the whole day chittering like school girls, except for the hour of silence. Steph had advised me to have an hour of silence every day, and seeing as I would be living in close quarters with others, it sounded a good idea.

After lunch, we set out in search of the source of the River Thames. A stone marker in a field tells us we have found the source of the Thames, but there's no water. The source of rivers moves slightly as more or less groundwater is available. When we do find the first water of the Thames, it is about half an inch deep and running absolutely clear over the pebbles. Miranda takes a sample.

"There are people all over the world taking samples of their rivers and then they are being combined and shared into one sample of the sacred rivers," she told me.

We follow the growing stream and suddenly it drops away into a deep, glass-clear pool. The day is really hot now. The pool looks freezing cold, clean and very inviting, except that is, for the mosquitos; hundreds of them are flying all over it. The idea of swimming with those little bug-ers in my face is horrid.

"We will get a swim though," said Miranda. I nodded, hoping she was right. A river clean enough for me to want to swim in is a rare thing. This high up the river we're above all sewage outfalls, so the only things that should be in it are agricultural runoff, and we hadn't had rain for a couple of days.

Following the Thames Path will miraculously take us near a friend's house in South Cerney. I've known Ben for a year from heart-to-heart chats at environmental meetings. A counsellor in his fifties, he's often the one to bring up the emotional aspects of group dynamics. I find it relaxing speaking with him as he is disarmingly honest about his personal emotions. He's been kind enough to offer to put us up for the night. As we walk down the road in the sunshine, Ben walks out to meet us and greets us like celebrities, with flower garlands for our necks and heads. We are all laughter and celebration. *Stuff it, I don't care if I look silly, someone just made me a flower garland!* Unlike me, Miranda wears hers comfortably as if she wears flower garlands all the time. Thinking about it, she often does.

We set out from Ben's after lunch the next day, only to stop an hour later at the Cotswold Water Park. We sit outside the lakeside café in the hot sun with our pots of tea; a holiday with friends. Strolling along the river we talk about what we would do if we won fifty million pounds. I feel a detached relaxation with other people talking; I don't have to talk as much and I don't have to think so much either. I delight in how safe and happy I feel. I feel like anything could happen and it would be OK, because we would face it together.

We pitch up for the night in a field next to the river, as far from any houses as we can. We check there's no livestock in the field and that we're out of sight. A little while later though we hear cattle being moved in a field on the other side. As the sun goes down, the orange glow lights up the dandelion balls. We're sitting eating the dinner that Miranda has cooked, talking and laughing. Suddenly, a large dog runs full speed at us, knocking over all the food and forcefully jumping on our backs. It seems more interested in us than the food. Ben tells us to stand up with our arms crossed. We pick the food up and stand as still as we can with a dog jumping on us, and after a few minutes, it calms down. There's a very quiet instruction, "come", from nearby, out of sight. Immediately the dog shoots off back to the owner as if it is highly trained.

We'd made quite a lot of noise when the dog was jumping on us but there had been no exclamations, or admonishments from the bushes. It seemed to us that the dog was doing exactly what the owner wanted, while they watched, and that its owner might well be the landowner. Whoever the dog owner was, they didn't come to speak to us.

"Because there're several of us we were laughing," said Ben. "If you were alone, they wouldn't have known."

A bit rattled, we finished the food and went to bed early to avoid the mozzies. With Miranda's extra warmth and presence in the tent I slept really well; the best night in the tent so far.

Waking up next to the river is heavenly, as is Miranda's porridge; beats the hell out of oat bars. We follow the Thames path slowly all day until we arrive at Inglesham, where Ben is friends with the farmer Mervin. This part of the river itself is not on the Thames Path, but will be soon and Mervin laments the impending visits of countless strangers across his land.

We will be camping right next to the river and Mervin describes to Ben the spot where we can have a campfire. Mervin shows us his CCTV which covers his lambing shed. He made it from junk he salvaged and now, in his seventies, it means that he can monitor the sheep from bed. As we walk down towards the river, a small plane crosses overhead then comes down to land in the field. We step quickly out the way as the man taxis along the mown grass to the little hanger where he stores the plane on Mervin's farm. It's a very surreal experience for me. I've never even known someone who *knew* someone who owned a plane before. Nipping out for a bit of a flight when you fancy it is kind of boggling to me.

With perfect timing, just as we approach our camp spot, Ben's girlfriend Kate arrives with dinner for the four of us. Ben and Miranda gather the wood and get the fire going and I set up our tent and things as Kate lays out the spread. As we sit on blankets all tucking in, the bizarre relaxation and luxury of the last two days has me in a bit of a daze, not wanting to talk much and feeling so grateful to just be here. Kate and Miranda run off to swim in the river while Ben gets the campfire going. I sit happily listening to the splashes, squeals and giggles from out of sight in the river.

After a spectacular sunset Kate and Ben head back home. With only a moderate amount of giggling fits Miranda and I fall asleep. No guns, no badgers, no shivering, just a great sleep.

In the cold morning air, a mist is sitting on the river and partly out on to the bank. No sooner have I finished munching the wonder porridge, than Miranda excitedly gets up and declares she's going for a swim. I enquire as to whether she knows the current temperature of the river. Taking the dishes to wash them in the river I call out that the river is indeed, as I suspected, "bloody cold", but Miranda is soon naked and swimming regardless. I valiantly fulfil my role as towel holder.

We pop in to say goodbye to Mervin on our way out.

"There's a difference between the country folk and the town folk," Mervin tells us. "They don't know how each other live. People park up here and throw their litter out the window. Or they walk their dog not on a lead when we've got livestock in the field. One man kept letting his dog chase sheep, which causes distress and they can miscarry. When Ben challenged him, he said it was the sheep's fault for running away!"

Over the next few days I heard an increasing amount of abuse from people towards their dogs, almost entirely from men, especially at the weekend. When the dog didn't do what the person (I'm intentionally avoiding the word owner) wanted, there was shouting, insults, swearing and hitting.

It felt like the same process of dominance, whether to an animal, a woman or a person of colour. When someone does something that the dominant group doesn't like, the blame is placed on the other party. It's the sheep's fault for running, it's the dogs fault for not coming, it's the woman's fault for speaking back; a very neat way of avoiding the morality of the dominators actions. In the dominant culture people seem to like siding with a winner. I once read an amazing book about case studies of abuse called 'Why does he do that? Inside the minds of angry and controlling men.' Counter to what we might like to believe about ourselves, people almost always sided with the abuser rather than the victim. Until we recognise and actively seek to counter that behaviour we are likely to continue it.

Our first stop that day is the 11th century church in Inglesham. It's a much less imposing church than others, shorter but more inviting. It remains intact today thanks to the support of William Morris in the late 1800's. William Morris was a multi-talented political theorist, fantasy writer and artist who believed in equality and socialism. He founded the Society for the Protection of Ancient Buildings, one of the first preservation groups in the world.

We gingerly push open the large wooden church door and inside find old wooden pens surrounding the benches. Neither of us has seen such things before and we decide that they must have been to keep the occupants out of the drafts. There are faded wall paintings from across the centuries, most not recognisable to me.

We had arranged to meet a friend Sophie in Lechlade for lunch. It's surprisingly busy in Lechlade by the river, and I realised it's the seventeenth of May, a Saturday; so many people were free to enjoy the sunshine. Although the sun was out there was a strong wind all day to keep us cool. We spotted a smiling Sophie approaching us along the bank and the three of us had just begun to seek a picnic spot when we found the floating forge.

Surrounded by displays of ironwork, metal art and pokers on the riverside, was a blacksmiths, on a boat. On the roof of the small narrow boat was a painted colour shop sign that read 'Brian Greaves Blacksmith' and on a blackboard further along the roof, a William Morris quote - "Have nothing in your house that you do not know to be useful or believe to be beautiful". Peering down into the partially open boat I saw lots of tins, tools, clamps, a small forge, and the man himself.

Pleasure boats and the odd row boat pottered past as Brian good-naturedly answered my questions.

"Why did you become a blacksmith?" I asked.

"Well I started out as an engineer over thirty years ago and moved into welding and blacksmithing. The thing with blacksmithing rather than engineering is it's quite a creative skill," said Brian.

"What made you decide to take it on to the river?" I asked.

"Well I bought the canal boat when I was about twenty six. Originally I just had the canal boat Emily," he gestured to a normal size boat in front of the forge boat, "and after a while I thought I would like to have a forge again, so I built Bronte, to take my work with me."

"Oh, wonderful! What are the solar panels for?"

"All our lighting, a small oven, and they also run the small grinders and the blower for the forge."

Sophie, Miranda and I walked on to Kelmscott where we passed William Morris' old manor house, now a museum. We finished the day with a drink at a pub in Radcot and Sophie headed home, leaving us to find a sneaky riverside pitch.

In the morning light the Thames is beautiful. An old stone bridge artistically frames it in a leaf-shape, reflected in the shining water. It's going to be another corking day, I'm certain Miranda has brought me good fortune and good weather. Next to the river is a concrete hexagonal box-like structure with small windows. It's a pillbox. They were built to defend the rivers in the Second World War in case the Germans invaded. How close we came to a very different existence. Along the wall in chalk we draw a smiling bee and the words 'Change the Culture, Not the Climate'.

A few hours later we're as far from towns as we're likely to get and we come upon a muddy beach. Having stripped off, we're just about to go into the water when I stop.

"Wait! What's that noise?" I ask in a half whisper, confused. We stand still listening, unable to place the sound. Suddenly the sound becomes a lot clearer.

"Boat!" I say with alarm and we both dive to the ground as it comes around the corner. We hadn't passed a boat for an hour or so and I totally forgot about them. My knickers and vest top are to hand so I put them back on. Turning around I can see Miranda's face and bum poking up out of the grass as she's marooned from her clothing. I wave nonchalantly to the boaters as they pass, before we both collapse in laughter.

Wary of more boaters I decide to swim with my vest top on, so I reach the water's edge first, and sink up to my ankle in the dark grey mud.

"Ug, it's a bit muddy!" I call laughing, but I stumble through and splash down into the cold water. "Waaaaahhh. It's fine, it's fine, just have to swim, just swim, just have to get used to it. Waa haaa."

Miranda stands frowning at the edge of the mud looking for the best footing. She can see my deep footprints. From my vantage point in the river, I've got a better view of the bank and I spot an area that looks more solid.

"Try that side, it looks better," I call gesturing. Miranda gratefully steps out onto the beach... Only to discover that what appeared solid, is merely a crust. In slow motion horror I watch her sink in past her knees and topple forward.

"Noo!" I shout, hands out in horror, as Miranda's arms disappear into the mud up to her shoulders. *Oh my god I've drowned her.* Finally she comes to rest, stuck horizontally. For the second time that day all I can see is her face and bum. Her face at first in wide-eyed shock, is then bellowing laughter.

"Ah HAA HAAA!" she says as she realises she's not sinking anymore. I swim towards the bank but she's already rocking, flopping and rolling to get free. A dark grey and white splodged creature, she climbs back out using a hummock of grass to get a knee up.

"I'm sorry, I'm sorry," I say in between laughs. "I swear it looked solid. I swear I thought it was better."

Miranda is now even more hesitant to enter the water and it takes a minute or two of poking with feet to decide on her route in. Once submerged, the mud is soon gone.

"I *am* really sorry," I reiterate, trying to stave off a dunking.

It takes a while to dress as we stumblingly use grass to scrape the mud from our feet and ankles. We're just about decent when an old man comes past walking his dog.

"Morning!" the ritual greetings are exchanged. "Beautiful morning!" "Isn't it just?" "Wonderful." "Enjoy!"

After he's gone I turn to Miranda, whispering, "I'd say that was pretty close."

We push on for several hours in the draining heat. We're aiming to meet a couple of friends in a riverside pub in Newbridge for lunch but we're late. The river path winds around a lot and it's much further than we thought. Having run out of water, conversation grinds to a halt, headaches are pounding and tempers heat up.

"You got the chalk?" Miranda asks at another pillbox.

"No time for that," I say. "Oh, you can but I'm going to keep walking." Begrudging the seconds it takes me to get the chalk, I walk on in sullen silence. Clumps of rustling poplars give us a brief respite of shade before we return to the glare of the sun.

My friend Mark walks out along the river to meet us and we arrive an hour late to meet Matt. Rewarded with large glasses of cool water we are all smiles and joy. Matt treats me to a Sunday roast. It's a carvery so you can serve your own vegetables and I stack the wide oval plate embarrassingly high. Around me, very overweight people are filling their plates to a similar size. I sheepishly return to my seat, and work my way through the whole stack, leaving the plate clean. I've never eaten that much in my life.

Matt and Mark bid us farewell and feeling well-fed and watered, the afternoon walk is much more jovial. We admire the buttercups and dandelions sprayed across a whole field. After the strong winds the day before, all the seeds have blown off the dandelions and they are bare nodding stalks. We redecorate another pillbox and sit to watch the mayflies.

There are hundreds of them. Mayflies only live for one brief day. Throughout May they can be seen flying straight up and floating down, up and down, constantly. Their aquatic nymph stage lasts for about a year, but as adults they have only one purpose - to mate, and only one day to do it.

"I knew it," said Miranda, about the immediacy of their lives, "but it's different seeing it." She seems profoundly affected.

The next day we approach Oxford without a map (since I'd lost it the day before in my excitement at seeing friends) but thankfully Miranda grew up in Oxford so we just head in the right compass direction and wait for a village name we know. Miranda begins to see more plants that she knows.

"Just a few days walk but the plants are different," she says.

On the river before Appleton we meet Judy and Don Reid on their boat Angonoka. The boat is named after the Angonoka tortoise from Madagascar. They spent ten years of their life in Madagascar as Don worked to protect the tortoises and stop them from becoming extinct.

"The biggest threat to them is poaching," Judy tells us.

I feel like I can't take a stroll without stumbling upon environmentalists. We cross the river at Northmoor lock and discover Barefoot Campsites which has the nicest composting toilet I've ever seen, complete with fake flowers. We gratefully bestow our patronage.

In Cumnor we posted off a card and little bee brooch to Kara, she had gotten a job with CAT (The Centre for Alternative Technology) in Wales and wasn't going to be able to join us. She'd also recently suffered bereavement. We let her know we cared and that her work, even if it was not with us, helped make a world we wanted to live in.

During a long descent down a hill, cows stared at us accusingly. "It makes me want to free them all," said Miranda, looking at the cows angrily, "but there's nowhere for them to go. It wouldn't help. It's the whole system."

"If I was serious about changing the dairy system," I said, "and clearly I'm not, since I still drink milk, I guess I would tell the awkward truth, that we have no right to enslave other creatures. It makes me think of being a guest at someone's house, back in the days of slavery. How many guests would challenge their host about their slaves? Is my moral authority close to nothing whilst I eat dairy products? Does being a hypocrite mean you can't say anything? In this culture, who isn't a hypocrite?"

"Well there're no perfect people, just people who want to be better," said Miranda.

"Mmm," I nodded.

We crossed several fields in the hot sun then realised we were about to enter the city. We didn't feel quite ready. As the noise rose, we became more irritable and distressed. Stopping in a shady spot, we talked it through.

Walking into Botley on the east side of Oxford the smile response is terrible. There are large numbers of children from at least two different schools, all walking home next to a very noisy busy road and having to cross four lanes of traffic. Not even the children smile back. *Surely this is not a healthy habitat in which to raise our young?*

Along Botley Road we get a lot of strange looks, almost no smiles and a couple of pained grimaces. I can't believe it. I used to live in Oxford, I never thought of it as an unfriendly town. *What could be causing it? Is it the traffic? Because it's a warm day? Because it's a Monday? Are our smiles not big enough? Because it's exam time for the students?* It's getting near summer season and Oxford has very large numbers of tourists at that time, which most residents don't like. Perhaps it is our large backpacks that are causing the displeasure? I resolve to do more smile tests around Oxford without my pack. As we pass the train station people are rushing and stressed. Despite the large numbers of people we've passed, the smile rate has been about 2%.

Then we cross the river. Flowing rivers all over the country cause an increase in smile response. For the short distance over the river the smile rate jumps to 40% (out of about twenty people) before dropping down to 5-10% through the town centre. I mention this because these are the lowest figures on the journey so far. In other towns and Bristol city, the smile rate varied from 20-80%, never reaching the heights of Totnes, but also not as low as this. Something was making people in Oxford either displeased with me, generally unhappy or culturally disinclined to express themselves through smiling.

Oxford seemed to have an air of pretension, of needing to look aloof. Is that because many of the people there are not from Oxford but are living there short term and want to fit in? Is it a consequence of the perception of Oxford University?

Several times in recent years I'd been confronted with having to re-see Oxford. When I lived there and was working, I saw certain sides of it, shaped by the people I mixed with. A year later when I returned and began to seek out activists I discovered new groups and activities I had never heard of before. All of the impressions we form of places are so incomplete, so personal to our own created world. Then on top of that they reflect just a moment in time. All the little cross sections of places in this book cannot tell you what a place *is*, merely my personal world of it on that day. If I went back in a different mood it could reveal itself to me differently.

We stopped into the Lush shop in town where the staff had been so kind to us. We were rewarded with tea and foot soaks. It was as we stood with our packs on by the shop, that none other than Sara bumped into us. Sara was the young MSc student who we had met at the Charity Pot Party fundraiser two months earlier. The chances of her walking past again at exactly the time that we had returned, were freakishly small. We all took it as a sign and she decided she would join The Buzz Tour as it left Oxford.

As we made our way to a pub to meet up with a group of Oxford activists, we separately bumped into three different people we knew.

"Eve! How was your walk thing?" one asked smiling.

"Good, I'm still on it!" I said waggling my enormous backpack at them. "Another few months to go."

"Well good on yer!"

The smiles of our friends were priceless. As we walked into the pub, we knew half the people in it. To be greeted with joy by people who care about the same things as you, is like being given a physical lift. Some of the people I'd met during the walk were working in semi-isolation without access to a group of allies nearby. Looking around I could feel the strength it gives you, to have friends.

CHAPTER 15 — Oil and money

The next day I set out from Miranda's house to meet Al and interview her about 'divestment'. Divestment or disinvestment is about removing investments from things that are harmful. A cancer research charity would not invest in tobacco, it would be unethical. A peace group would not invest in weapons. If we want to create a healthy future we can't invest in unhealthy things.

It was Al's first day in a new job and she was going to squeeze me in, in her lunch hour. It would take about an hour and a half to walk to the other side of town, but in sharp contrast to before the tour, that seemed like a very reasonable and normal thing to do. Along the way, I restarted my smile tests. The results were equally as poor as the day before, despite no longer having my backpack. But I did have a rather uncool bumbag on. I had become utterly attached to the bag, which contained a compass, tissues, lighter, phone, suncream, chalk, snacks and several other things which I deemed essential. About five of the people who frowned at me did so with a significant glance at the bumbag. Perhaps that was the root of their displeasure?

After an hour I felt my smile beginning to flag. I gave myself a shake and began to chalk smiley faces onto the pavement at intervals with the words 'Keep Smiling'.

I stopped outside an allotment and began to chalk. Through the metal fence a Chinese lady called out to me with suspicion and anger from her plot,

"Hey you! What you writin'?!"

"Keep smiling," I said smiling up at her. She stood leaning on her hoe, and then began to smile.

"You should come ev-yday. Keep us smiling!" she said. We chatted for a little while about what she was planting and I walked on feeling I'd 'chalked up' a minor success.

"Just keep smiling, keep going, someone will smile back. Please, come on, someone. Just keep smiling," I thought.

About ten minutes from Al's office, a man on a bike smiled back: a genuine, human connection.

"YeeeeSS! We have a winner!" I thought as I walked on. Then, after a couple of minutes, the man cycled back to me. He was carrying some flowers.

"These are for you," he said handing over the bunch of wildflowers. "How did you know?" he asked.

"Erm, actually, I didn't. I've been smiling at everyone for the last hour trying to get someone to smile back, and then you did. Thank you." We stood opposite each other smiling.

"I really needed someone to smile at me today. I picked these for the office but when I saw you smile... I thought you should have them," he said.

In a moment we had become connected, not in a flirtatious way but as a human to a human. For ten minutes we stood either side of his bike, as Robert told me about his struggles since coming to Oxford as a foreigner with an American accent. He had felt that Oxford was a difficult place to enter into socially and that very few people smiled on the street. I felt that all those smiles had been worth it, to find Robert and to show him that I saw him. We parted with heartfelt good wishes, and I knew just what to do with the flowers.

"Thank you so much for these, they're lovely!" said Al as she looked at the flowers with emotion. I felt very strongly that I was supposed to meet Robert, so that these flowers would reach Al, the intended recipient all along. For my part in the workings of the universe, I got the gift of receiving and the gift of giving. It is a little piece of work, to smile, but it is a work of joy and fulfilment. Al's first day at the new job had been a struggle, she was following her heart with her divestment campaigning work but she had been forced to return to a nine-to-five to support her children.

"In its simplest form, the Fossil Free divestment campaign is about asking institutions to move their investments away from fossil fuel companies," she told me. "It's asking them to say publicly, 'What you're doing isn't okay so we're going to take your money away.' Their business plan depends on burning several times more fossil fuels than can safely be burnt to try to stay below two degrees global warming."

The figure of 'two degrees' that Al mentions comes from the Copenhagen Accord, which was signed in 2009 by nations at the Conference of Parties (COP) to the United Nations Framework Convention on Climate Change. Two is the only number in the document. Countries were able to agree that global warming must not go above two degrees Celsius, but not what to do to prevent it. The accord is not legally binding.

"One of the things that is preventing policy solutions is the concentration of economic and political power in the hands of the fossil fuel industry. They lobby governments mercilessly. The fossil fuel industry is also continuing to explore 'unconventional fossil fuel extraction' which is ever more socially and environmentally destructive. Tar sands, Arctic drilling, fracking," she said.

"Why do you believe in divestment as a tactic?" I asked.

"Divestment from South Africa was part of bringing about the end of the apartheid policy in the 1980s. So there's evidence that it can be successful, which makes it really exciting. There's a strong moral and economic case for divestment. There's evidence of the 'Carbon Bubble' and stranded assets. It's looking like a no-brainer really."

At this point some explanations are perhaps in order. The 'Carbon Bubble' is the term for the over-valuation of fossil fuel stocks on the stock exchange. The price of fossil fuel company stocks is currently determined by their known reserves, but if we are to avoid catastrophic climate chaos we cannot burn all of these known reserves. Estimates of how much we can safely burn range from a fifth to a third. But when you're playing Russian Roulette, do you really need to take an extra pull? So if we assume that we are not going to kill ourselves, the stocks would be overvalued by as much as five times. That's one hell of a bubble when it pops.

In 2014 the UK's Committee on Climate Change warned the UK government of the dangers of overvaluing these investments and World Bank President, Jim Yong Kim, warned that governments and businesses should consider removing their investments.

"Divestment is attractive to me because I'm a mum of two small children. I feel a huge sense of urgency, climate change is happening now, it is with us. We need to take immediate and transformative action on it. I'm absolutely in awe of people who climb gas station chimneys and camp out there, and risk arrest, all those sorts of things. My family responsibilities at the moment mean that that doesn't feel a terribly attractive option.

"Our particular campaign, Fossil Free Oxfordshire, is targeting Oxford City Council and Oxfordshire County Council. The county council has over forty two million pounds directly invested in fossil fuels, but it's only 2.8% of their overall pension fund. So we think it's a very reasonable thing to ask them to move that."

"So how would someone start a divestment campaign?"

"350.org and People and Planet have provided a lot of information and advice. It's then really about finding out about the institution you're targeting and where the levers of power are. Trying to build a groundswell of support amongst the community, whether it's religious or educational. There's an online petition tool that you can use, for example. Next week we've arranged a rally in the town centre, there's a meeting later about it actually if you want to go?"

"Fantastic, yes please," I said. "How did you get involved with climate change action?"

"Why would anyone in their right mind not be concerned about climate change? I've been involved for around fifteen years. I did the easy things like stopping eating meat and driving a car, then that didn't feel like enough. It felt like to take effective action we really need to challenge the vested interests of the institutions that are pushing climate change. Initially it seemed like an issue of social justice, it seemed deeply unfair that the people who are suffering the worst and earliest effects are the people least responsible for bringing it about. I've an added concern now that it's affecting us all, we've seen the floods, even in more advantaged societies."

350.org is the organisation behind the global divestment movement for fossil fuels. For most of human history the concentration of carbon dioxide in the atmosphere has been around 275 ppm (parts per million). In 2013, the concentration reached 400 ppm. We are not talking about emissions per year remember, this is the total concentration in the atmosphere. The name 350.org comes from climate research which suggested that in order to have a good chance of keeping the planet's climate from passing two degrees Celsius of global warming, the atmospheric concentration of carbon dioxide must be brought down below 350 ppm by the end of the century. This now seems optimistic, as it may need to be brought down much earlier.

Carbon dioxide causes a warming effect in the atmosphere. For the last 650,000 years the CO_2 concentration in the atmosphere has always been below 300 ppm yet we have suddenly made it go above 400 ppm. We increased it by a *third*. Looking at one of the NASA graphs on CO_2 you see a sudden almost vertical line, shooting up beyond the normal scale. How could that *not* affect the climate?

Bringing down global carbon dioxide levels in some ways has a very simple solution. Stop doing what we're doing, now. But our culture has become entwined with fossil fuel use and to stop its use overnight would cause an unknown number of human deaths in industrialised society. Of course failure to stop emissions, leading to climate chaos would kill far more, largely people who did not cause it.

You may have heard government targets to bring down carbon emissions (not total atmospheric carbon) by X amount in say, ten years time. But there is a very big difference between making the bulk of those reductions this year and making all the reductions in emissions in the final year.

This is because it is not the emissions in any one year that matter, but the total carbon dioxide present over time in the atmosphere. And carbon dioxide stays up there for decades. Every unit of carbon dioxide in the atmosphere adds to the warming effect, for all the years that it stays there.

Chemistry and ecosystems are full of buffering effects and tipping points, beyond which there is a sudden change. I remember a chemistry experiment at school, using acids and a buffer solution. We could add quite a lot of acid to the mix and the buffer solution would mask the effect so that the solution did not become more acidic. Then we would near the threshold and each drop was crucial, above the threshold the buffer solution was all used up and the acidity would suddenly change. Another similar experiment used potassium permanganate which was a vivid dark purple colour (my favourite colour at the time). When the magic threshold was reached the solution would turn a transparent light pink. My classmate and I proceeded to decorate our lab coats liberally with the deep purple colour. It was only later we learnt that potassium permanganate oxidises to a poo-brown colour.

For another one, imagine you have a glass, full of iced water. When you heat the glass, the ice will begin to melt, but importantly the *temperature* of the water does not rise. This is because the heat energy you are putting in, is being used to melt the ice. When all the ice is gone, the temperature of the water begins to rise...

Carbon dioxide creates a mildly acidic solution when it dissolves in water. As the ocean warms, it is less able to absorb carbon dioxide. The ocean has been buffering our emissions by absorbing about half the total carbon dioxide we have emitted. This has prevented the atmosphere from warming a lot more, but has instead caused ocean acidification. In the last 200 years the ocean acidity has increased by 25%.

There is a limit to the acidity that the ocean can take and still sustain sea creatures that have shells; this is because the shells are made from calcium carbonate and acid partially dissolves them. Unfortunately for us, and most other life on the planet, the shelled sea creatures are a vital part of our global ecosystem and carbon cycle.

There are hundreds of other natural effects, feedback mechanisms and buffers that maintain the delicate balance of our world. I believe that we as individuals do not need to know all of them to know that we should not be messing with them.

As a result of the hard work of Al and many others, in September 2014 Oxford City Council became the first UK council to pass a motion to divest from fossil fuels. In February 2015 Bristol City Council became the second. In the spring of 2015 the Guardian newspaper began a high profile divestment campaign. Several universities have begun to divest. The race is now on to see who else will be on the right side in history.

I head back into the centre of Oxford to find the meeting about the Fossil Free divestment rally and am greeted by four people in a small room discussing email contacts, strategy, leaflets and creative stunts. One of them is Danny Chivers, author of The No-Nonsense Guide to Climate Change.

The first time I met Danny was at a Shell Out Sounds protest in London. Theatrically exuberant and expressive, Danny had cheerfully welcomed me to the singing rehearsal. Although I was joining at the last minute, most of the rest of the group had put a great deal of work and thought into planning the performance. The singers took it very seriously and we did warm up singing, practiced the notes to pitch perfection and worked on our presentation and performance. Performance protest; it's protest Jim, but not as we know it.

Our troupe of about twenty had gotten tickets for a classical concert sponsored by Shell at the Southbank Centre. The centre was receiving about five percent of its funding from Shell and in exchange was giving Shell cultural legitimacy and promoting it to the wealthy.

Just before the Brazilian orchestra came out, we rose in unison from our seats behind the stage and began to sing 'Oil on the Water' to the tune of Wade in the Water. Shell had recently been forced to withdraw from purchasing ethanol from lands taken from the Indigenous Guarani people, but had succeeded in purchasing Brazilian oil fields in a bad deal for the Brazilian people, with serious risks of offshore oil spills.

At first it seemed that people, including the theatre staff, were unsure if our song was part of the performance. The audience respectfully paid attention to the performance and after the second verse we unrolled a banner protesting Shell over the balcony, to cheers from the crowd. Security had gradually mobilised but made no attempt to stop us. As the song came to a close we slowly processed out to applause from the audience. That was a definite first for me.

Shell Out Sounds is part of a movement to oppose oil sponsorship of the arts through the use of that art. At the same time another group emerged - the Reclaim Shakespeare Company, now 'BP or not BP?'

"The Reclaim Shakespeare Company was set up to challenge oil sponsorship of theatre," Danny tells me as he moves energetically, hunching and unhunching his shoulders and pushing up his glasses. "That's how it all began. Back in 2012 we found out that BP was sponsoring the Royal Shakespeare Company and World Shakespeare Festival. This made us quite upset, some us who really love the theatre, really love Shakespeare, *really* hate oil companies," his hands gestured dramatically emphasising his indignation. "These companies who are doing so much to wreck the environment and human rights, are trying to present themselves as lovely, friendly and socially responsible; and sponsoring the arts is a big part of their PR strategy.

"One member of our group had a theatrical background and we suggested that he could do a performance about BP in a Shakespearean style. So before the show, he jumped up, in doublet and hose and it was things like 'What country friends is *this*, where the words of our most prized poet may be bought to beautify a patron so *unnatural* as British Petroleum?' At the end of the performance another one of us asked the audience, if they agreed that this was a problem, to rip the BP logo out of their programs in protest, and a lot of people did. There was a lot of applause in the audience when they performed and ripped the logos out, and this made us think this was potentially quite a powerful tactic.

"We're going into these spaces, but doing it in a way that brings people with us. So we're challenging the decision makers, the companies and the institutions, but we're doing it in a way that builds support amongst the people who also care about the arts.

"We went on to do a lot more stage invasions, at different plays, with different people doing it. It was pretty nerve wracking to get up in front of an audience that aren't expecting you to be there, to suddenly do something that is challenging the space. But it felt really powerful and liberating. The corporations don't own these spaces. I think that's what's interesting. They are infiltrating them by sponsoring them, and a lot of people are uncomfortable with that. What for me is so powerful about this tactic is it allows us to connect with those people whilst challenging the decision makers.

"We've seen some successes already. The BP sponsorship of Shakespeare has been massively downgraded, they don't put their logos all over the plays anymore, and so we started going and doing it in other places as well: the Tate Gallery and he British Museum."

"So what are some of the challenges with this tactic?" I asked.

"It does take quite a lot of work and preparation to pull off a proper performance. In the case of the British Museum it was the BP-sponsored Vikings exhibition so we took a hoard of Vikings and re-enacted a Norse saga inside the museum and we had hundreds of people watching and got on to the news. Remembering your lines and not getting thrown out by security, there's lots of things to think about, but it's all the more satisfying when you pull it off."

I parted from Danny with a stack of posters which I promised to put up in the Headington area the following day.

Back at Miranda's I found her housemate and landlord, Rupert, in the kitchen, stacking crates of apples juice. If he's not being an engineering wiz and fixing something, Rupert will be doing something with apples or bees. On a Saturday in Cowley area you can find him at the East Oxford Farmers' Market selling his apple juice. He helped start the market seven years ago and every time I go it's thriving. Rupert and I first got to know each other when I helped out at harvest time and he let me stay.

There are unwanted apples in orchards around Oxford and Rupert climbs up the trees and shakes them, then we pick up all the apples, peel them and he shreds and presses them. He sells the juice and the trees' owners are given some of it in return. He seems to know the personalities and appearance of dozens of varieties. The Tiddly Pommes apple juice is unusual in that each batch is made from a different variety, so they each have a very different taste. Having never had anything but standard apple juice I didn't know it could taste like that. No matter how many apples or how much honey Rupert eats, he still seems to relish it every time.

Sama, her friend Julia, and Sara all joined Miranda and me at the house for a vegan dinner so they could all have a look at the maps and prepare for their departure the next day. I would be taking a break for a friend's wedding and it was a great relief and joy to think of them continuing together.

Watching the four of them set off the next morning was one of my proudest moments. They looked fantastic, four colourful, light spirited women heading off for adventure. I could do a walk, but they made it look *good*. Hugs and excited laughter all round, I waved them off and couldn't turn my teary eyes away until they were out of sight.

CHAPTER 16 — As Brill as a cow

This was the moment that I, Sama, had been looking forward to for ages – joining the Buzz Tour. There has always been this voice inside my head telling me that I should give as much of my time and energy as possible towards creating positive change in this world. But mixed up with it is another voice, a more healthy and hedonistic one, telling me that this should include pleasure. So although walking around the country was not originally within my life plans, when Eve came up with the idea, I could see it ticking so many boxes that I had to jump on board.

So here we are: Miranda, Julia, Sara and I will be keeping the Buzz Tour going while Eve is taking a few days for a friend's wedding. Eve looked at me with pride.

"Sama, you look fantastic! That fabric wrapped around the tent and that flower! Julia, those red sunglasses, you lot look like rock stars. You make this walk look *good*," she said.

Covered in black and yellow fabric, bee antennas wobbling and various necklaces and bracelets hanging, we look like we're on a buzzing hen do. First, up the hill to Headington, with a bit of pavement chalking and some photos along the way. The packs weigh nothing to us at this point.

"Aren't you supposed to stay back to get the techy side of the walk done, and prepare for the wedding?" asks Miranda when she realises that Eve is going to come with us. "You've definitely caught the walking bug."

"I will, I just want to see you off and I need to put up these Fossil Free posters," says Eve in excuse.

So we all get to it, each taking a bundle of flyers to spread the word about the divestment march. We divide the shops amongst us and each go in to ask if they would put up the flyers in their windows or keep some on the tables. Between us we get through the stack in less than half an hour.

A couple in a café see us come in with the flyers and ask what we were up to. They call after us as we're leaving, "Bee ladies! Bee ladies!" and give us £5 on the spot. I was bewildered by the generosity that came without any hesitation. I knew at that point that everything would be fine. Although we live in a world that is presented to us as harsh and individualistic, the reality of things is much more communal than we usually believe.

We reached Headington Park and here it was time to separate. We attempted our first bit of self-interviewing with the video camera and just ended up laughing helplessly while it gave me brain-freeze. The four of us were waved off by the first Bee as we took her dream, her project, our adventure, and continued on in the direction of....Cambridge.

How slow it was! Being so used to getting around by bike I wasn't very adapted to walking speed. I was, however, ready to embrace the experience as that was one of the main reasons I had decided to join this walk. I was in sincere need of slowing my life-pace down, starting to appreciate my surroundings and my own being within it.

The appreciation didn't take long to come! As soon as the sound of cars was replaced by that of birds, I was thriving amongst all the wild garlic, nettles, hawthorns and many other plants that Miranda and Sara were educating us about. Very quickly we felt like we could be in the middle of the countryside. The way the hills were, meant that you couldn't see the city at all for a while, which was blissful as the bugs buzzed and the sun beat down on us. Four women marching through magical paths and fields filled with yellow flowers and old oak trees, felt like the epitome of freedom and happiness.

We went through a cattle field and had our first opportunity to put our training into practice.

"Okay," said Miranda. "All stick together like one giant cow and we'll fool them."

Julia was fairly terrified and it was quite scary, if ridiculous. We were all shouting "Mooooove away, moooooove away!"

We believed without a doubt that they understood our cow language. They dutifully moved and left us alone and we felt we had connected.

We approached some farm buildings as we were in need of water. As we drew near to the building we saw that it was closed, but that there were definitely people still around. We walked forward and were confronted by a recorded message telling us to leave and that we were being recorded on CCTV. Julia called out to see if anyone was there, and we got a response from a man wearing a white coat, covered in what looked like quite a lot of blood.

Miranda looked vaguely sick, but we needed water, so we went into the building and met his colleague. We filled up our water and explained a bit about what we were doing and were rewarded with an offer of fruit and ice lollies. Miranda went to sit outside away from the smell of meat and a few minutes later we joined her, with our arms loaded with fruit. I now knew where the cows ended up.

"It's really good you didn't see inside that fridge," I said.

We walked on and found a fantastic field surrounded by woods to camp in. As we started to get our tents out, Miranda suddenly exclaimed,

"The tent poles! Oh no! I must have left them in Eve's bag!"

I started giggling. What followed was some excellent MacGyver improvisation with a different tent's poles, a bungee cord, a stick and some string.

The next morning we emerged from our surprisingly still-upright tents into the high grasses surrounding us. "This is brill!" shouted out Julia with a smirk on her face. Indeed, we were camped just by the village of Brill.

Brill is on a hill; a big hill. The view is worth it though. We headed for Brill because we had been contacted by a man who was very interested in what we were doing and wanted to meet us and show us around the famous windmill and the environmental education centre. Peter Davis met us at the windmill and gave us a fascinating tour of Brill from an environmental perspective.

According to him, it wasn't a particularly extraordinary effort to take care of the environmental wellbeing of his village, all the residents did so and it was just common sense. With a population of 1300, he considered it a perfect size to be a sustainable and liveable area. So when I asked what the consequences would be if the fracking industry tried to come to this region, he answered without hesitation, "They would have to be prepared for a war!" That seemed pretty clear.

The skies opened and down came proper rain that continued for the rest of the afternoon. It was then time for Sara to catch the bus home and get back to her studies. Although we didn't want her to go, we all agreed that if we wanted to carry on being flooded with amazing information, we had better let her go back and acquire some more. Sara very generously left us with her tent, so that we would have a complete tent when Julia went home the following day.

We ducked quickly into a real local country pub. They let us stay and dry off and we ordered some chips and got comfy to wait out the rain. We looked at our maps and drew quite a lot of interest from the locals. A group of women with large backpacks, walking sticks and maps definitely gets noticed.

As Miranda, Julia and I left Brill, the sky began to clear and we walked down the hill starting our hour of silence. Quite quickly we were back onto the footpath and into the quiet, apart from the squelching of mud and the dripping trees.

Somewhere near Kingswood, as we sat in a magical woodland covered in moss that dripped, we chatted while we ate, about what we would like from the universe that evening.

"I would like somewhere to dry my socks," said Miranda.

"I want a hot shower," I said.

"Wouldn't it be great if we had somewhere to pitch our tent where we could feel completely safe too," added Miranda.

"And the person whose garden we would be camping in will be completely aware of the sort of thing we are trying to do and will have an amazing story!" I giggled.

"And we can cook our breakfast in the dry in the morning," said Julia.

We stopped at a pub, which looked quite posh with its clean marble floors. Walking in, we immediately felt out of place in our muddy boots and huge bags. There were two women chatting and drinking wine sat on a sofa near the door who smiled at us in an inquisitive way as we left. We got outside and were about to start walking to the other pub, when Miranda decided to go back in and give them both a Buzz Tour business card.

The women were enthusiastically chatting to her for several minutes then Miranda came back out grinning.

"Umm, so... we have a place to camp if it's not against our ethics to get a three minute lift in a car?"

"Yes!"..."Great!" Julia and I shouted simultaneously. Although we hadn't been on the road for too long, we knew the importance of seizing every opportunity for drying wet socks, taking showers and drinking a warm cuppa.

The sun set on our pleasant safe campsite and we fell asleep in the rain after I read a bedtime story from The Hitchhiker's Guide to the Galaxy.

In the morning our wonderful host Sarah told us about some of the research she had done on the feasibility of banning recyclables from landfill, while Miranda cooked an epic breakfast. It seemed that banning recyclables definitely was feasible and Scotland was considering taking it forward.

Then it was Julia's turn to leave the bees. So it was just Miranda and me, joyfully marching along with probably little direction in mind. We happened to go through the village of Steeple Claydon and ended up chatting in the library with Pat and Betty about the HS2 (High Speed Railway) that would be crossing through here - that is, if it doesn't get stopped by the inhabitants of course.

One aspect of the Buzz Tour that I instantly started to love was the fact that we weren't in a rush. The whole idea that meeting people was a fundamental part of the walk, which meant that we were always with a very open attitude and on the lookout for whoever may be of interest and interested to speak to us. I have to admit though, at times over the weeks I got tired of all the meeting and talking.

Then came another field of cows. But with just the two of us this time our cow impersonation did not have the same effect. One by one they started to stare at us, breathing louder and louder until we found ourselves being charged at full speed by the whole herd!

We managed to jump a barrier at the very last moment, and Miranda and I exploded into laughter with relief.

"Let's take the other route, shall we?" said Miranda wisely. And it was worth it! We were both becoming more and more aware of how beautiful the English countryside was. Just like the generosity that reigns in this society, it is another element that is rarely portrayed in the news or other mainstream media.

We were walking along a disused railway, when suddenly Miranda tripped over and tumbled down the bank. She lay struggling to get up with her pack dragging her down and a very pained look on her face. As she tried to rise again it was obvious that she'd badly hurt her knee.

"Ow. Bugger," she said.

By that time, my hands were so frozen I couldn't even undo her backpack from her waist and I struggled with my teeth to open the first aid kit. She was in quite some shock and the pain remained with her for the rest of her time on the walk. Luckily, we had a pre-arranged stay in Winslow that night, where Miranda's friend lives. Eve rang for the daily check-in and I overheard Miranda,

"...great!...Yes...Well I had a little fall...no, fine, just a graze," she said, lying.

The day ended up being quite eventful all in all. After the cows, the fall, and Miranda and her friend reuniting, my best friend rang me to tell me she was pregnant!

Every morning you wake up on The Buzz Tour you can be sure that a new adventure is about to start. Boredom was one element that never appeared. And that was something I loved! The structure of the walk was the stable thread running through our days, and all around that, there were the exciting uncertainties that led to so many new experiences and discoveries.

We passed Clophill Eco Lodge for walkers on the Greensands Ridgewalk. The rectangular block buildings with pine cladding were still under construction but would be ready in two weeks. After some lovely time spent with just Miranda, we were joined just of Milton Keynes by another woman who, over the time, I grew to become very fond of and full of admiration for - Mel.

Mel is a very humble and timid person, with a great sense of dedication. She's also highly intelligent. She is the kind of person you can rely on and will look towards when a situation needs grounding a bit and bringing back to reality. She had decided to leave London for the weekend and become a Buzz Tourer. Unfortunately, a lot of the walk she was part of took us through endless monocultures where the growth of only one crop, usually rapeseed and wheat, spread from field to field... to field. We saw this as a great issue for the environment as it causes a lack of variety of soil nutrients, and biodiversity, which harms natural cycles. The plants grown purely for cash, rather than for feeding a person, have a great cost on the environment, especially when it comes to pesticides. We experienced the spraying from the front row when we were walking by a field and had to run to avoid breathing in the horribly potent products that were being sprayed.

The next day was much more pleasant. We hula-hooped in a churchyard and walked through a little village where we decided to do our first skip of the Buzz Tour. There was a little Tesco supermarket in the centre that looked like a good possibility. Skipping is the practice of going into the skips, the bins, behind the store and collecting food or any other products that have been thrown away.

The amount of waste in the UK is huge! We waste half our food and that isn't even taking into account all the packaging that gets produced and thrown away with it. So in a time of environmental destruction, a widening wealth gap and the increasing use of food banks, it seems absolutely ridiculous not to put your arm in a bin and come out with food that many wouldn't usually be able to afford. This quick treasure hunt treated us with smoked salmon, bagels, cheese, fruit and much, much more. We had the best lunch in a long time!

We knew by smell that we were passing a landfill and thought of our host Sarah's research on banning recyclables from landfills. We felt pleased that we had reduced the landfill load a little.

To add to the great discoveries of that day, we met Barbara. She was out walking her dog when we bumped in to her and she invited us to her house down the road. We all started sharing stories from our lives, her telling us about her past travels across the world and then laughing at our "young idealism" that she too once had. That night, after a warm dinner and shower, we cuddled up into bed and I read Miranda and Mel some chapters from The Hitchhiker's Guide to the Galaxy, before falling fast asleep. Away from the rain and the cold and feeling extremely blessed once again.

Like a train that stops and starts with passengers flowing in and out, the Buzz Tour waved Mel off the next morning, and welcomed Eve back on just a few hours later.

"Ladies!" that was the Bee. In the distance we could see her jumping up and down in her yellow and black outfit, a massive grin on her face. She was back with us, and it felt good.

142

CHAPTER 17 — Bright pink knitting

Trying to meet a moving pair of walkers who aren't sure where they will be when, can be tricky. I accepted a lift from my parents to track down Miranda and Sama. But in an age of mobile phones, as long as you can get signal, you can arrange anything. So mid-afternoon, in a car park by a woodland, near Old Warden, we pulled up shortly before Sama and Miranda came triumphantly down the lane.

"Ladies!" I shouted out with delight as we rushed together for backpack-restricted hugs. I thanked my parents and waved goodbye as Sama and Miranda skilled me up. They had written extra verses for a song Ben had taught Miranda and I when we walked the Thames, and they wasted no time in teaching me. The first verse I already knew:

"As we tramp, tramp, tramp, along the winding road, with our dusty hiking boots and heavy load, we will sing merrily sing, till the woodlands ring, with a song that was made, for us all to sing!" we enthusiastically bellowed. Then came the treat.

"As we skip, skip, skip, along the woodland paths, with thoughts of firesides and bubbly baths…"

"Genius!" I said laughing

"…we will laugh merrily laugh at a thousand cars, with oaty bars and musclely calves. As we dance, dance, dance, along the country lanes with a hoola hoop and a walking cane we will dance merrily dance, through the woods entranced, with hawthorn leaves and smelly farts."

"But, that doesn't rhyme!" I said in protest, smiling.

"That's what makes it even better," said Sama confidently.

The pub marked on the map was inexplicably closed so we sheltered in their smoking area to eat our dinner.

"It is so good to be home," I said looking round at my friends. "Oh...what a strange thing to say...but it is. This feels like home."

I had said it before thinking, and I knew it to be true. Whatever makes a home, it was here with these two women.

"Paula lent me a book when I was in Oxford," I said, "called We-Think, it's about collaborative creativity. I think that's how I want to do the book. Anyone who walked can write if they want to, and we can post drafts online so people can comment."

"That sounds great!" said Miranda, "I've not done any writing before though."

"Well none of us have but we can help each other," I said.

A little later we were checking out the cricket ground as a possible camping spot when we saw a man and boy out walking their dog. We explained our search and asked if they might be able to fill our water bottles. He kindly agreed that on their way back with the dog they would take us to their house to get some water, as it was only a couple of doors down.

After consulting with his wife Debs, John offered us their garden to camp in and the use of their sink and washing machine. Before we knew what we were about, Debs appeared with tea and homemade cake. Sama got out an offensively bright pink ball of wool and began to knit as we started on the tea and cake.

The offer of the garden changed to the use of their caravan. It turned out that their son Charlie was autistic and he had asked for the caravan as a space for him to be. I wanted to be really sure that Charlie was happy for us to be in it and when John and Charlie confirmed they were, we felt quite overwhelmed. Miranda became unusually quiet and seemed to struggle with the unexpected kindness and generosity.

"We home school Charlie," Debs explained.

"That must be hard?" asked Sama, as the pink thing grew.

"We used to have him in a special school but it wasn't working out well at all," Debs said. "With a lot of education of autistic children there's an emphasis on stopping them doing what they do, so that they will fit in. But if there's something physical they are doing there's usually a reason."

"What sort of things do you mean?" I asked.

"Rocking is quite common, for example," said Debs. "But it's a physical way for them to deal with something that is overwhelming them. Rather than judge the way they view the world, other approaches are about entering into that world to communicate. We discovered Son-Rise, which is a programme you do at home, based on play. If they are rocking, for example, you might start rocking too, until they notice you. By not judging them and trying to force them to change their behaviour they can slowly build skills in a safe environment."

"Wow, and you do this yourselves?" I asked.

"It's been a lot to learn, and it takes a lot of energy and creativity with all the games but it has made a really big improvement, he's doing much better. Well, I'll leave you to get settled in the caravan," she said kindly as she cleared away the tea and cake debris. "Take a couple more," she said, gesturing to the cakes smiling, "you might want a snack." We didn't need our arms twisting.

Sama unfolded her hula hoop from its small ring and clipped it back together as one large ring. She then began to brush her teeth whilst hulaing. After putting some things in the laundry and brushing our teeth, Sama, Miranda and I were snuggled in our sleeping bags together on the caravan's double bed. The bright pink knitting came out again.

"What's that going to be?" I asked, fearful that one of us might end up wearing it.

"It's for Wool Against Weapons. People all over the country are knitting pink squares and when they are sewn together they'll reach between two nuclear weapons factories to protest. AWE Aldermaston and AWE Burghfield. AWE is the Atomic Weapons Establishment."

"Ahhh. Very cool!" I was extremely impressed that Sama was being so productive. And grateful that that colour would not be on our persons.

"Pheeewww," said Miranda breathing out heavily. "I can't believe they let us stay in their caravan." Tears began to break her words. "And, their, son. People, are, *so* kind."

Sama and I nodded. "YES. Yes they *are*."

After a pause I began to sing. "There were three in the bed and the little one said, roll over, roll over. And they all rolled over and one fell out, there…"

"Hang on, hang on!" shouted Sama. "Who's the little one?!"

"You are of course!" I said with certainty. "You're the smallest, and the youngest...There were two in the bed and the little one said roll over, roll over, so they all rolled over and one fell out, there was one in the bed and the little one said 'Gooood night!'" We laughed and wriggled.

"Storytime!" said Sama, introducing me to a new Buzz Tour tradition. Every night Sama would read a chapter of the comedy sci-fi 'The Hitchhiker's Guide to the Galaxy' to us. The fantastic story and characters, so far removed from the concerns of climate change, were a delight and a medicine.

Before sleep, Sama planted a big wet kiss on our cheeks. The kind of kiss your grandma might insist on and you would violently struggle to avoid. I scowled and leaned back as far as the pillow would allow.

"Night night!" we each said to each other.

In the morning Debs brought us out a cooked breakfast, tea and more cake. I glanced over at Miranda as she tried to hold it together.

In Ickford we passed the village maypole, carvings and a plant sale, on our way to Sandy. Sandy was our destination that day because the map showed a nature sanctuary, but when we arrived we discovered with surprise that it was actually the headquarters of the RSPB (Royal Society for the Protection of Birds), as well. Luck, as usual, was with us.

We wandered the reserve in search of Peter, the senior site manager for Hertfordshire and Berkshire. Exploring one hide, Miranda and I looked across a small pond at lots of different birds, and had a go at identifying them with the picture boards.

A strange noise drew us outside, and on investigation it turned out to be the Sama Bird, up a tree again, having us on.

At the reserve shop we were able to catch Peter before he went home and he explained some of the changes at RSPB.

"We've just had a big rebranding," he told us, surrounded by the books and bird boxes in the gift shop. "'Giving wildlife a home.' We have been focused on habitat for quite some time but this was just saying it publicly. The change to industrial chemical farming practices, has led to a big loss of birds.

"RSPB has over two hundred sites around the country," continued Peter, "and is one of the biggest landowners in the country. We lobby to protect rare habitat, join up habitat areas and help reconnect children with nature. With the changing climate, we need a more joined up approach to habitat for ecosystems to survive. Partly we're just creating pockets for rare species, because otherwise they don't even have that. You can't think only of some species though, they all rely on each other. As the climate and society changes we have to help the rare species hang on."

We made our way up the hill as evening drew in and when we arrived in Potton, we smelled chips. After that, no other food would do, and they even had tables and chairs in the chippy. Well fed and warmed by our chips we went to the large church to investigate camping. Sama went to ask at the house next door to the church if they knew who the reverend was, but instead returned with an offer for us to camp in their garden.

Lesley and Nick lived in a grand house full of strange artefacts of life, stuffed animals, family photos, unusual art, a big piano, and expensive looking ornaments. They showed us to a large section of the large garden where we could pitch our tents and then we all trooped in to use the bathroom.

We all wanted to be together for the story so the three of us squidged into a two-person backpacker tent as Sama read to us again. It was just about possible, if two of us stayed on our sides, and didn't laugh too much.

Sama's parents are English so she has a perfect English accent, but she was actually raised in France, so her English has some holes in it. Sometimes she stumbles over pronunciation or doesn't know more unusual vocabulary. Every now and then this would lead to a confusing moment in the story where we would have to try and work out what she meant to say. I tolerated the wet cheek kiss when it came.

In the morning we breakfasted with our hosts around the large farmhouse-style wooden table in the kitchen. Sama's favourite cereal put a smile on her face, as did the toasts and jam on pretty blue and white china.

"It's taken our whole lives to earn enough to get the house as you see it now," Lesley told us. "When we bought it, it was partly ruined but we've gradually renovated it, bringing up our three children here."

With us three visiting, it wasn't long before the conversation turned to politics and the environment. Depending on our moods or experience each of us could lead a conversation; Miranda's spiritual connection, Sama's humour, my data.

"It's the balance of our three different energies that makes the walk together flow," said Sama, putting my thoughts into words better than I could have.

Lesley and Nick told us about the Eco Hub at Gamlingay so, not quite sure what it was, we headed there.

The Eco Hub was a community building where we found local residents using computers, coming and going and volunteering behind the desk. One long wall was lined with bookshelves which extended out into the room as the local library. They were cleverly designed so that they swung shut on themselves and could be locked safe when the building was hired out for events. The hub had been built three years earlier, renovating and extending an existing building which had fallen into disrepair and disuse.

"We wanted it to be a multiple use space," one of the parish council clerks, Kirsty, told us as she showed us around. "Before, it was just the hall and people rented it out privately, but no one wanted to use it. It had leaks, smelled awful, and we spent fifty percent of the income just heating it. Now we've got this great kitchen for events, different rooms which can be used separately or in combination, the computers, the library, it's a real community space. Day nursery, parish council, dance, yoga, drama, children's activities, parties, people working, and now, it's *well used*! There will be a recording studio out the back in future too," she said with pride."

"So what makes this an eco hub?" Sama asked.

"We have rainwater harvesting equipment on the roof which is used in the toilets. We also have solar water heaters and photovoltaics for electricity on the roof. We have recycled plastic cladding and a *large* amount of insulation. We also have a ground source heat pump, which is under half of our recreation field. There're lots of water pipes and you get the heat from that which goes into our large tank and delivers it to the underfloor heating and hot water."

Kirsty put us in touch with Brycchan from the Gamlingay Environmental Action Group (GEAG), who came to the eco hub to speak to us. Gamlingay Environmental Action Group really stand out in my mind.

"How did it all get started?" Sama asked.

"My wife and I saw that film, The Age of Stupid," he said, "and we felt like we should really do something. Then we were talking with our neighbours and they said they really wanted to do something too, so we decided to organise a film screening. We put out a thousand leaflets for a public meeting, with a film screening of The Age of Stupid. We had a good turnout and it really motivated people to do something. It was from that meeting that we ended up forming the group."

"What sorts of things does the group do?" Sama asked.

"We've really brought together all the different people in the village who are doing wonderful things to help the environment," he said. "Bringing things together, making the village feel like we have a real energy and *mission* to change things. We promote low carbon living, get speakers in, protect habitat, hold events and campaigns and influence planning. It's *so* hard to resist development. Developers want to build low density housing in the suburbs because that's where they make more money. Strategically supporting development on brownfield sites has helped, with careful negotiation. We managed to get a new park, wildlife area and allotments as part of the development. "

Everywhere I've walked around the country I've seen new houses being built on fields; large areas of towns expanding out. My few months working in a planning department told me loud and clear that councils don't stop development, only manage it. There appears to be no limit, no line that cannot be crossed. Green belt is reclassified when a council wants to build on it. The current Conservative coalition government has also given councils targets to get new houses built quickly, making it very hard for local residents to have influence so the achievements in Gamlingay should not be underestimated.

"The village is influenced by being near the RSPB and Cambridge," said Brycchan, "so there is a higher concentration of environmentalists and academics than you might get elsewhere. That's really helped."

Gamlingay also now has a community owned wind turbine, supplying 10% of the village's energy.

"Most people bought shares in the wind turbine," said Brycchan, "but those of us who couldn't afford to, some bought it with time. I do the website for example." We take a walk with Brycchan to see the wind turbine. It's a smaller version than the large projects you sometimes see. It doesn't intrude on the landscape and is owned by the community, so it feels good. The new community park includes an orchard, where Miranda coos over the different apple trees that have been planted. Rupert's apple juice business has inevitably rubbed off.

"Thank you Brycchan," I said as we parted, "for being so generous with your time to us. It's really impressive seeing what the village is accomplishing."

"It's a pleasure. Do check out the allotments on your way

out of town, and the woo woo toilet." I raised a quizzical eyebrow of alarm. Brycchan laughed. "It's great," he said.

The pre-existing allotments had only eight plots with a waiting list of over forty people. The new allotment had eighty plots and they seemed to be largely occupied. Standing out on the allotments was a strange curving box with a chimney.

"That must be the Woo Woo," said Sama.

"Well woo woooo! Cause I need the loo!" called Miranda as she made her way to the door.

I took out my ipod to take some footage of the toilet and had to include Sama, as she refused to move – instead, she draped herself against the wall in provocative poses. The Woo Woo toilet is waterless and works by using sunlight and wind to dry the sewage. The sun heats a black part and air is heated and drawn through. Once the sewage has been dried, it is odourless and takes up very little space.

After we had all had our fun I met Michael, an elderly gentleman on his plot, and asked his opinion about the new allotments. I hoped he hadn't seen us with the Woo Woo.

"I had an allotment a long time ago," he said, "and now I'm retired, it gives me time to myself. And gets me out from under the wife's feet. You can see just by looking around, that most of them are taken."

That night we pitched up on the sports ground in Bourne, after asking several people where they thought would be best. "No one will mind on there," we were told. As we pitched up for the night a group of teenagers began a heavy drinking session on the other side of the park. Sama was brushing her teeth whilst hula hooping when one of them shouted insults at her, from a safe distance. Then came a chorus of Happy Birthday and several hours of drunken shrieking. I wish I could judge, but my own teenage years included a fair bit of drunkenness in parks (not being abusive though, that's just mean).

The tents were pitched front to front so I could hear the story as Sama read. As we settled down we were all wearing cosy socks. The rain had rotted more socky victims, and one of the houses we had stopped at that day for water was owned by someone who works for a sock company. As well as our full water bottles, we were each presented with a pair of thick, hard-wearing socks.

After a late start from the park, Eve, Sama and I came across a small arts centre on a quiet road towards Cambridge. I was delighted to discover an exhibition that I had read about.

"Wow! I wanted to see this exhibition!" I said. Sama also wanted to see it.

"So why don't Miranda and I stay and you carry on?" Sama suggested to Eve.

We waved off Eve and walked into Wysing Arts Centre and awkwardly asked if we could leave our bags by the door, gently fighting the feeling of sticking out in a very clean space. The exhibition was fascinating, the paintings by Soheila Sokhanvari using egg tempura and Iranian crude oil were what I had wanted to see. We stayed for about an hour and then started trying to hitch a lift. After about fifteen minutes a car turned out from the arts centre with a woman driving, and it pulled over straight away. We got talking and discovered that the driver was an artist, and none other than Soheila Sokhanvari herself! She drove out of her way to drop us off and we sat chatting in the car once she had pulled over, then arranged to do an interview at her studio over the weekend. What wonderful synchronicity!

CHAPTER 18 — Two places at once

Our host in Cambridge was to be a lady called Anna, from Transition Cambridge, who was going to walk out to meet us at the edge of the town. As we approached the south of Cambridge from Grantchester we walked alongside the river Cam, having our hour of silence. I had had some time to walk alone, whilst the others were at the arts centre, but there always seemed so much to think over.

My hour had me contemplating the nature of responsibility. Do you take, give or create responsibility? How is the sphere of our responsibility related to our sphere of influence? In the English language we have no pronouns to distinguish between ownership and responsibility. 'My' does not tell you whether you are expressing ownership or responsibility, but there is very different behaviour which can stem from the two.

We all smiled at each other to signal the end of our hour of silence and prepared to meet our host. Anna met us with her bicycle, and a stack of posters for a Repair Café event. As we walked slowly to her house, she put them up along the route.

"It was really Transition that made me stick here," she told us, "once you get to know your community it's like you've put your roots down."

"What's the Transition Cambridge group like?" I asked.

"You'll get to meet some tonight at the pub! About half the people who started Transition Cambridge in 2007 all used to go to the same Five Rhythms dance classes. I heard about it though The Work That Reconnects, by Joanna Macy. Now we have a hundred active members."

That night at the pub we were greeted by nearly a dozen people from Transition Cambridge, to listen to our tales and to tell us what they were working on. I was so grateful to have Miranda and Sama there to spread out the effort of talking.

When we settled down at Anna's for the night I primly presented my cheek to Sama for a kiss.

That weekend in Upton, near Chester, there was to be a gathering of Reclaim the Power climate change activists to plan the summer camp in a couple of month's time. To make the best use of our time, we decided that Sama and I would hitch up to the meeting, whilst Miranda stayed to interview people in Cambridge. Setting off on the hitch, I had a delightful and strong feeling that we were in two places at once!

This particular Reclaim the Power gathering was hosted at a protection camp. A protection camp is a temporary camp which is guarding or blockading land to try to protect it from environmental harm, in this case, from fracking. A large marquee had been erected in the field for the sixty or so activists to meet under.

The meeting was conducted using a process called consensus. A facilitator takes points from people who have raised their hands to speak. To avoid duplication, if anyone agrees with the speaker, instead of saying the same point, they wave their hands, like jazz hands. When someone feels that the discussion has generated a possible way forward, they make a proposal. The facilitator invites people to ask clarifying questions. Then they ask if there are any blocks. A block prevents the proposal from going ahead and is only used if the person believes the proposal violates the ethics or purpose of the group. Next, people are invited to raise their hand if they 'stand aside'. This means that they do not want to be part of the proposal but will not stop it. If there are too many stand asides, there must be more discussion. Finally the facilitator checks for 'active consensus' and all those in favour do the jazz hands. It can be a long process, so normally working groups are used to generate the detail of proposals that are then brought to the wider group. Thankfully that weekend we were blessed with warm sunny weather, to soothe the discussions.

So I was on my own in Cambridge while Eve and Sama went north. It felt sad, exciting and a bit like we were defying physics by being in two places at once, as if we were collectively one person. Anna who had very kindly offered to put us up in Cambridge had also organised events that we could go to. I quickly realised that I had too many events pencilled in and would have to choose from the incredible array of events over the next two days.

I was again overwhelmed by the continuous kindness of people throughout the Buzz Tour. Axel, Anna's housemate, arranged to get me picked up and taken to Waterland Organics at Willow Farm about ten miles out of Cambridge. The rest of the group were on bike, and as we arrived, I knew we were somewhere very special.

There were new and old volunteers there to work with the farmers Paul and Doreen as part of Crop Shares. Crop Shares came about through Transition Cambridge, and volunteers come every second Saturday to work in exchange for veg and a big shared lunch. I was so excited, I had heard a lot about it from Anna and others and I was ready to do some work!

We were shown around and the work divvied up; I headed off with Paul and a few others to do some planting with the mini tractor planter. Three people sit on seats at the back and load seedlings from a tray into the slots that rotate down into the ground as you drive along. I think we planted about 1500 seedlings. Hot and happy, we sat together for a pot luck lunch with sixteen of us at a long table out near the horses. Then gloriously there were three different types of homemade vegan deserts! Over lunch I chatted with one of the volunteers about why they got involved.

"Well I spend pretty much all my time sat in front of a computer," she said, "so getting outside at the weekend is really important to me. You get to meet the farmers and you can see how hard they have it. You appreciate the food a lot more. It helps me meet people with similar ideals to me too, which I struggled with when I first came to Cambridge."

I asked Paul and Doreen, about the impact on the farm.

"Our life's changed quite a bit in the last four years because of the help of Transition Cambridge," said Doreen. "They're a fun bunch that come and with their help we've also been able to donate food to St. Pauls Church for the meals for the homeless."

"It was getting harder to earn a living," said Paul, "but as a consequence of their help I can still grow a large range of organic crops and I've got more customers for the veg box scheme. Although we're getting old I've got lots of young people now to help me out."

I was dropped back in Cambridge and went to see if Anna wanted help with the event she was coordinating; Transition Cambridge's first ever 'bring and fix it' Repair Café. People brought all sorts of things, from clothes to computers, and people donated their time and skills to set up stations to show people how to fix their broken things. After a short while I found myself in my comfort zone serving tea and biscuits, which is also a great place for meeting people. This is where I met Jackie from Transition Cambridge.

Jackie had been involved with Transition Cambridge since 2008 but before that she had been inspired with others at The Big Green Gathering and a talk that was given by Rob Hopkins, one of the founders of Transition.

"I think my whole life has been about food. My business is a cheese company. I got involved with outdoor foraging and it dawned on me that I could teach foraging, which is what I then brought to the food group. We did garden shares, and Crop Share and all sorts of projects. It's really been about community in Cambridge for me as I'm not originally from here. I've put down roots and that's priceless."

The following day, I decided to take up Anna's generous offer of a bike to borrow (my preferred mode of transport at home in Oxford). Returning to the Wysing Arts Centre, Soheila explained how she came to be an artist.

"I worked for Cambridge University for a while researching into human leukaemia and then I decided that I wanted to follow my dreams so I left and studied Fine Art. I've been a professional artist since then."

156

"Why do you paint with crude oil?" I asked.

"Well I think I have always been drawn to art that has some underlying political narrative," said Sohelia. "I brought half a litre of crude oil from my home country of Iran and I put it in the hold on a British Airways flight from Tehran to Heathrow via Istanbul. I was expecting to be arrested but I wasn't! It's exciting as a material, plastic and versatile, but it smells really bad and I'm sure it's extremely dangerous. So the inspiration for my project was to paint with the very blood of the Middle East - a blessing and a curse that we can't escape from.

"My 'negative space' self-portraits I painted on calf vellum to talk about the sacrifice of the individuals, like me and the many people like me who are victims of this political situation, which in my opinion stems from having the crude oil. Since these pieces I've moved on to using all sorts of ancient pigments that are natural."

Next I went in search of The Missing Sock pub. As you get nearer to the pub, you start to spot small pink sock symbols on the road signs and the signs on the bike route. After getting quite lost, twice, and on the chain coming off the bike, I eventually found it. It was definitely worth seeking out with its surreal decorations and lovely atmosphere.

As I approached the bar I was offered some cake to share with the lady behind the bar and when I declined she asked whether I would like a vegeburger and she went to get me one. A burger and a few amazing conversations later and I felt like I had been a regular there my whole life. They were planning a festival for the autumn called 'A Kinda Happy Festival.'

"How did you start being environmentally aware?" I asked Anna over dinner that evening.

"It was gradual but there were some key moments too. A lecturer was talking about the change in the crops we grow caused by the emissions into the atmosphere. For me that was like 'one step too far' that we've really changed things we shouldn't have. It was one of the big moments where I realised we need to do something. I got involved in

Cambridge Carbon Footprint and also The Work That Reconnects. I went to a bookshop and this book fell out at me. It felt like a really significant moment. Joanna Macy was the author and she's the founder of The Work That Reconnects. I read the book and then did one of the courses.

"The Work That Reconnects is a series of practices that help you reconnect to the Earth, to the people around you and to what is important to you. It was amazing but also really difficult. Finding all the pain from being part of this world and then having the opportunity to say 'Now what do I want to do to make things better? Which part is the part that I can engage with?' So that was really powerful."

Transition Cambridge has a lot of spin-off projects in various areas of community life to create a more sustainable culture in Cambridge but one of the aspects that Anna feels helps a lot with generating that culture is the weekly newsletter.

"We have, say, a couple of thousand people who receive that and each week there's this reminder that there is a community of people working together to create a sustainable city. I think that's really powerful and very much part of the energy to move forward as a city."

That day Eve and Sama had hitched back as far as Oxford. They had a lift to Cambridge the next morning and wanted some time to explore the city, so we agreed I would walk on in the morning and they would catch me up later in the day.

Leaving Cambridge early the following day, I felt elated and superbly excited. I had never gone off with a bag and a compass on my own before in a place I didn't know. As I walked, I thought about why this was and started to break down some of my fears. Walking in silence through the city I thought about how it might be different if I was a man, and what those differences mean. I wondered if my progressive parents would have allowed sons to go off exploring beyond the garden. I walked along the river Cam excitedly reading all of the tourist boards about the area, with no particular rush to get anywhere, but a thirst to really take it all in.

I kept to the shade as much as possible in the heat. After stopping for lunch and a five minute lie down on a big log, I trundled along and turned to leave the river. I soon hit a stile into the fens. I noted happily how much better I was at getting over fences with my pack on than I had been when I started.

I wondered at the hugeness of the sky, the sky really is bigger in some places. It wasn't long before I started to speak to myself, then sing quite loudly. I turned a corner and smiled shyly at some fellow walkers who had caught me!

It felt so free and empowering to be walking through fields with my map and compass to guide me. Soon I stopped to check my landmarks – as I had diligently learned to do – only to discover that I couldn't see any at all. There was just flat as far as the eye could see. No church spires, no towns, no roads...nothing!

I wondered how long I had been walking and tried to gauge it by where the sun was in the sky and then gave up and turned on my phone. I tried the GPS, but that didn't really help, as I was just a dot in a vast expanse of green. I decided to head for a line of trees in the distance, as I figured that trees planted in a specific way may mean humans.

I let Eve know the nearest village, with the hope that we would be able to find each other before night time but I was starting to worry, as I was also running out of map. Sitting under a tree, drinking some water whittling my walking stick some more with a small leaf pattern, I soon calmed down. I decided that if I was lost, then a map wasn't much use anyway, and that I would just walk in the general direction that the village might be.

The line of trees turned into a beautiful dappled shady tunnel of old oaks and hawthorn and I wondered who had planted them and sent thanks into the past. "*I really must plant some rows of trees for walkers in the future.*" I mused to myself, when up ahead I saw a person walking towards me. I stopped him and asked for directions and discovered I was just one field from the village.

I sat in the pub waiting and wondering where we might pitch up for the night. I was super excited to see Sama and

Eve, it felt like such a long time had passed since I had seen them and I missed them.

"The signal is really bad here...you're where?" I asked Eve.

"No that can't be right, hang on, we are somewhere near I hope...Stow?" I could hear Eve sounding confused.

"Ummm, I think I'm in Stow Cum Quy," I said, looking around for signs.

It turned out they had been dropped about 200 yards down the road from the pub I was in, within 45 minutes of me getting there! Thank you universe! What a joyous reunion it was, with so much hugging and laughter. I must remember to trust my feet and the universe more.

CHAPTER 19 — Silence of the lambs

Sama and I arrived from Oxford and wandering around Cambridge for the first time, we were drinking in the sights; the old university buildings, the river, the punts, the alleys, the tourists. I hadn't really known what to expect of Cambridge, having never been, or even seen footage of it. I had a friend who went to university there, but the only thing they ever told me about it was that it was cold, because of Siberian winds.

It all had a shocking similarity to Oxford that I hadn't expected at all. I knew they were both old university towns, but I didn't think they would look alike. What was noticeably different was the height of the buildings - unlike Oxford, Cambridge was only two stories high and the buildings were not necessarily terraced.

Sama and I had a coffee at a table outside a café and felt for all the world like we were on holiday. Then I had an ice cream, at the busy Friday market, and I *knew* I was on holiday. An ice cream makes it so.

Wandering back to Anna's house we had a compass, but I didn't exactly know where I was going. I felt drawn to a road and then as I was passing a building, I noticed a sign saying Cambridge Hub. Curious, I opened the red door, and was shocked to find it opened directly into a small office with three people working in it.

"Um, hello." I said quietly, with a wide Wallace and Gromit smile. I wasn't sure if I was making a fool of myself, but being no stranger to that, I carried on anyway. "I was just wondering what sort of things...you do?"

We were kindly ushered in and sat down as Emily explained what we had walked in to.

"The Hub provides opportunities for Cambridge students to get involved in social and environmental issues," Emily said.

"Wonderful! What's happening at the moment?" I asked.

"We've got an art fair that's coming up tomorrow to bring together artists in the local community with artists in the university. There're all sorts of things, some of it is supporting existing groups around things they're doing about say climate change or international development. Some of it is running our own projects, like the edible garden at one of the colleges. Young people are figuring out what they want to do with their lives. What I enjoy is helping people find what they're passionate about and channel that to have a really positive impact on the world."

What's behind red door number one? Another awesome person, doing wonderful things. *Love* those mystery doors.

We caught a lift out of Cambridge in the direction of Miranda and managed to hit the target at a roadside pub. Miranda had managed to navigate on her own and was feeling rather aglow. We walked on for the next few hours updating each other on the things we'd been doing.

Suddenly a creature like a giant guinea pig ran past in a field next to us.

"WHAT is THAT?!" I cried, but none of us have any idea. It was a couple of days before we got the answer.

"Oh, I've been here!" Miranda said as we approached a pub. This is the pub I was telling you about where the owner is going to put on a festival about happiness! You should meet them, and they might let us camp. I can't believe it."

The Missing Sock had a giant sock painted on the side of the building and in the grounds around the pub were brightly coloured surreal ornaments and shapes. Since no one was home, we sat down in the car park and began cooking our dinner. We were just tucking in to our couscous when the owner and the rest of the crew arrived back. We pitched our tents in the children's play area, next to the pirate boat and rubber tyres. I presented my cheek to Sama with a smile for my goodnight kiss.

Over breakfast we met Stefano an Italian in his fifties who was working and revisiting England to refresh his English.

"I am writing a book also, it is about love," said Stefano, "and what it means to be European. I am going to revisit Germany and Spain also." As we parted, Stefano said he was very interested in the walk and might even like to join for a while, so we exchanged details and they waved us off with heartfelt good wishes.

Cambridgeshire is flat. Field after field seemed to go on. We approached a stream and a sign informed us that we were entering the fens. This also appeared to be flat and I wasn't really sure what fens were. It's one of those words that I knew meant some sort of landscape or nature, but I couldn't have really described it. The river is weirdly several meters above the height of the field, which reminded me of the Levels in Somerset. The information sign was by the National Trust, so I figured fens must be special somehow. A little later on, Martin the Countryside Manager for Wicken Fen enlightened us.

"Wicken Fen is a wetland national nature reserve, first designated in 1899. The nature reserve is quite tiny, only about 300 acres. It's part of fragments left of the Great Fen that used to stretch 3800 square km around the wash basin."

"So why has it reduced so much?" asked Sama.

"It was waterlogged peat, and peat is a very good growing medium for food. Over the last 200 years vast tracts have been drained for farming. About 99.9% of the original habitat has now been lost. The peat underneath the arable farming is disappearing too because when you drain it, oxygen can get in and organisms break it down. We've lost at least four metres height in 300 years. It takes peat a thousand years to accumulate one metre. As it decomposes it emits large amounts of carbon dioxide to the air. Because it's such a vast area it's emitting vast amounts of carbon dioxide, which is terrible for climate change."

The National Trust has about four million members and conserves landscapes, coastlines, large buildings and habitats so it's got a very broad remit. They're the second biggest landowner in the country after the MOD and at Wicken Fen they have a big plan to help protect the area.

Most organisations seem to think only a few years ahead but The National Trust have a hundred-year plan to buy up all the land around the fen and restore it to fenland, locking up carbon and protecting the habitat.

"By making it a long term plan it's less scary for the farmers because we're buying it when they pass away," said Martin. Martin has worked at Wicken Fen for nineteen years.

"Things have changed a lot in The National Trust in the last four years," he said, "and a lot more autonomy has come down to the properties. The organisation as a whole has become more outward looking. I think it's fair to say that the things I'm involved in now, far, far exceed the things I got involved in nature conservation to achieve."

We asked Martin about the strange guinea-pig-like creature we had seen in the field the other day and were rewarded with the answer. It was a roe deer. Shockingly, it is a native species in our country, yet none of us had ever seen it before. The commonly seen muntjac deer is not actually native.

After another night of wild camping and a day of walking we settled down to celebrate our final dinner together before Miranda would depart the next day. So, in a metal shelter, in the corner of a park we made our temporary home and Miranda and Sama began the cooking. I decorated the metal benches with our waterproofs and the metal posts with our strips of yellow and black coloured fur. I hung up a colourful Reclaim the Power poster. Dinner was a triumphant mix of spinach, chopped tomatoes, veggie sausages, couscous and laughter, with blueberries for dessert. A protein feast compared to the usual couscous with a tin of vegetable soup. It may not sound like much, but it felt like a celebration, like a moment together to cherish.

That night, in the garden of a friendly carpenter, Sama continued the bedtime story.

"The deadly missile attack shortly to be launched by an ancient automatic defence system will result merely in the breakage of three coffee cups and a moussécarj, the bruising of somebody's upper arm, and the untimely creation and sudden demise of a bowl of petunias and an innocent sperm whale."

Being an avid science fiction fan, I'm very used to the suspension of disbelief required by it. There are often situations or words that don't make any sense but are explained (or not) later and you just have to go with it. But I was a little confused so took a glance over Sama's shoulder.

"Ha, haaa!" I laughed with my hands over my face. "Mousecage! It's a mousecage," I said as Miranda and I collapsed into the giggles. Sama checked back, frowning at the text, before she too succumbed to the giggles.

I made sure I got my kiss before Sama went to her tent.

Miranda was to leave The Buzz Tour the next morning. It didn't start well. She was upset...and angry.

"Don't laugh at me!" she shouted.

"Darling! I'm not laughing *at* you," I said, "I know these feelings will pass and you will be okay."

And after a cry, she was. We were going to have to part at lunchtime. After a couple of hours we were back to normal, and fondly cherishing the last bit of time together. We found a garden centre café and enjoyed our final Tour tea together... and some brunch...and an apple pie and custard. Afterwards, Sama and I walked one way up the street, and Miranda the other; a silhouette with a walking stick, slowly getting smaller. She had finally finished all her whittling and carving and the staff looked rather magnificent.

I missed her almost immediately and it started to be real to me that Sama too would be leaving in another day, and then I would be alone. In our hour of silence, Sama and I passed wild pink roses and then came upon a small beautiful stone bridge. Sama stopped, and motioned me into a silent game of Pooh sticks. We tried a few rounds with different sticks and then smilingly continued in silence.

Out of Chippenham the road was quiet and the fresh tarmac strong smelling. Then the smell was replaced by pigs and bare earth. Too many pigs and no tree cover, just metal huts. I felt strongly that such an environment would never bring out their souls. Then I wondered why I had been so sure of the word 'soul'. I thought of the dead look in the eyes of slaves and how their masters used to say they were not real people, that you could tell it by looking at them.

If those slaves no longer seemed human, it was their treatment that made it so. What habitat are we creating for ourselves and other species? How much value is there to being alive without fulfilling the nature of your species? What does it mean to be a fulfilled human?

I heard a regular bang. As we walked along the lane we came upon two women banging in fence posts on their land with a heavy metal tube with handles. I was impressed. We greeted them cheerfully on the hot day and they invited us in. Orange juice, cheese sandwiches and cake followed, which was a blessing, as we hadn't passed any shops.

Ahead on the map was a large green patch which, as we approached, we discovered was Cavenham Heath in Suffolk.

A small off-road motorbike passed us on the path just before the gate into the heath. The path went nowhere else so he must have come through the reserve. We nodded and smiled.

Ask any child of five and over, and they'll get this one right: what noise do sheep make?

As we came into the heath there were sheep all ahead of us with their lambs, all being really noisy. Sheep noise. Grass stretched off ahead of us, with low shrubs, and some trees, all under glorious sunshine. We decided to sit and eat our lunch and afterwards I lay face down and stared at the 'grass'. Only it didn't bear any resemblance to a lawn. I slowly noticed that it was absolutely full of different species of plants. Apologies, I come from an age of general botanical ignorance, but I think there were liverworts, mosses and over thirty different tiny plants just in the foot square in front of my face. From walking height I would never have seen them.

Have you ever seen Honey I Shrunk the Kids? I could almost imagine myself down there amongst it. There were tiny little flowers, white, purple, blue, pink. Different delicate stems and strangely shaped pods. One I recognised as a miniature version of daisies. It was like an incredible diverse jungle, but absolutely tiny. I'm sorry, I'm utterly incapable of showing it to you with words.

Since the walk I have tried to look into heathland a bit more. This is a definition I found on a free dictionary site, just underneath an advert for 'Ecologists for developers'. "A tract of level wasteland; uncultivated land with sandy soil and scrubby vegetation. Wasteland - An uninhabited wilderness that is worthless for cultivation." No wonder English heathland is an endangered habitat.

What does the UK government website have to say about it to encourage us to protect it? In plain text with no pictures:

"Much of Cavenham Heath NNR is typical Breck heathland with dry, acidic sandy soil supporting acid grassheath, heather heath with patches of bracken and sand sedge... Between March and October adders are found in this area. They are quite timid in nature and will not usually bite unless they feel threatened or cornered. You should keep dogs on a lead during this period. If your dog is bitten, seek prompt veterinary attention." Feeling the love? Want to go there?

After about twenty minutes of looking at the plants I noticed that the noises of the sheep were different. They were no longer all baaing. Now there were just three distinct voices. I looked around to try and identify them. Two of the voices belonged to two lambs on the outside of the reserve fence, and the third to an adult female about thirty meters behind us. When the motorbike came through, the lambs must have run and got separated. It now appeared that they couldn't work out how to get back through. In fact I couldn't see anywhere for them to get through. Had the gate been open when we entered? I couldn't remember.

When Sama saw, she got up and went to guide the lambs back in. She managed to get them to the small gate, which I was holding open, but they were scared of me. One bolted back past her and the other then went sideways into the next field over, still separated from its mother by a long gate. The mother went up to the long gate and continued to call to its young, which came right up to the long gate but could not get through. By this time Sama had managed to run ahead of the second lamb which also bolted into the adjacent field. Still running, Sama came back through and opened the long gate.

Now on the one hand I wondered if the lambs would find a way, without us there, but on the other I felt responsible for them. We couldn't leave a gate open, and we couldn't see how they had gotten out, so we had to try to get them through. Sama went into the other field and managed to get one through and reunited with its mother. It was like watching a difficult game of dodge. She finally succeeded in driving it to the gate. The lamb took a heroic bound over the threshold of the gate high into the air and gambolled over to its mother. It looked so happy.

After Sama had shut the gate she came back for a triumphant high-five and we sat back down smiling hugely. The sheep were all silent. What noise do sheep make? If they're happy, apparently none.

We sat for a while longer, enjoying the peace. Then the motorbike passed up a lane on the other side of the reserve. And set all the sheep off again. The lambs scattered around, and then tried to get back to their mums. Their calls subsided much quicker this time, after just five minutes. I doubt the man on the bike had any idea the chaos that must have caused when he rode through the reserve. At speed, with a helmet on, watching the ground, the noise of the engine. We rarely see the consequences of our actions these days. Don't we have a responsibility to try and see?

"How do you want to mark the end of the walk? To celebrate?" asked Sama as we walked.

I was silent for a while.

"That's a really good question. I hadn't thought about it. I'll need a minute," I said. We walked on for a little while.

"OK," I said, "I'd like to have a big party and invite all the people I visited to come and share their stories with each other and help each other. I'd like them to connect and I'd like to help them with their work. Give awards out, have a meal together, some dancing. Yes, that would be lovely. What an awesome question. Thank you!"

"Wow, that does sound awesome...I was expecting you to say have a meal with your folks or something."

We talked it over for a little while and gave it a name - a Pollination Party. We walked until evening and camped by a wood, eating the last of our food under a beautiful sunset. The temperature dropped after the sun set and the next morning was bright and sunny and quickly got hot again. With no food for breakfast we headed on. At lunchtime we passed a builder doing some work on a house and asked him if there were any shops the way we were headed.

"No, there's none for miles that way," he said.

"Sorry, strange question, but do you have any food we could buy off you?" I asked.

"No, I was going to drive home after finishing here. I tell you what, I can give you a lift to Elveden, they've got a Post Office, should have some things?" he offered.

Sama and I exchanged a look.

"Yes please!" I said. "That would be great, thank you!"

In Elveden we dined on crisps, muffins and chocolate in the churchyard of an incredibly beautiful old church. After lunch Sama missed a turning so our next stop was accidentally Thetford, which we didn't mind. It seemed to have a great history and a pretty river but a strange present. The smile test results were OK. Most voices were Polish or Portuguese and there were a lot of out of town retail park shops and factories. A couple of people we had met in the preceding days (the builder and a mole exterminator) had mentioned the high number of immigrants but I'd thought they were exaggerating. Apparently most people came over as seasonal agricultural workers. After stocking up again we sat by the river and I ate an ice cream (on holiday again).

That night we were due to stay with an artist, Ben, at 'Heaven' in Coney Weston and with our Thetford detour we were running late. We walked out of town to hitch the three miles along the busy road to Euston. I had just put down my pack to eat oatcakes with tomato paste (yes sounds weird but Miranda put me on to it and it's actually really addictive) when we got a lift and were able to restart in Euston.

The day was a scorcher by now and I was in shorts with a head scarf over my hat to keep the sun off. The geology in the area was sand and clay and there were wide open ridged crops that looked very drying to the soil. We arrived at Heaven at sunset. Heaven is a field where several artists work in makeshift outdoor workshops, carving wood. It's also where Ben lives, in the biggest bender I've ever seen.

A bender is a structure made by bending poles and then covering the dome in waterproof covering like tarpaulins. The wooden composting loos were a little way away from the bender and separated urine and poo.

"The urine is used in the green compost," said Ben, "and the poo manure is left to mature. Without the urine it's fine."

We fell asleep to the deep booming of Ben and his two friends drumming in the bender.

Thunder woke me.

CHAPTER 20 — Right door and day

"**Let's** get up!" I said to Sama. "It's going to rain, we might just have time to get the tent down dry." When we put our heads out we could see the black cloud coming and the haze of rain underneath it and some lightening. We grabbed the stuff out of the tent and put it in one of the open-sided workshops then took the poles out of the tent as the first spots of rain fell. No time to fold the tent, we just picked it up and ran with it to the workshop. Just in time. The heavens opened on Heaven. Thunder, lightning and torrential rain kept us sheltering in the workshop. When we made it to the bender for some tea and breakfast we found Ben's friend, looking soaked. He'd decided to sleep over in a hammock between two trees and had gott caught in the downpour. Hugging teas, we sat cosy on the sofas near the wood burning stove. If you didn't look up at the insulating duvets, you would forget you were in a bender.

We levered ourselves off the sofas at lunchtime and headed to East Harling which had a good range of independent shops and even a house with solar thermal water heating on the roof. I felt so enthused and really wanted to talk to them but felt embarrassed to bother them.

"Eve, you're walking the country, you can be brave enough to tell them you like their roof," said Sama.

"Of course...yes...you're right, I will," I said. Sadly they were on holiday the neighbour told us, so I left them a note.

Clouds of mozzies met us along a wooded path, so we turned back and I scrambled to get out of my shorts and into trousers before we attempted it again. It felt like some of them managed to get me before I had changed. After struggling through the path, mud, overgrowth and mozzies we eventually reached a part of the wood that was wholly flooded. With no way around, we had to walk all the way back. Back at the start of the lane leading to the path we met a group of boys on their Duke of Edinburgh walking challenge and told them about the flood, but they confidently ignored us and carried on. Ah well.

We passed large spray-jet irrigation in fields. Huge long hoses with water spraying high into the air across the fields.

As we came into Eccles something weird happened. Along a woodland path there were lots of tree trunks stacked, some really wide and many just rotting away. We fell silent and hurried on then we came to a harshly built brick house with some rubbish in the yard. Still silent we quickened our pace. It wasn't until after we were out of the woods that we spoke.

"That house really gave me the creeps," said Sama.

"Yes, I got a really powerful feeling that someone was hurt there. It's not safe," I said.

"Weird, I got the really strong feeling someone died there."

Who knows? Not us. But if my gut tells me a place is not safe, I'm not hanging around. Ahead of us in the bright sunshine we could see a beautiful pale stone church tower; the memory of the dark woods receded as we made our way towards it. The church was surrounded by green fields in front and a wood behind. The wood seemed established and comfortable with itself. By the church we met a cheerful lady geocaching whilst her son was at a children's party.

"What's geocaching?" asked Sama.

"People leave things hidden all over the world and they post the coordinates on the website and you have to find them," she said. "But I don't think I'm going to find it today, the GPS I've brought with me today isn't accurate enough. It can be the size of a film pot, up in a tree, anywhere."

"Sounds fun," said Sama smiling.

We set up our tents in a gap, away from the gravestones as the sun streamed sideways through the trees in the churchyard. Sama brushed her teeth, whilst hula hooping. Then she read the final chapters of the book. Peaceful and undisturbed we slept safely by the side of the church.

Sama's pink knitting for Wool Against Weapons was nearly forty centimetres long when she left the next day. I hugged her hard for as long as I could before I walked on alone.

"What is home? It was home with Sama and Miranda...But now it's just me...on a walk."

At the edge of town leaving Attleborough I realised I had forgotten to fill up my water bottle. Searching for a friendly house I dismissed several - too set back from the road, large closed gate, no personality on display. Then I saw a newly tended garden over a low fence, and stained glass on display in the windows of an end of terrace cottage. There was a woven wooden heart hanging on the front door.

"This is the one," I thought. But when I knocked, no one answered. *"No, that's not right."* I thought slightly petulantly. I tried again and waited, then reluctantly and frowning I tried others and came back to the first door, but there was still no answer. *"No, it's definitely supposed to be this one."* I was now quite in need of the loo and starting to do a slight jig. I saw movement in the garden and called out over the fence.

"Hello?! Hello?" I called.

"Oo, hello, sorry did you knock? I didn't hear the door!" said a lady in her thirties with blonde hair. I explained my need and she immediately invited me in, with embarrassment and utter kindness, as if we were already friends and she had forgotten our appointment. After I had used the toilet she offered me an iced drink and showed me around the house and more stained-glass artwork, of which she was the creator.

"We only moved in a couple of weeks ago, so we're still getting sorted," said Elaine. I looked around the beautifully arranged lounge in disbelief.

"But it looks like you've been here for months!" I said.

Elaine shyly invited me to join her in the garden for a drink. As we sat in the sunshine chatting it quickly became clear why this was the right house. Elaine worked for WREN managing their biodiversity fund and she was delighted by The Buzz Tour. She was also a week into a permaculture course...with the same people I was due to stay with, in a few days time.

"How amazing!" cried Elaine. "What a wonderful coincidence, what are the chances?! That never happens."

"It happens to me all the time," I said...and immediately regretted it. This gentle, generous and sweet person, and I had just belittled the experience of meeting them. Elaine just nodded and smiled shyly as if what I had said was fine.

"Oh Eve! Badly done," I thought, mentally shaking my head at my arrogance. But I couldn't find the way to apologise as the conversation moved on.

Elaine's newly planted garden was the result of only two weeks hard work and she told me about what she'd been planting with delight.

"You're supposed to observe for the first year," she said guiltily, waiting for judgement. "But I really wanted to get some vegetables started so we've got some of our own."

"I think it's incredible how much you've got done. It's fantastic," I said. "What made you decide to take the course?"

"I wanted something to change the way I was living. To learn more skills, growing my own vegetables, harvest water, little things like that. That'll hopefully help my contribution and make my life more interesting while I'm doing it. I'm really enjoying the course; I've met some wonderful like-minded people."

Heading through Norfolk it seems that the grass verges are less diverse than other counties and they have been cut. Overhead the screeches of swifts are comforting.

The outskirts of Wymondham have a new housing development and soulless business parks, deserted on a Sunday. Entering the centre of Wymondham, the style of houses gets older and more pleasingly arranged around the shops. There is a large ruined abbey but nowhere for a tent. In the distance a large solid grey cloud is approaching and a barmaid suggests I try a nearby farm.

I see some lightning in the distance and wait nervously for the tell-tale temperature drop as I hurry to the farm. It is early evening on Sunday 11th of June as I approach and there are signs to an Open Day. Julie the farmer has had an intense and exhausting day - over one thousand three hundred visitors have come through the doors for the eggs, animals and the café that day.

"No, we don't have a campsite... but you could use the field. You're here on the right day we've got a portaloo from the open day. You're in luck, it would be gone tomorrow." Julie shows me to a field at the back of the farm with a standpipe and a little gazebo with hay bales under it.

"I won't take any money," she tells me firmly as I reach for my bag. Julie leaves me to set up camp, but when I return from the portaloo she's just walking away again.

"I've left you some snacks on the hay bale. Come and see us in the morning before you go and we'll sort you out with food for tomorrow."

Earlier that day I was alone and in truth rather scared about what lay ahead. My life feels like falling with each step, stumbling on, but people keep catching me. *"When you travel, providence will protect you."* No kidding. And today providence's name is Julie from Cavick House Farm.

On the hay bale is a tray, with cake, flapjack, a small packet of biscuits, pizza, yogurt and fruit (*a snack?!*). Sitting on the hay bale, under the gazebo, I watch an amazing sunset unfold as the storm passes me by to the North West.

The gazebo keeps the dew off, and my tent is perfectly dry in the morning. When I pop my head in at the farmhouse Julie invites me in for breakfast with the family, hot tea and scrummy things. The farm is part of the High Level Stewardship (HLS) government grant scheme.

"We've always tried to be environmentally friendly with the farm and then a few years back we went into free-range eggs," Julie tells me as we're sat at the table. "We sowed wildflowers on the margins and planted 2000 trees. Hopefully if all the farms do it then it will join up all the countryside with wildlife corridors. My husband added a wind turbine which generates about a third of the farm's electricity, and solar panels. The wildlife around has really increased over the last twenty years. Back in the seventies farmers were ripping out all the hedges and creating these enormous fields."

The town centre of Wymondham feels much friendlier and less threatening today with its Monday bustle. There are a lot of independent shops. Although very few people are smiling, when I smile at them they respond very quickly and it's a high proportion of people. The librarian, Sue, is very friendly and her daughter works in the Lush shop in Norwich, where I'll be visiting. Leaving Wymondham on the other side, the depressing industrial estates return. It is all men on the streets here. Although there is a park just the opposite side of the road it's separated by high hedges and there are no paths into it or benches. I doubt many women want to work here.

I approached Norwich from the south and spent my first night in a campsite next to a railway line and river. The next morning I was walking the path along the river at the campsite, when I got a very emotional text from Sama...to thank me for the changes that The Buzz Tour had caused in her. Sitting on a bench looking at the river, I started crying, again (yeah I do it a lot on this walk), but this time with happiness. Happiness that I changed my life, that I met these wonderful friends, and that this whole project worked out.

I write in my notebook. *"My hope is usually an exercise in willpower. For me hope is a choice. But today, I believe. That maybe, just maybe, we can do it. There's a lot of things to change, a lot of behaviour to change, but maybe if we keep at it, we can find the tipping points...and give it a shove."*

The damselflies (or are they dragonflies?) are flying around in quite large numbers, and two graceful swans float towards me under drifting willow seed-fluff that's bright white in the sunlight.

CHAPTER 21 — Boats and boots

Norwich is surprisingly busy, the city centre shopping area is packed, like a Saturday, and there is a permanent outdoor market. I don't have the difficulties that I had in Bristol. Perhaps there are less adverts or perhaps I'm not observing as much anymore or not so tired? My first stop is the Lush shop where I'm warmly welcomed and pampered.

With renewed energy I seek out the Green House. Inside it is a wooden-panelled, wooden-floored café and an organic eco-friendly shop. Then upstairs there is a meeting space and a gallery. Through the café I see a courtyard garden, and when I take my drink out, I find that the roof is covered in solar panels and the shade of the pergola is provided by a type of small squared solar panel strip that I've not seen before. The Green House has been going for twenty years now. It began with thirteen students campaigning against nuclear weapons.

"People kept saying, you're always against things, but what are you for?" Tigger told me. Tigger was one of the original students and is still supporting the project twenty years on and living above the Green House in a flat. The flat is classed as a Superhome because of its energy efficiency and energy generation. Meeting rooms and a gallery are on the first floor, with the shop and café on the ground floor. Buying and renovating the building was not an easy task.

"We wanted to show what you could do, not with a new building but with all the restrictions of an old listed one," said Tigger. Even with the combined resources of the thirteen students, it was only with the help of a wealthy benefactor that they were able to buy it. Like many a wealthy benefactor, this one prefers not to be mentioned by name, but I'd like to take a moment to celebrate the shadowy benefactors. I've come across several groups, projects and protests which could not have happened without access to resources. Most grants are restricted to things that are not political, but anything that is about change is political. In late 2014 'The Gagging Law' came into force, restricting what charities and NGO's can say or spend money on, in the run up to an election.

"I'm not very good at the detail or going to the protests, but I'm good at earning money, so that's how I help," one anonymous benefactor told me. Access to non-grant funds, especially for more radical groups, can make the difference between success and failure, so here's to the benefactors.

Next I arrive at the Green Party office in Norwich. And think I'm in the wrong place. It's a terraced house on a residential street. I double check the address and ring the bell with some nervousness. The volunteer coordinator Spin, and communications officer James are men in their twenties and they show me to a small cluttered office that must once have been a lounge, with a map of the districts of Norwich on the wall showing where they have been campaigning. In a tiny kitchen at the back of the house, with piles of unwashed mugs, four people are having a very focused meeting. A key issue for the Greens in Norwich at the moment is fighting the proposed Northern Distributor Road (NDR). In the last general election they tell me 15% of Norwich voted Green.

"It'll be so much easier for people who want social change if there are green politicians that agree with you," says Spin.

"You might as well try and change the system from within whilst simultaneously disagreeing with it," says James. Spin and James arrange a meeting for me with a local Green Councillor, of whom I'm told there are a whopping fifteen.

In the centre of Norwich is The Forum a large glass building which hosts a fantastic public library (with all the maps I need), shops and council offices. Outside in the sunshine at a café table I wait for one of the County Councillors, Richard. He's wearing a fluorescent yellow cycling tabard and a white t-shirt when he arrives.

"I didn't chose to get involved with *politics*," Richard tells me, "I got involved with *Green* politics, which is very different. I've lived in Norwich for twenty seven years and when I came here I was keen on organic gardening and cycling. Then I realised, we were beavering away, trying to change our world, yet there are people making decisions in county halls, town halls, and Westminster, which actually make a difference to your life.

"I discovered The Green Party in Norwich. It's now been quite successful, at getting fifteen city councillors and four county councillors. I've joined the establishment for a very good reason; because I want to make a difference in what kind of decisions they make, but there is a need for public protest to show other parties that there *is* public interest!"

During 2014 and early 2015 the Green Party has seen an unprecedented membership surge, outstripping both UKIP and the Liberal Democrats. The additional funding has meant that MP candidates can now stand in more places than ever before. After UKIP was invited to join the leader debates and the Greens were not, there were months of fierce campaigning. In late January 2015 the Green Party was also permitted to join, along with the Scottish and Welsh national parties.

"What made you care about the environment?" I asked.

"The writing is on the wall, it's pretty clear we're adding to the temperature of the planet," Richard said. "Ten years ago I worked out that anybody who relies on petroleum products is going to be in real trouble in the future. I moved to a different house, I got a south facing garden, and installed eco-renovations and grow my own vegetables. I walk or cycle into town. I've cut my energy bills by over fifty percent and I make a profit on the energy I produce...Ah! The other councillors are coming out."

Behind me a procession lead by the mayor had emerged from the council chambers. The annual ceremony to welcome in the new councillors had just finished. Richard stood up and waved and two women broke away from the line and joined us.

"That's enough of that!" said one, as they sat down.

"Lesley," one said shaking my hand.

"Jo," said the other smiling conspiratorially.

Lesley had been involved with The Campaign for Nuclear Disarmament (CND) since she was fifteen but only realised the importance of environmental issues in the last ten years.

"One of my favourite quotes," said Lesley, "is this: If I act alone it will be too little. If I wait for the government it will be too late. If I act with others, we might just make it. The Quakers showed me the importance of equality. "If you realise everyone is equally important you don't trash their resources. Political campaigning is a great way to campaign on all issues at once."

Jo came to politics differently. She had been a sheltered housing manager. "When I met the local Green Councillor I thought, 'How brilliant!' I saw how they were helping people and that's what I was missing," she said.

My host that night Benj, is a student activist with People and Planet. Approaching along the street of terraced houses I can hear the sound of a guitar drifting through the summer air. Pleasingly, following the sound leads me to Benj, sat in his back garden under the washing line.

"I study at East Anglia University," Benj told me when we were settled back down on the colourful rug under the washing line with a drink. "I'm doing International Development with Anthropology and Politics."

"Wow that sounds cool! So what is People and Planet and how did you got involved?"

"It's a democratic student network campaigning on environmental and social justice issues," said Benj. "It has all these people who are like minded and trying to work on the same sorts of issues."

"So what are you working on at the moment?"

"The main thing is campaigning around fossil fuel divestment, to get our universities to divest their endowment funds. We've got 5.2 billion pounds in the fossil fuel industry from UK universities. It's pretty empowering and inspiring, at times frustrating, but ultimately it's quite rewarding."

The next morning I wander slowly across the city heading to find the TCV (Trust for Conservation Volunteers) office. I hadn't made an appointment, but gave them a call and hoped for the best. The office was in a rather run down area. There was a square with small closed business units and a band practicing on an old sofa outside in the sun. The TCV office building itself was a one story block like a large portacabin with a greenish tinge growing on it. As I arrived so did a minibus full of volunteers back from a work trip.

Debbie is the volunteer co-ordinator who takes volunteers out to work on public green spaces.

"I used to be a banker," Debbie tells me, "and I gave up work and did an environmental science degree. Then I did a masters and volunteered for six months. I wanted to work for TCV because I wanted to do practical conservation but also use my brain. So I do things like publicity, finance and marketing too. This is my dream job."

Debbie offers to let me stay for the night and I explain that it wouldn't just be me - I'll be meeting another walking companion that evening. No problem. She tells me that her husband is a marine biologist working down in Ipswich and he'll pick us up this evening after he gets back on the train.

I've no time to eat and must rush to an appointment at the Norfolk Wildlife Trust. Nik Kandpur is the head of development at the trust, which is one of the largest in the UK, having around 4000 members and about fifty reserves.

"You should definitely visit Cley Marshes if you can," Nik advises me. "It was the first reserve that founded the Trust nearly ninety years ago. Two years ago we had an incredible opportunity to purchase land between Cley marshes and Salt Marshes which would increase the size of the reserve by nearly a third. We've had the most incredible response from the public and the lottery. We decided to build a new conservation education centre as well and we managed to raise the whole amount. With the National Trust land too, there's now 8 km of protected coastline there. It makes you realise what you're doing, in terms of land and just how much it means to people. It's been a very moving two years.

"I'd spent sixteen years working in the arts and prior to that I'd been working in corporate education, so coming to the trust was my big career risk, but it was the best one I ever took. I do wake up every day and feel proud of the real impact that we have for habitats in the future. I think the thing about changing your path and saying 'right this is what I want to do' it comes to us all at different points in our life."

The land around Cley marshes was previously used for commercial shooting. Now the reserve is home to the rare Avocet. The birds had left Norfolk entirely and began to return in the 1980's.

"You give that back, the space for the species and it's almost immediate. The habitats should all connect," said Nik.

I walked by a lovely river on my way to the cathedral in Norwich. If I followed the river out it would take me to the Norfolk Broads. I had no idea that the Broads were man-made from a system of peat removal. The cathedral is visible from a little distance and then in front there is a large grass square. Lying on the grass, I relax against my bag and wait for Stefano. I met Stefano at The Missing Sock pub with Miranda and Sama and he had decided to join the walk for a few days. When he arrives, his pack is clearly causing him some pain - it's hanging off at a worrying angle. He takes everything out and we repack it and adjust the straps to get the weight angled better. Then it's time to meet Debbie's husband, Ollie.

As we get settled in to Ollie's car I need to satisfy my curiosity. "Ollie, Debbie told us that you're a marine biologist?"

"Yes that's right, on a research vessel down in Ipswich."

"...It wouldn't happen to be called Song of the Whale would it?" I ask, feeling a flutter of excitement.

"Yes, how did you know that?" asked Ollie.

"Ha ha, YES!" I exclaimed with delight. "I spent a month on Song of the Whale delivering it back to Ipswich last summer."

"You're THAT Eve! When Debbie said the person coming to stay was called Eve I thought that would be too much of a coincidence. I remember the owner saying that someone called Eve who was trying to reduce their carbon footprint would be on the boat," said Ollie.

"I took up sailing to stop having to fly, so that I could get around for free," I said nodding. "I delivered yachts for several months. That time on Song of the Whale though was some of the best memories of my life. The whales, using the hydrophone, sailing and the dolphins! The phosphorescence at night as they swam by the boat, it was so beautiful!"

"I flew back to start on the data," said Ollie.

"Oh, you're THAT Ollie!" I said. "Ha! I left you some messages in the data! They showed me how to listen on the hydrophones to identify the sounds but when I didn't know what it was I would put a description in the comments. You'll see when you go through it. Some of them got a bit surreal;" I said laughing, "two squeaky gates fighting, that kind of thing."

I had been shocked to discover the noise pollution in the sea; there are big tankers and cargo ships that sound like a freight train even though they're miles away. There is frequent blasting and underwater construction. Then there are other mystery military noises and a massive range of boats; the deeper the hull the bigger the noise. I remember a couple of times having to remove the headphones because of something uncomfortable outside my hearing range. It's no wonder mammals beach themselves – they've no fingers to put in their ears and sometimes it's enough to drive you bonkers.

When we arrived at Debbie and Ollie's beautiful cottage Debbie was cooking dinner.

"Thank you so much for letting me stay also," said Stefano in his Italian accent. "You have a most beautiful home."

Over dinner and later in the lounge the conversation travelled through politics and the recent results of the European elections which had included a rise in UKIP.

"I'm very surprised at the British people," said Stefano. "How could they fall for it? The manifesto reads like Mein Kamf! It is very worrying, the rise in fascism across Europe. They are joining together also."

Debbie decided to walk out with us the following day and I listened gratefully as they walked slightly ahead of me.

"I've been very lucky with my relationship with Ollie, he's really helped me develop. That's the key to life really, is people," said Debbie, "but lots of people think it's things."

"Love is everywhere, if we are capable to see it," said Stefano. "How we look at a person makes a difference and how deep my greed is related to possession. Every time we keep something we close. We must remain always open."

My route from Norwich was back West and then North to the Norfolk coast. So this was a rare occasion when I returned to a place I had already been, Wymondham, and it made me feel so confident! "*I know this place,*" I thought, smiling inside. Debbie left us at Wymondham and I headed to the library to check for maps.

When I arrived at the library there was a circle of ladies knitting, so I went over to chat. About a minute after I sat down, the cakes came out and they offered me one. I explained about the tour, and that no, we didn't have anywhere to sleep that night. Immediately a lady across from me, Diane, offered me a bed for the night. I explained that Stefano was also walking with me and she said that was no problem. When we arrived at Diane's house her husband Keith opened the door and exhaled.

"Where did you find these two?" he asked unruffled as he took a step back and gestured us in.

"*Uh oh,*" I thought. "*She hasn't told him.*"

"The library. So this happens a lot then does it?" I said.

"Yes," said Keith with a shrug and a smile.

And indeed it does. Keith and Diane have two spare rooms and regularly take in waifs and strays as well as frequently having friends to stay. Diane used to be a nurse and Keith was in the army then worked for Windsor Palace. They became used to putting up groups of people and looking after others, and they never lost the habit.

In the garden, every surface has a bird feeder on. Every fence panel has something which is for the birds. Decorative teacups, ladles, plates, everything that can be put into service

184

for the birds, has been. Every evening and morning Keith fills all the feeders. They know the behaviours and personalities of their visitors as they watch from the conservatory. The jay, the blackbirds, tits, pigeons, the hedgehogs.

"At our last place I would feed the foxes and they'd come when I called. If they got mange I would send off for the free medicine. But we moved to be near Mum," said Di.

I gave them Buzz Tour badges and a packet of lavender seeds for the garden. Such caring people, I hoped that good things would always come to them.

In the morning after breakfast, Keith asked about my boots, which I admitted had split quite badly. The leather was coming away from the sole and it had splits across the top. Keith offered me a pair of his walking boots and I said they'd probably be too big.

"I don't think so, I'm a size six," he said.

"What? How was that in the army?" I asked.

"Tricky," he said. "I had to have special boots made. These aren't though, they're just walking boots, but I can't walk much anymore because of a knee operation."

"Wow. Thank you! That would be fantastic."

Stefano was to leave me that morning.

"What has been most important is to find how people can be so nice and kind when asked for help," Stefano said. "It's a very good, touching experience because it's a slow way of living, like slow cooking. This kind of slow walking can make a bridge and feeling with human beings. And this difference is going to be perceived by other people, it's like an energy to get nearer, nearer, to the people. The better we will be able to establish, to create a new alliance among people that should bring all together to a more beautiful world. Above all with more love, love, love. Love is at the end what we need."

Ah, Italians.

In the afternoon, I leave my old blue boots. I'd carried them in case the new boots were uncomfortable but they were too heavy to keep carrying, so I placed them beside a bin. I kept looking back at them as I walked away. Sixteen years.

In the village of Rocklands I stopped at the community shop and café which seemed to be thriving. With shares owned by local residents and staffed by local volunteers and employees the café was the hub in the village. The young lady working there told me that she was going to have to move out of the village because she couldn't afford to buy there. I'd seen several 'sold' signs around the village.

Early evening I was headed to a church in a village when someone called out to me from a pub garden table with eight men, asking what I was doing. When I explained, he offered to buy me a drink so I joined them for a lemonade. Rob was curious about the changes I'd made in my life and how I'd lived with so little money the last couple of years.

"You'll have to return to real life at some point," Rob said.

"I never left," I said. "This is my life."

After a short time one of the other guys at the table offered to let me camp in his garden. But as the evening wore on he kept drinking and his friends teased him more and more for offering a strange woman his garden.

"Aren't you frightened walking on your own as a woman?" someone asked.

"Sometimes, but everyone I've met has been lovely," I said.

"I wouldn't let my daughter or girlfriend so something like that," said Rob. "Do you have a boyfriend?"

I exhaled slowly. "I'd rather not answer. I'm not being awkward but I don't exist in reference to a man. What he would think or wouldn't think isn't what matters."

Rob nodded thoughtfully. Others began to offer me horror stories of the dangers for a woman alone. The conversation turned to tales of women who had been attacked or murdered locally and a woman murdered and dumped in the lake. Someone joked that I would end up in the lake.

"Come on. That's a bit too dark!" I said starting a new conversation with Rob as people agreed. The evening drew in and I was getting tired. I went to the toilet, but when I came out... my host-to-be was gone!

186

CHAPTER 22 — Kill Owen Patterson

"**It** all got a bit too much for him - the teasing," said someone. *What to do?* My host had disappeared and it was getting late. I sat back down to think. One of the guys asked about weapons, did I carry any? I explained that no, it would be a bad energy, it was easier for people to trust me as a woman and knowing that I meant no harm. After ten minutes one of the guys said he lived above the pub and he would put me up in his spare room. After showing me the room, he retired to watch TV, and in the morning he had already gone, so that was the last I saw of my saviour for the night.

Walking out of the village I can see huge stacks of hay bales in the distance. The mayflowers are gone now, not surprising I suppose since we're into June. In Wooton there is a charity on the high street for motivating young people... right next door to a bookies.

"Are you lost?" someone asks me. I turn in surprise.

"No. I'm found. I mean to be here," I said.

I had contacted a permaculture site, but forgotten to confirm a few days in advance so I left a message for the owner, Ben, and headed there in hope. When I arrived Ben wasn't in, so I decided not to chance it and to keep walking. The poppies were out and the soil sandy. Feeling a bit low and in need of a hug I remembered the rule about walking: if you feel low, have some water and food. Biscuits and raisins did indeed help.

I had been walking for a couple of days across the flat and that day I reached a very slight incline. The gentle slope would normally have passed unnoticed but by the side of the road at the top was a warning triangle, telling drivers to check their brakes! After hours walking alone, it completely set me off. I actually had to grab my knees I was laughing so much.

In the evening I found myself a space out the back of a village hall, and just before I put up my tent I got a call...from the permaculture farm. Ben had got my message. When I told him where I was, he exclaimed, "Well I'll come and get you!"

Back at the Grange we had some dinner in the big bright yellow open-plan kitchen. There were family photos, colourful paintings hanging as well as directly painted on the walls. Musical instruments lay around. In the hall we had passed lots of photos of visiting groups to the house.

"We're already seeing the effects of climate change, but the next thirty years we'll see a lot more," said Ben as we washed up. "Not just climate change but the impacts of the growing economic inequality and uncertainty in resource peaks."

"How did the Grange get started?" I asked.

"I have friends who had survived torture, which changed my perspective on what a life problem is. I worked on the Copenhagen climate change COP negotiations and I was disillusioned and emotionally burnt out by it. Partly because I didn't think it was going anywhere but partly because too many people had become institutionalised by it and lost the integrity of what they were doing. None of the NGO's were offering any solution which came anywhere close to the reality of climate change. Knowing where we are currently headed, I decided to focus on resilience.

"That's what we're doing here in two words - building resilience, for ourselves and for others. We've been here two years and we work with people who've survived torture and trauma. Initially the idea was therapeutic retreats, but more and more we're realising what people need is to be welcomed into a family home.

"There are therapeutic activities of different types depending on the needs of people, but often it's just about being outside, feeling safe, getting involved in activities where you're contributing to something. We've had over two hundred people come and use the space and we're learning as we go. Most of all here, it's a lot of fun, it's the best job in the world. We sit in this kitchen with people from all over the world, eating great food that people have cooked, playing music, singing, dancing, and laughing. There's no greater therapy for anyone really."

The next day Ben showed me their garden and chickens, then drove me to Willow Farm where he was teaching a permaculture course with his friend Lee that weekend.

"Last year there were a few people whose life fundamentally changed during the time of the course," Ben told me in the car, "to be part of that is a real privilege."

We found Lee picking some veg in the garden for the lunch. The land at Willow farm includes barns, a tepee and a growing orchard. Inside one of the barns, the materials from the previous day's teaching were taped to the walls. One wall had dozens of colour coded post-it notes with intriguing things on: Seven Hat Thinking, Input output analysis, S.W.O.C., Wild design, and Mind maps. The core principles of permaculture were on a poster: People care, Fairshare, Earthcare.

"I've been here about eleven years," said Lee. "I spent the previous twelve years travelling around the world as a fashion photographer with, maybe fifty to sixty international flights a year, using a lot of carbon. I was looking out into the world, waiting for everyone else to do something. Then I realised that nothing was going to happen unless I did something. It's very different to have gone from this other lifestyle, earning thousands of pounds a day, taking pictures of beautiful people in warm exotic countries, selling lies to people, to actually facing up to the hard truth that, we're all human and part of this planet and we need to cooperate.

"I began to slow down and to find ways to observe myself. Realising what my own truth was, rather than the truth I'd been creating for others through the media. People say 'I can't stop, I have all these things, I have a mortgage'. I did it one thing at a time. I stopped watching television. I stopped reading newspapers. I stopped listening to any kind of media. All of a sudden I realised I didn't want anything anymore, I had everything. My work before was to create this illusion of something being desirable and slightly unobtainable.

"It's been a very difficult journey to get there, it just takes patience and just to believe in yourself and to love yourself. Just to do one stage at a time, to do one small achievable bit and then another after that and to just keep on going. And before you know it that will be your life!"

As the students began to arrive, I instantly recognised one.

"Elaine! It's so great to see you again," I called.

"You too!" Elaine said smiling.

"How's the course going?" I asked.

"Good, we've got to put together a garden design today in our group. We did the surveying and interviewing yesterday."

I wandered the site as the students began their work again. The wind chimes rang in the open-sided shed kitchen with colourful benches and rocket stoves. Young trees have been planted all over the site.

Sitting outside in the long grass I felt how fortunate I was to have met so many people who are changing their lives for the better. Permaculture seems a very good way for people to transform because it's got very wholesome, holistic principles which relate to everything we do. Living in a balance and recognising that you are part of a system and that you are dependent upon that system. Once you get those principles inevitably you start to look around and view things differently.

Around the farm are a number of semi-derelict barns and there's a feeling of space where things are possible. Many of the things I've seen, seem to happen on the margins, giving me the feeling that if you are too imbedded in the existing way that things are there's more inertia to stop you from changing.

An hour later the students were back in their groups.

"How are you doing with your design?" Lee asked one of the students as they passed.

"Not very far," came the reply.

"Well good, it's good to have somewhere to travel to innit? Just enjoy the journey," said Lee as he followed the student back to their group. With his voluminous hair and exuberant personality, Lee reminds me of Zaphod Beeblebrox from the Hitchhikers Guide to the Galaxy.

After a lunch of homemade dishes brought in by the students and teachers I set off north towards the coast. I stopped for water in a pub and the landlord told me about a local farmer that was keen on orchids. "I'm sure, he'd love to show you."

Nick owns Old Hall Farm and part of it has been designated a County Wildlife Site. As we walked around Nick pointed to different orchids with pride and told me about the surveys on the field. I was surprised by how small orchids are; tiny delicate flowers in a column.

"There're areas that used to be ponds in the past, but were filled in and we put some back. We restored an old orchard. We planted new trees for habitat and wild bird seed planting to help with the hunger gap. I don't know what'll happen if they stop the funding for the bird habitat. Ponds are quite neglected in the payments schemes but the pond work was paid through a research PhD," Nick told me.

As we wandered around the land Nick pointed out different plants and beetles. He explained that he had apps on his smartphone for identifying bird calls, dragonflies and orchids.

"How did you become interested in conservation?" I asked

"I've lived on the farm since I was seven. After university I was a plumber but when my Dad died I took over the farm. I've always been interested and I think the payments scheme is a good way to farm *and* do conservation. It's nice to have a good field of wheat, but it doesn't excite me, but then if you find some great wildflowers..."

The afternoon was drawing to a close so I walked on to Dereham where I found a Scout Hut. I was relieved to be given permission to camp, under a nice big oak tree next to four fire pits. A steep bank of trees shielded me from the road.

"If the ladies were with me, I would light a fire in the fire pit, but I won't on my own," I thought. *"Oh go on. This is the perfect spot, where you're allowed. If not here, where?"*

I scavenged little pieces of wood and was relieved at how dry they were. I wrapped a frayed piece of wood in a piece of cardboard and made a lattice of kindling above it and was rewarded with a small blazing fire to read next to. Earlier on in the walk I didn't have the mental energy to read after walking but these days I found I could stay up and do something.

The smile response walking into Derham is a little slow in the morning but maybe my own smile is not convincing enough. Breakfast in a café strengthens the smile. After a day's walk I arrive at the Foxley Wood Norfolk Wildlife Trust site. It's ancient woodland, but it doesn't have old trees, which confuses me. The warden, Steve Colin explains.

"Ancient woodland is where there has been a wood on that land since ancient times. All the soil and species are adapted to woodland, but it doesn't necessarily mean the woodland hasn't been managed. Species have evolved to take advantage of mankind's old management practices, so we mimic these and create a range of habitats."

"In the way you cut the trees?" I ask.

"Yes, cutting lanes and removing the trees with horses," says Steve. "The broadleaf trees grow from the base and so when they are felled it will regrow rapidly in multiple stems. The 'standards' are the remaining large trees. We coppice the bushy habitat about every ten years. The semi-natural landscape gets more wildlife, which you need in these small isolated woodlands. In an ancient wood most of the magic is under the ground, the bacteria and the fungi maintain it."

A young man called Lee arrives to talk to Steve and I discover that he's a woodsman.

"Steve convinced me to get in to it," says Lee with gratitude. "I started on a traineeship, Skills for the Future, to work in the countryside and Steve encouraged me. I had a vague interest in woodland, but coming here really sparked my imagination. I see the value of coppicing for wildlife but I'd also like to bring back some of coppicing crafts."

Some of the things that Lee makes from the coppiced wood are hurdles (for sheep farming and fencing), bean poles, lampshades and faggots. Faggots I discover are a bunch of sticks for burning.

"They would have been used in all the ovens in the past," says Lee. "The idea of using timber for fire is a modern one.

In the past it would all have been faggots. The phrase 'by hook or by crook' comes from getting dead wood out of trees."

"Ash is the best for firewood," says Steve. "But sadly with Ash Dieback they won't be around in the future."

"There's a cultural loss too," says Lee. "I've never worked with Elm, and in future people won't be able to work with Ash. Acute Oak decline is creeping up the country too."

Steve was the first in the UK to identify Ash Dieback and he finds it very saddening to see its spread. It begins with a blackness at the branch tips which slowly spreads back to the trunk and kills the tree. Steve takes me to see a few Ash that have the disease. I'm pleased to now know what they look like. It's strange to think I'm looking at a species that probably won't be around in the next generation. Elms, died when I was a child and I don't know what they look like.

A few birds are calling around us. "It's difficult to protect migratory birds, many are shot in other countries. Like cuckoos in the Mediterranean. That's the thing with migratory birds," says Steve, "when they are here we think they are ours and when they are there, they think they're theirs."

There are lots more bird calls the next morning, but I don't know what any of them are. One seemed like a symphony, such a varied song that went on for ages. I am looking anew at the wildlife and plants around me. I've seen several flowers in Norfolk that I've never seen before but only four different looking butterflies, three of which I've seen lots of times before. Cabbage whites, peacocks and another orange one a bit like the peacock. The wild roses don't usually have a smell so when they do it's a real treat. The hazelnuts are starting to form already, but they're really tiny. Other seeds are forming too, on red leaves, but I don't know if they are sycamore or field maple. Small things hidden in the verges often rustle away from me.

I pass several concentration camp style farms and lorries with animals in. The big metal warehouses are more like factories than farms; dark threatening places with unfriendly business signs and a feeling of exploitation.

Half an hour later up a quiet lane I see a 'community speed watch' sign. I slow to a tiptoe... and edge past grinning.

In Cley I find a village hall where I can camp and I stash my backpack under a hedge and head into town. Walking around I pass house names that are like tombstones. The Old Forge. The Post Office. Joinery. Rectory. Bank. A local resident tells me that rich Londoners are buying up holiday homes and renovating, pushing up prices and depleting the community.

The next morning I arrive early at Cley Marshes visitors centre but there are already twelve people in the glass-walled café. The visitor's centre is a new eco building which looks out over the marshes. Its energy is supplied by a wind turbine and the roof has been planted. There are meandering streams amongst the spongy green of the marshes, pools of water, edged with curving plant mounds and beyond them, the sea.

Jonathan, the reserve manager, used to be a warden at a wood near Manchester. He'd played there as a child and the previous warden's ashes were scattered on the nature trail. Now he was at Cley.

"The new building has been really successful," Jonathan told me. "Last year we had 108,000 visitors. Most don't go onto the reserve though. They have something in the café and watch the reserve with binoculars. There was a man who came who had heart problems and it was his lifelong ambition to see a marsh harrier. He sat down with a coffee and one flew right past the window. He was nearly in tears. The new land we've acquired will mostly be protected from visitors but we'll have more educational things.

"You've still got some serious bird watchers, but not like in previous generations. When there's a rare bird in town nothing else matters. They tear up to the car park, leaving the cars anywhere, see the bird, and then go. A local person heard there was a rare bird in town and knocked a hole in his roof to see it! The church made £4000 when a rare bird turned up and people wanted accommodation. It paid for the stained glass window."

As I sat drinking my tea, one of the long term volunteers came over to speak to me.

"I really admire what you're doing," she said, "we need it. Now if you could just kill Owen Patterson, we'd be set."

I looked up in surprise then laughed. Sandra had, long white hair in a ponytail, a warm manner, glasses, bright eyes and she was also a nun. "Being a nun I don't have money, which I find so relaxing." I looked at her blinking. Now even the nuns are advocating killing the environment minister.

I had thought the marshes were salt marshes, but actually they are a freshwater habitat created by underground springs. The levels are managed by the warden to maximise the habitat. The length of grass is managed for different types of birds at different times of year and reed is taken for thatching.

Bernard is the reserve warden, as was his father and great grandfather before him. When the sea floods the marshes it actually damages the rare freshwater marsh.

"We're working with the sea now though," Bernard told me, "no longer trying to hold it back. Over time it will flood more and the habitat will change and the wildlife will adapt."

Bernard was born in Cley, sixty five years ago, in a house owned by the trust but Cley has changed a great deal.

"The first bit of the reserve was purchased in 1926, it was the first county wildlife trust. Soon as I could walk I was out on the reserve with my father. He built hides from timber that washed up on the shore. The scrapes were dug with private donations and the boardwalks came in the eighties. You had to be pretty fit before then."

"What about the village?" I asked.

"It's gone from a community of people to a community of holiday homes. There's no one in the village that works on the farm now, it's run by contract. Cley's like a building site with renovations and new places that locals can't afford to live in. There was a school my son went to but it's closed. There were four pubs and lots of local shops."

Walking through Cley now, there are still two pubs but the rest is only galleries and tourist shops with one delicatessen that sells expensive goods.

"You didn't need to go anywhere other than Cley," said Bernard. "It was almost self sufficient, except for clothes. There were also a lot of cottage industries and people selling crabs and cockles at their windows. There used to be a café called Gulls, where all the twitchers (bird watchers) went. The phone at the café would constantly be ringing with sightings. They'd sleep rough, the younger guys. I used to row out to Blakely Point to fish with friends and go babbing for eels with worms on thick wool so the eels teeth would get stuck. Or we'd go creek jumping and end up splat."

In the visitors centre there are identification keys and I discover that the pink flower I've been seeing around is called the Red Campion. As I leave the centre every table is full and people line the window. I look at the marshes again with new eyes. Humans can be a wonderful force of disturbance and change if we act in harmony. Sometimes doing it right means you can't tell we've done anything at all.

Setting off along the coast I aim for Wells-next-the-sea and a grey cloud follows me all day. The marshes seem vast and peaceful. People I chat with that day and subsequently seem sceptical about the offshore wind farm.

"They don't pay for themselves," one person tells me. "Because of the sea salt erosion it's much more expensive than building it on land."

There seems to be a lot of tourism ahead along the coast and I wonder how strong the communities are when there is a high proportion of tourism? The length of my detour around the Norfolk coastal path starts to seem unwise. Although it was worth it to get to Cley I decide to use a bus to get me back on the main route. In Wells-next-the-sea every person I ask for directions is a tourist. I can't find a single person that lives there. With a few minutes to spare, I arrive at the bus stop and pay my £3.10 for the last bus that day (early evening). I've never enjoyed a bus ride so much! It feels so fast and so incredible to go sixteen miles for just £3.10. We're travelling fast enough that we escape the grey cloud and break out into dazzling sunshine. Passing so many villages so fast and none of them mean anything to me. It feels naughty but fun as the bus shudders and thunders along. I overhear the driver's conversation with a passenger. "In the winter most of it's closed, you drive through and it's all holiday homes."

As we turn the corner the sea is blinding in the evening sun. A packet of chips later and I'm pitched in a holiday park campsite amongst line after line of empty caravans. I had managed to catch the lady before she put the chips in polystyrene and asked for it in paper. She had looked at me confused and didn't know how to wrap it in paper. Over the last five years I've seen a big change, all the fast food places are using polystyrene now. One place when I asked for chips in paper, measured them in the polystyrene, tipped them out then threw it away. Mercifully, these chips come guilt-free.

At the resort bar I'm hit with déjà vu. The children are being entertained in a mostly empty dance floor whilst the parents sit around the outside drinking. I walk to the beach past a depressingly closed funfair and a shut sea life show. In fact almost everything near the beach is closed. It's late June.

The beach is almost deserted as I take off my clothes to paddle in the sea. From this distance no one can tell a bra from a bikini anyway. I watch the clear sunset and head back to my tent, through the long stretches of carbon-copied resort, to wash some clothes in the sink. For what you get at the caravan park it's still fairly expensive for families and now I understand why. For the majority of the year, the place is empty - they have to charge enough in the brief school holidays to cover the whole year. But it keeps the kids happy and safe, for many this is the only holiday they will get. That's what my parents always used to say - as long as the kids are happy and occupied, you're happy.

As I had bent my leg to get up into the bus I'd discovered it was very stiff and rather painful. Undressing revealed that a series of mozzy bites I had received, had taken a turn for the worse. Over the previous few days I'd watched them increase from the diameter of mugs to that of side plates. I'd had to hobble a bit as I left the bus until my leg unstiffened.

The luxury of hot water and a proper toilet for my night time pee are a significant plus. In the morning I enjoy a warm breakfast and make use of the swimming pool, causing a bit of a disruption. Having no swimsuit with me I decide to swim saggy-boobed in a black top and knickers but the lifeguard loudly disapproves, telling me that it will have absorbed all the chlorine. But by then I'm already wet, so there's not much to be done. I mutely keep looking at him apologetically until he stops. The sight of my angry swollen leg is a bit alarming. Friendly people in the sauna chat to me and all in all I leave the campsite feeling like a million bucks (the male deer not the money) and smiling hugely.

The second bus journey is nowhere near as enjoyable as the first, it squeaks like a kettle all the way to Kings Lynn. The library in Kings Lynn is a beautiful old intricate brick building near a lovely park, but it doesn't have the maps I need so I'll have to just aim for the towns. I don't find any leads in the library or a café. "*I wish every town had a 'green' place. It would really speed things up.*" Perhaps sometimes it's just about walking and hoping.

There is a nice wide river in Kings Lynn and the port is still functioning. The riverside buildings seem to be restaurants rather than working for river commerce though. It takes a while to walk to the bridge, my leg feels very hot from the bites. To get out of town I pass a derelict quay, full of weeds. A faded swastika has been sprayed on the concrete wall. I get out my chalks and draw designs, obscuring it.

In the village of Clenchwarton, Ian gives me food although it's against company policy. My smile is back and my stomach is full, of pasties and cakes. There is about £75 left in the bank to last two months. Now that it's just me the money lasts longer but I must be stricter with myself about not using campsites. £75, two months. Every free sandwich makes it seem possible. *Thank you Ian.*

CHAPTER 23 — Permaculture pause

"**Mick** The Hat...but the hat's in the car." Mick The Hat is a kind elderly gentleman who buys me a lemonade. I highly recommend lemonade to restore you after walking. My leg feels tight as I sit on the bar stool. Mick The Hat's wife is in hospital, he's lost without her. He loves the robin next door, who he always greets every day, and watching the wren.

"You can't buy that. You *cannot* buy that," he said. "Since I retired, if my wife's health were better, I'd say it's the happiest I've ever been."

The evening is drawing in as I approach Sutton Bridge through a field. The gap in the crop that I'm walking in has thirty sticky spider webs across it that I have to sweep aside with my stick. In Sutton Bridge after calling up the church I'm taken in by Christina; piano and violin teacher, dog trainer, and vicar's wife. Arriving at the door, I'm greeted by a cacophony of barking from three dogs, one of which is a white Great Dane. "Hello da-ling, hello da-ling!" I say petting them. All pets, children and close friends are 'darling' to me – it's descriptive and it simplifies names when looking after new acquaintances.

Christina protested against a local biomass power station where wood would have been imported from Canada.

"I thought, oh no, I've just arrived, am I going to be 'angry vicar's wife'? But another power station when the village already has a gas fired one - really, NO," said Christina. "I don't want to be lying down in the road but I will if I have to."

As Christina moves around the house there's a constant dialogue with her dogs. The dogs were all rehomed with her after the owner's couldn't keep them. Soon after Christina and her husband arrived in the village, one of the residents told them about 'Pet Service'. It's a monthly church service where parishioners bring their pets with them to church.

"One person asked to bring a horse!" she said.

I have a suspicion that the residents are pulling the leg of the new vicar but how would I know. Christina says they're going to honour the tradition. I wonder about that horse.

Christina gave me dinner, breakfast and a pack lunch. I'm eating a lot less these days. I guess my body has put on whatever muscle it needed to. Over breakfast we talk about the empowerment of people.

"For them to become themselves and be part of the body that is the community of humanity," said Christina. "It's about equality and honouring all the parts."

I'm struck by how much we can be at different starting points but going in the same direction.

As I walk on the next morning there are school children everywhere and black bin bags by the road. It's been a long time since I've seen bin bags. Everywhere else has wheelie bins now. Some of the bags have a rip in them. The bags are surprisingly less intrusive than wheelie bins, but more likely to let litter out. A lot of the common litter I see in rural areas is drink cans and bottles, snack wrappers, tobacco packets and lottery scratch cards.

I find that lots of places have free wifi to access the internet now but no computers. When I was in my late teens the first internet café opened in our town. There was an explosion of cafés around the country for a while but now there seem to hardly be any, except in areas with a lot of immigrants. It seems everyone owns a device themselves now. Unfortunately I don't have a device so it's hard to try to find people ahead to visit.

I realise I've left my stick behind when I reach another field and am covered in sticky spider webs.

Roger lets me in to use his toilet and gives me a coke.

"I watch a lot of news," said Roger, "and I think the world's gone mad." His daughter has cancer and I surprised myself by saying I would pray for her. I don't know what I'm praying to though. I recommended he read Positive News instead.

"You can read it online," I said.

Roger lost all his pension and later savings when the companies went bust.

"I left school at sixteen and I've always worked," he said.

"Wasn't the money protected? Don't companies have to protect pension funds in some way?" I asked. I remember seeing on the news years ago about company's stealing from their employees' pension funds. My first big protest was a union one against the government taking public pension money to pay off national debt. You've taken someone's money and told them you'll look after it until they are old. How can governments or companies steal it?

"I don't know about all that, legal stuff, all I know is I lost it all. I paid £300 a month for years and it's all gone," he said sucking on a cigarette.

At the Chestnuts garden centre Dave and Rick give me packets of seeds to give to hosts as gifts. The day is really hot by now. In the future, all roads and paths should be tree-lined to protect us from the sun as we walk.

The last time I was at a computer I'd tried to put some requests out online for hosts and after only a short walk I am to be sheltered by Johnny and Beth in Holbeach. Just as well, my mozzy bite is the size of a dinner plate and makes walking difficult. Over dinner Beth tells me about growing up in nearby Spalding.

"It used to have the most amazing flower festival, people would come over from Holland for it. But the last one we went to, there wasn't a single real tulip, it was all crepe paper on all the floats! It's become so commercial we don't go anymore."

It turns out that Beth and Johnny travelled to Vancouver at the same time as I did. They notice my tattoo of a blue drop and I tell them it's about the blue drop movement that was happening at the time in BC.

"Against the tar sands oil pipelines!" Johnny exclaims. "We went to one of those protests! People made a giant blue drop by holding big blue drops each over their head."

"Ha! Yep, I was one of the people holding a blue drop."

"Small world! It looked so good from above."

"During the public hearing about the Enbridge pipeline, I was giving out a couple of hundred blue drop badges a day, for people to show support for clean land and water."

The Canadian tar sands mining operation is the biggest industrial project on the planet. The bitumen is extracted either by mining or with underground steam injection. The tar sands sit underneath the Boreal Forest, so in order to mine them the forests must first be cleared. After extraction, the bitumen is melted and mixed with solvents like benzene to make it pumpable. When it spills in rivers and seas however, the solvents evaporate and the bitumen sinks. The synthetic oil is hugely more carbon intensive than crude oil. The current Steven Harper government in Canada wants to maximise tar sand oil production and sell this synthetic oil to China. When I last heard, there were applications to build nine new oil pipelines to take the tar oil to the west coast for shipping to China. The tankers would have to pass through some of the most precious marine coastal habitat imaginable and through narrow straights amongst islands. The route is so worrying that when Enbridge made a promotional video, they edited out sixteen islands to make it look easier to navigate.

Walking to Spalding there's no option but to take the main road. For the first time on the walk I use my headphones and iPod. On the walk I normally don't want the intrusion of music (unlike every other time in my life) or to waste the battery but I have the volume up full. A large car or truck will still entirely drown out the music. It's shocking how loud cars are when they go fast. A pack of cyclists go past raising money for cystic fibrosis and I applaud and cheer. An ambulance goes past, and I silently wish them luck.

The sun is hot today and I can feel the tight pressure of my leg skin where it's throbbing from the bite. I lose concentration for a second and scratch it. *Damn.* There are lots of dead birds and bees lying around.

"Well the birds and the bees around here won't be getting up to any nooky". I laugh slightly guiltily.

I can't see any flowers around for the bees to eat, perhaps that's it? Perhaps the birds were hit by cars? Pesticides? I don't know why they're dead.

Entering Spalding I notice that quite a lot of cherry trees are ripe now, but many are too tall for me to reach the fruit or next to busy roads with fumes. All that food, out of reach. The smell of barbeques is on the air tonight, it makes me long for friends and hot food. I see my first No Parking sign in three languages. I guess there must be a lot of immigrant agricultural workers in the area. I walk on through the flat land but don't find much enthusiasm.

The church I was aiming for is now houses so I have to keep on. It's another hour to the next village and there are only a couple of farm buildings before it. My leg hurts and I feel I really don't want to go further. The farm I'm next to has what seem to be newish fruit trees planted near the house, and chickens. Good sign. I knock at a farm and they agree to let me camp in their garden.

Annette, the farmer's wife invites me in for a tea. When I explain that I'm finding people doing things for the environment and community, she exclaims, "Good luck finding that in the Clough!" The Clough, Annette explains, is this area. The more I talk with Annette, the more unravels.

Annette is involved with Women in Rural Enterprise and is a midwife. She's trying to get yoga classes for pregnant women. She's starting her own business in aromatherapy local products like soap. She's planted fruit and veg in her garden and is rearing chickens. She supports more natural medical therapy like herbalism and wants women to have more choice and power over their pregnancy. Good luck finding someone doing something for the environment and community? Well luck is with me my friends, cause I found her, she just didn't know it.

"We're illegal at the moment, independent midwives."

"Why?!" I asked, shocked.

"They changed the law to say that midwives have to get a certain type of insurance like dentists, but there are no insurance companies who offer the insurance."

There are no flowers around so I give them the rest of the packets of flower seed that I have as I leave in the morning.

In one of the villages I passed previously, people sold their allotment produce but around Lincolnshire there seem to be lots of little driveway stalls with people selling things. There are big flat distances between each farmhouse and long straight roads. Some cars come past like a rocket, doing about 80 mph. The sun is hot and I reach around behind into the side webbing of my pack for my cap, but my hands find a chocolate bar first and I have to give that my full attention. Other than chocolate I'm still eating a lot of oatcakes and tomato paste.

I passed a lot of men out mowing their lawns and I didn't pass many flowers. Why not let it grow? They'd have more time for other things and the wildlife would have food.

Late afternoon I was walking down another long empty straight road, approaching a solitary house in the distance, when I got a bad vibe. A man came out with a sack barrow and into the shed and the vibe got worse. What sounded like a generator was going. I needed a break but I didn't want to stop in sight of the house. I kept walking and as I got near I saw that the black pillar on the side of the house was a slightly bigger than life-size statue of a woman. Then I got close enough to see that the woman was chained up, with her hands above her head. My shoe lace came undone. *No bloody way I'm stopping to do it up here.*

The permaculture teachers Ben and Lee had told me about Hannah who taught them. "If you get the chance you really should visit her," they said. Since it was on the way it seemed that I really should. I arrived at The Inkpot and waited for Hannah and her family to return from a day out.

There were two portacabins which were the large kitchen and dining area for the students, and an office. A set of compost toilets, a yurt, a marquee for teaching in and a fire pit with wooden benches around. In the marquee were the remains of the course that just finished that day - flipchart paper notes and writing on the whiteboard.

When Hannah arrives she gives me a tour. Around the buildings there are several food-growing areas with interestingly arranged plants as well as food growing out of large tyres as raised beds. There are ducks in one of the gardens and amongst the grass, white bobble clover flowers are higgeldy green clumps. Next to the greenhouse are a couple of sets of wooden outdoor table and chairs.

"I did a Masters in Organic Farming and went to New Zealand to go WWOOFing (World Wide Opportunities on Organic Farms) on large-scale organic farms," says Hannah. But I kept ending up at small, messy, very abundant places. They were all talking about permaculture and I thought 'interesting, but it's not going to solve the world's problems.'

"One of the farmers said that there was a permaculture course happening. I was just like 'well what could they tell me that I don't already know', you know the arrogance of youth! Ah hem. So I thought I might as well get a certificate in my year off, it'll look good on my CV. And...nearly left on the first night. They were like 'oh permaculture, it's going to change your life, it'll be amazing.' Yeah right, OK really? Then within the first couple of days, the hair was up on the back of my neck. It wasn't anything new but it was just everything that I already knew, that made total sense. And suddenly it was like, 'ah, yeah, of course, yeah, I knew that! Why didn't I think of that before?' That was eleven years ago.

"Daniel and I came out of our house and mortgage when the girls were one and moved into a yurt on a friend's farm and worked there for rent. Then we started hunting for our land and moved into our lorry. So it was two adults, two babies, two dogs on tour for a year as I taught permaculture.

"We'd got these absolute things that we wanted, like it had to be within two miles of a train station, above thirty meters above sea level, about thirty acres, within an hour of public transport from my mum...and we compromised on all of those! This land was at rock bottom when we bought it, there was no diversity. The soil was completely compacted, completely sprayed. It had been a conventionally managed oilseed rape arable field for decades and then it was sparingly planted with ryegrass and pumped full of fertilizers and pesticides. And in three and a half years it's now this buzzing place, so much diversity of insects and birds. We love it."

The sun was setting behind Hannah and we sat around the bonfire. In the field there was the skeleton of a large round wooden structure which is to be their field shelter and part time classroom. I could see why she loved it.

"We're running an introductory course this week. If you wanted to stay and help prepare for it, you could come on it for free?" said Hannah over breakfast.

Losing three days walking time was a significant decision, but getting a free permaculture course, letting my leg heal and learning from Hannah would also be fantastic.

"There's a group coming from a land project on the way to Nottingham, they might be able to give you a lift there afterwards, to make up the time," she said. That swung it.

The next few days were spent cleaning and doing bits around the land. I'd read a permaculture textbook during my time in Canada, but all it really did was open my eyes, I didn't internalise much of it.

Stefano got in touch to say he would like to rejoin me on the tour for a time. I explain about the permaculture course and he decided to join. He arrived the night before and we sat by the campfire.

"The digital divide has created a cliff that some will never climb," he said. "70% of Italians don't have an email address."

"I had no idea it was that many," I said.

"I think policies have to reshape different models of life not their model of rich. Stop saying wealthier, start saying happier, more peaceful," said Stefano.

We talk about the ideas of a free university, some of which are appearing online. "The excellence is not in the building but in the will to love knowledge and to search for it," said Stefano. It's several hours before we make our way to our tents in the dark.

The next morning as the students arrive, so do their dogs. Adding to Hannah's dog and the neighbour's one which comes over, we have six dogs working out the order of the pack. Most work it out quite quickly but two can't agree; one spends the next several hours trying to mount the other.

We begin the course by defining permaculture.

"The conscious design and maintenance of agri-productive ecosystems which have the diversity, stability and resilience of natural ecosystems."

Then we go straight to the ethical basis of permaculture. It's rather thrilling for me to find something where ethics are the first thing that gets taught.

- Care of the Earth - provision for all life systems to multiply
- Care of People - provision for people to access those resources necessary for their existence
- Setting Limits - to population and consumption

In permaculture design the principles used are:

- Work with nature not against it
- The problem is the solution
- Make the least change for the greatest possible effect
- The yield of a system is theoretically unlimited
- Everything gardens. Every species has an effect

Hannah tells us about eight generational thinking. Knowing your history for 200 years, how did people live in this place before? Will your decisions still be good in eight generations?

One of the other students Dan, is doing a course called 'A Year in Transition' to help people transform their livelihood.

"I'd travelled a lot," said Dan, "but I wanted a purpose for my time, so I offered to help some friends who were starting a smallholding. I was reading a copy of Transition Free Press when I saw the course advertised. To have a year to take control of where your life is heading is powerful."

"What's the course like?" I asked.

"It's a very alternative way of learning things. We've done storytelling and meditation for example. It's changed how I've thought about a lot of things and quickly," said Dan.

As we move on to the twelve principles of permaculture, Hannah's twin daughters arrive back from school. One sits on a chair near to Hannah and asks to help, so the principles are written up neatly onto the board by a young child. I wonder how many times she has heard these principles.

- Use edges and value the marginal
- Observe and interact
- Use and value renewable resource and services
- Design from patterns to details
- Catch and store energy
- Obtain a yield
- Creatively use and respond to change
- Integrate rather than segregate
- Produce no waste
- Apply self regulation and accept feedback
- Use and value diversity
- Use small and slow solutions

"The amazing thing about the principles of permaculture design is it isn't just used for your garden, you could design other things with these principles," said Hannah.

As Stefano and I part the next day he leaves me with a note of inspiration pollen written on a Buzz Tour card.

"Life is a walk. Ask love to move your steps. Ask your steps to move your heart. Ask your heart to embrace love to move your steps."

Several of the people on the course are from the land project Indigo Brave, and they agree to take me west with them to hear what they do there. The journey is alarming to me - I've become unused to being in a car.

"I don't normally drive like this Eve!" Leila calls to me in the back, as a truck swings out in front of us. "I need to shave five minutes off the satnav so my daughter isn't abandoned."

"I'm sure she won't mind ten minutes," I laugh nervously.

"It isn't her, it's the ballet teacher!" says Leila, "She's a fearful woman, she rules with an iron rod and rebukes parents for poor hair bun construction."

CHAPTER 24 — Book by its cover

Indigo Brave is a very large area of fields, with three temporary buildings. Two couples bring up two children and they have a volunteer to help around the farm.

"I'm their godmother," Vanya tells me, "Phil and I help take them to school etc. We all share tasks on the farm."

Vanya shows me the gardens and two of their pigs.

"Aww...I have to go in to say hello," she climbs over the fence to stroke and pet them affectionately. She points out the hot box composting which has me confused for a moment. The only hot box I know isn't to do with those kind of weeds.

"It's a very fast way of composting even human poo into high grade compost." Nearby is the beginning of a straw-bale building and past that, a stream. A rocket stove is being used to heat their outdoor hot tub.

Sat at the table outside, Leila tells me about the work of Indigo Brave. There are pots of herbs and vegetables around and a few leaning sunflowers.

"Behavioural change is about inviting people to examine their choices. We work with people on what they're thinking, what they're believing. Hopefully at the end of the process, there is the opportunity to go 'I get why I did that and I want to reach for a better choice now' and people are able to take that very deeply into their lives. Their habits shift.

"Indigo Brave started back in 2006. We started working with what we called children at risk of exclusion from school or who were behaving very inappropriately. We work with them creatively through a lot of drama, expressing their own story. What they believe. And the teachers said, 'OK, these kids are behaving differently, what are you doing?' So we started training the teachers. Then we wrote a play called Strong At The Broken Places, which won a millennium award.

"Then we started taking our work to adults with mental health histories and different issues and the same thing happened. We developed what we like to call the Robin Hood school finance and started to work with corporate organisations; things like stress management, communication and emotional intelligence. That funds the other work."

"What did it take for Indigo Brave to happen?" I asked.

"So how did we end up in a field?" said Leila laughing. "On May 13th 2010 at 11.45pm, an arsonist set fire to our home. Smoke alarms, taking the kids out of their beds. He had set a total of seventeen fires in the area before he was caught. Even after the fire there was the trial and the insurance bonkersness. We moved six times in eighteen months. When it was all done we sort of sat back and went...'well, now what?' It was so clear that instead of talking about the eco build and watching Grand Designs it was time to just bite the bullet and do it in any way we could."

Their daughter Esme sits with me after dinner and tells me about her favourite Disney films that I haven't seen.

"That sounds nice," I say. "Does it have a happy ending?" with shock I realise I'm about to cry and I have to turn away so she doesn't see. I can think of nothing I'd rather do now than curl up on a sofa with a child and watch children's films.

The next day I'm given a lift into Nottingham and I start walking across it from Sneinton. A Turkish-looking man with a slight accent greets me.

"Hello love, are you travelling through many countries?"

"No, just England," I say smiling.

"Well, welcome!" he says cheerfully with pride.

It's a strange mix of emotions that I feel. Grateful to be welcomed into Nottingham, annoyed to be welcomed in my own country by someone with a foreign accent, pleased that this is the sort of reception a visitor receives and wondering how much ownership, if any, I have of Nottingham. My father grew up in Nottingham and I went to university there, but I never integrated. No one else welcomes me. Only that man took ownership to be friendly and welcome someone. There is terraced housing and lots of ethnic diversity, a waft of cannabis from a passing white man in a tracksuit. The people mostly look fairly prosperous and content in themselves. Only a few look unhappy with themselves.

I see a sign to a Green Windmill and when I arrive I discover that it's green because it was owned by a famous Mr Green who was a mathematician and it is now a science centre. As I stare through the gates nearly an hour before they're due to open, Graham takes pity on me and invites me in for a cup of tea. "We have an ounce of humanity between us," he says laughing as he unlocks the gate. Graham is a short energetic man with a neat beard and bright blue eyes. He clearly loves his job and the history of the windmill.

The windmill was built in 1807 by a local baker. His son, George Green, only had a year of school before he had to leave to help with the business. It wasn't until his thirties that he was able to join a library and start to explore his passion for maths. Then in his forties he went to Cambridge University for seven years, producing all sorts of calculations that have helped the development of physics, technology and engineering. Greens essays lay forgotten until four years after his death. Things that you use everyday exist because of the mathematics of George Green.

Graham takes me up to the top window of the mill.

"There were huge riots in 1800, the Nottingham Food Riots," he says. "People thought millers were hiding grain. In the 1830's the only buildings here would have been the church and the duke's palace. The major industry was lace and average life expectancy was around twenty! There were five times more people than the city had been planned for."

They now mill biodynamic flour with the mill that they sell in the shop. At one time there would have been 10,000 windmills across England. Many were made of wood so haven't survived.

In the 1970's the government wanted to demolish the derelict mill and build a road but a group formed to protect it. In 1979 the mill was bought by the George Green memorial fund who gave it to the council to restore. The science centre now hosts spinning and weaving classes and an amateur radio club. At first glance it might have seemed that a science centre is not about the environment, but so much of what they are doing is positive for our future. Some of the volunteers have social difficulties and the purpose and support is hugely positive in their lives. Lots of people doing fantastic environmental and social work in our communities might not be labelled 'environmentalists' or 'social workers'.

As I walk on into town an old man in a tweed jacket and flat cap gets off a bus with a cane. He passes a young girl wearing very short shorts with patterned tights, who is dripping with jewellery and on a smartphone. He shuffles past housing tower blocks that would have gone up when he was in his thirties, and a lady sucking on an e-cigarette.

When the smoking ban came in, it was amazing how quickly we all adapted. Considerate smokers had been smoking away from non-smokers for quite a while but people said that the pubs would lose all their business, but of course they didn't. Shelters began to appear outside pubs for smokers to use. Outside shops and office buildings now you see guilty, rather pathetic looking smokers, tucked in a dirty doorway. Electronic cigarettes have only become big in the last year. First there was just one or two, now they're everywhere; a talking point, novel, so many flavours. I see the adverts on bus shelters everywhere. They don't miss a trick.

St. Anne's allotment is one of the oldest allotments in the country and one of the few remaining in the Victorian hedged 'detached town garden' style. The allotments are each surrounded by a hedge with a locked garden door. It has community groups and over 550 individual allotment holders.

"St. Anne's Allotment has undergone massive changes in the last seven years," The Partnerships and Volunteers Officer told me. "It was quite an abused and neglected area."

A few years ago the allotments were a hotspot of drugs and violent crime, so the council wanted to sell them.

"A group of the tenants got together and formed a group to protect the allotments and they were able to get funding.

They were also able to get the allotments historic listed status. Around five million pounds was invested in the new building, security, staff and restoration. It's completely used again. It's a really exciting time. There's always been a really impressive array of wildlife, considering we're near the city centre. As part of the restoration we've been able to manage plots that can't be used, as wildlife sites. I've worked in this role for only about three months but been a volunteer for seven years. So it was an absolute dream come true when the job came up."

In the visitors centre I meet Diane who does the accounts part time. She used to be a full time accountant but gave it up when she realised that it was gardening that made her happy.

"I just wanted to be happy. So now I'm a happy poor gardener, not a sad rich accountant," she said.

All the allotments are different, some have chickens or rabbits, and there is a community orchard. Hundreds of different style doors with mystery things behind them. So many keyholes; looking through them is like a game.

So far, walking into Nottingham I hadn't recognised anything. Suddenly with a shock of recognition I find myself at the Victoria shopping centre. Gradually I see more and more buildings that I recognise. A cashpoint that I used to use, a pub I used to go to. It's like seeing ghosts.

I've met a lot of students in the past couple of years who have amazed me. They have been so politically aware, so active. My university days seem quite different, full either of study or drinking, but then we are all on different paths. I remember in my first year, two male student reps came to ask for nominations to be our student rep. I looked around to see who it was going to be, and I counted six men. That doesn't seem right I thought, there ought to be at least one woman, so I put up my hand too. It then turned out that the competition was to be a drinking contest race.

"I...can't," I said halfway through the contest, feeling rather sick. Looking across, the men were still downing theirs.

Where was the voice to say, hang on a minute that's not fair? Would the young men who innocently but ignorantly set the competition say something? Would the other competitors, engrossed on their own task say something? Would a spectator break ranks and say something? Thinking on it years later I realised that the voice to say something should have been mine. I was the one who saw that it was wrong, yet I was silent. I didn't want to seem like I was whining. My instinct was to trust to an arbitrator. If you're waiting for a voice to stand up for what YOU think is right, you need to open your mouth. It is what it is, until you change it.

The Alley Café is down a little alley with a stylized painted mural on the wall; orange, black and green on white. I'm there to meet Gregg from Frack-Free Nottinghamshire.

"Frack Free Nottinghamshire is one of the many Frack-Free groups that are going on all over the UK. Basically we are defending Nottinghamshire and raising awareness about fracking. France has banned fracking in France so the French company Total has invested an awful lot of money in the East Midlands. We've already had Dart Energy do some exploratory drilling in north Nottinghamshire. We weren't really very prepared but we locked the fence and raised awareness. Out of that a new group has formed up there. So next steps are film screenings and public debates."

After the café we head to Nottingham's Critical Mass. Dozens of cyclists gather in the city market square and music blares out from a speaker system on one of the bikes.

"It's a community of cyclists," one of the participants tells me. "We want peace on the roads for all road users. We want better cycle routes and junctions for the cyclists cause let's face it, petrol is not going to continue. Critical Mass happens all around the world on the last Friday of the month, usually from 6pm onwards and the object is to do a two hour cycle ride around the city to try to reclaim our bit of space."

After the sun goes down, the group all head to a pub, stacking dozens of bikes outside. The city seems quiet for a Friday and I realise that the students will have left at this time of year. Passing the canal on my way to the station to meet Paula and Rowan, it's more beautiful than I remember.

"Hey lovely!" calls Paula. "THIS is Rowan, I'm so pleased to finally be able to get you two to meet. It's so lovely to be able to introduce two of my favourite people to each other!"

Rowan has short grey hair and a gentle way about her. She works for an eco renovations company as well as doing activist training in strategy, direct action and support. She's also an absolute legend. We get chatting over a pre-bed drink.

"I feel," says Rowan, "that everyone should be as radical as they can, at any point and that way things will shift."

Paula tells us about her efforts to bring mindfulness into her workplace. "People were demotivated, the boss just didn't get what motivates us. My colleague said to me 'I wouldn't get out of bed for funding, but I would for civil society.'"

The next day I don't seem to want to get out of bed, for civil society or anything else. My head hurts. Rowan suggests a morning meditation, which seems a great idea. I do my best to concentrate on my breath for the half hour but my mind slowly goes to sadness. Rowan asks how our sits were. Paula and Rowan describe theirs, but then I just burst into tears.

"I'm sorry," I say in between jerky-breathed sobs with my hands over my face. Paula strokes my back and Rowan my foot as I curl into a ball on the bed.

"Don't be sorry, it's good, just let it out," said Paula.

I feel embarrassed but safe and the barriers that were holding back the tears are down, like water rushing over the top of a dam.

Our first stop that day is to be the Five Leaves independent bookstore. With gratitude I take a backseat for the day and let Rowan and Paula do the talking.

It was so nice to share a room with Eve and Rowan. I miss that. It makes you feel so connected. It is such a beautiful thing to fall asleep, be perfectly still and quiet, and recharge.

Eve had a big cry in the morning. I think when someone lets you see their vulnerability, it brings you closer.

"I'm relieved you have a breaking point too," I said joking as she smiled snottily from between her arms. She is such a force, so much energy and positivity, I felt almost reassured that even she got overwhelmed with it all.

I cycle everywhere and it was strange to think I would be walking so much. First we visited the 'Five Leaves Bookstore', an independent bookstore that opened six months ago. They made us a cup of tea as we explored the books.

Thich Naht Hahn – the Vietnamese engaged Buddhist monk – first introduced me to the idea that what we read is also a form of consumption. What we watch on TV, what we listen to, what we look at and what we read – are all things that we consume through our various senses. When you think about it like this, it is clear that all of these things that we consume can affect our minds. Just in the same way that what we eat affects the health of our body. Our thinking often drives our actions and our actions turn into habits.

Everyone gets the same living wage at Five Leaves. Ben who works there told me they wanted people to be able to access books that the mainstream bookstores may not sell but that are important. Five Leaves is full of books about counter culture, politics, climate change, sexuality. On their website they make their perspectives clear: "We are radical in that the shop supports those who want to change the world for the better. Personal change, political change, understanding history, understanding the world we live in…anarchist, socialist, green…we are not prescriptive. Independent publishing, independent thinking, independent writing."

One of the things I learnt over a cuppa with Ben was how much damage Amazon is doing to the book industry. With their aggressive tactics, Amazon squeezes publishers down and avoids tax, allowing them to sell books at lower prices, threatening independent sellers and reducing the publication of small presses and radical titles. I was inspired by their commitment. It's not just a bookstore, but also a place for the community to come for talks, book groups and other events. It is a place to be engaged, inspired and to challenge the status quo. The cherry on the top for me was finding a hugely inspiring book that was previously only available in Spanish called 'Let me Tell you a Story' by Jorge Bucay. Just the sort of healthy consumption I need in my life.

As Paula, Rowan and I journeyed on from Five Leaves, heading for a community centre, Rowan remembered a journey of her own.

"I'd almost forgotten it. It was A Pilgrimage to a GM free Britain. Lots of people from all over Britain either cycled or walked and one farmer from Pembrokeshire even drove his tractor, and we all converged in London and did a big march. It was a sort of pilgrimage to sites in Britain where GM crops had been grown and we'd been part of that resistance. I cycled on my recumbent and joined up many of the sites where I'd pulled up GM crops, visiting the communities that I'd met at that time. It's nice to be reminded of how much we did actually achieve."

"Welcome to the SUMAC centre!" said Laura as we arrived at the community centre. Laura came to England through the European Voluntary Service. "Because I couldn't really strive in Italy," she said. The three of us sat down with Laura and another volunteer Mia, all with our cups of tea.

"When I googled vegan Nottingham," said Laura, "and found the SUMAC centre I realised that maybe my political views were to the left. I came first for a film night because it wasn't very scary. I didn't meet to talk to anyone, then I started coming to the People's Kitchen and after three months I started to talk to people. It is sometimes a bit hard.

"The SUMAC centre has been set up as a cooperative, part of Radical Routes, which is a network of cooperatives all over the country for radical social change. Veggies is based here. Veggies started with a van in town about thirty years ago selling veggie burgers and now they are at Glastonbury selling veggie burgers and campaigning. SUMAC also has a bar set up with members as a social club because it's easier for selling alcohol. That also pays towards the mortgage and upstairs there is a flat which pays too. Different community groups use the building and contribute.

"We're in one of those groups. We give free English language lessons to women and we offer childcare. It's also a social event to get them out of their houses. It's men that provide the childcare. The women at first were a bit surprised and like, 'oh, can they do it?' and we said 'yes of course!'" said Laura with a big smile. "So breaking down stereotypes and getting people more involved and say that it is possible. We're planning more activities like art or going to the woods to do environmental education."

Laura and Mia tell us about a repair café, skills shares, a community circle, the food bank, the SUMAC youth club, an apple planting group, local market and community cafés. I like the picture they paint of their life in Nottingham.

"Tonight it's the People's Kitchen, do you want to stay for the meal?" Laura asks, and we nod enthusiastically. "It's every Saturday. Volunteers cook an affordable vegan meal to raise money either for SUMAC or different causes."

Laura lives at a Radical Routes housing co-op a street away and she invites us to stay the night after the meal.

As dinner is nearly ready I get chatting to two people that from first appearances I judge to be ladies, until they set me straight. One is on their way to becoming a man and the other identifies themselves as 'Queer', gender non-binary. I invite them to join us at our big round table for the meal... then put my foot in it straight away by introducing them to Rowan and Paula as ladies. *DAMN IT! Autopilot.*

"Pan gender or pansexual means that someone doesn't want to be defined by their gender or sexuality," Sandy is explaining as we get settled with our plates. The meal being served is a delicious Indian one with naan, rice, curry and dal.

"You can't put people into boxes," says Sandy. "If you find yourself in one box, suddenly you're in another box too. If you're on the margins and you form ghettos you'd weaken yourself. If we worked together we'd be a lot stronger wouldn't we?" I'm marvelling at how trusting they both are to explain to us. It must be wearisome always explaining to people.

Sandy continues, "About one in 200 children are born intersex, without clear gender and doctors give them surgery. The law requires children be assigned a gender at birth."

After the main, I'm surreptitiously hugging a large teddy bear under the table that I found next to the seats. No one seems to mind, at least no one comments. Dessert is cake and custard, I help finish up some of the leftovers. The whole meal was only a stunning £3.50 each.

After the meal Rowan, Paula and I follow Laura to her place, just around the corner. In the porch are Ecowork veg bags. A sign on the door says 'Solidarity', another says 'Opening the door? Beware of cops and bailiffs.'

The building was a crumpet factory before it was converted into a co-op house, so there is a lot of space to create or meet. Ten people live in the house. They have a bike repair workshop and there are lots of bikes and books; books on all sorts of social and environmental topics. The communal meals are vegan and people sign up to eat and to cook. There is a tea towel hanging in the kitchen which lists the seven Radical Routes cooperative principles. The kitchens, bathrooms and carpets everywhere are all clean, nothing like university communal living. Paula and I are sleeping on the third floor. Up a lot of stairs. *Why did I eat two desserts?*

I wake at seven to the comforting sound of Paula snoring gently. I feel rested and sit up making bee badges for Laura, Paula and Rowan. When I head downstairs I find Rowan in the lounge, with colourful throws and cushions, a woodburning stove and lots of informative books. Over breakfast we discuss books that changed us.

"Small is Beautiful," said Rowan. "My father made atomic energy, my step father worked for MI6 so I grew up surrounded by right wing politics. When I read Small is Beautiful it opened my eyes to a whole new range of ideas. What woke you up to things?" Rowan asked Paula. Paula had been staring fascinated at the curdling soya milk patterns in her coffee. Her long brown hair was in a plait. She looked up with her open-mouth wide smile.

"I started reading about Buddhism quite young but never got the full meaning of it. The Power of Now by Eckhart Tolle was one of the first books that started to shift how I thought about the mind. When I read mindfulness in plain English that is when it all started to fall into place...The reason I feel so passionate about mindfulness is it has literally transformed my life and changed my inner critic into something more manageable. It's like thoughts are buses and you can spot which ones you are getting on, and get off if you need to."

"In this secular culture," said Rowan, "I think we've missed a trick. We've thrown everything out including the things that help us, stripped ourselves bare and ended up with nihilism."

"That's my journey," says Paula, "to find those things that help me live a better life, be kinder to other people, to the earth, and to have better relationships...What was the start for you Eve?"

"I'm a late starter I'm afraid," I say hunched on my kitchen stool. "I didn't have much interest in politics until after I left my job. I read a lot of helpful books when I was in Canada though. One that got me angry was A Blueprint for Survival, written by a bunch of ecologists. It's written logically and succinctly with good science and contains a straightforward set of actions to stop us killing ourselves and our planet... But it was written in 1970. I felt so betrayed. They knew...They knew in 1970. About climate change, about all of this, and they didn't do anything about it. It made me realise, no more denial, governments *will not* do the right thing, so I must."

As we walk out to the north of Nottingham, Rowan tells us about her belief in accountable activism. Eighteen years ago Rowan was one of six women involved in the destruction of a hawk jet bomber that was bound for East Timor. They planned the action for a year beforehand and the four women who did the physical destruction stayed to be arrested. They were all ultimately acquitted based on their defence that they were preventing a greater crime. Before that, Rowan was involved with actions against GMO crops, again always staying to be held accountable for her actions.

"We wrote to the council, the Environment Agency and the police. We told them about the crime for the GMO's and asking them to act. We didn't receive a reply. We wrote saying that if they did not act we would. Then we went and began to pull up the crops. When one of the police arrived I said, 'no, no you've got it all wrong, we're not the one's committing the crime, we're here to prevent a crime.' He looked so confused! I told him to go and ask his superior and he did and I carried on pulling! When you ask people to do the right thing, with a genuine expectation that they will, it can really reach them."

The rain was coming down and we reached a tram station. Decision time. Rowan looked exhausted so Paula and she caught the tram back to the centre of Nottingham and I waved them goodbye, tearful as the doors closed.

I found a chain pub and went in out of the rain for a hot drink. I looked around and realised almost nobody was smiling, even though there must be close to eighty people. Everyone was looking around bored, not talking, disappointed, as if to say, 'Is this the weekend? Is this all we get?'

I realised how foolish I was being. Although at times I'm upset by the things I've learned, I feel alive and free. I wouldn't change my life back. I enjoyed the warmth, the drink and smiled at more adventures to come. I remembered to give my smiles away. After all, they cost nothing.

CHAPTER 25 — The steel city

Josh from the tea rooms in Linby gives me a rose lemonade and four big scones with jam and cream. *Yes! Dinner is served.* Many people in bigger stores won't give away waste food because they say they don't have the authority. Josh packs it all up with a drink and cream and makes me feel he's pleased to give it to me. There is a difference when we give wholeheartedly. Sometimes being helped or given things can make you feel small. If I give, I must decide that I can give and do it unreservedly and with all my heart. Then it is a joy to give and joy to receive.

I don't know where to go but there is a village called Pilgrim's Oak and a road called Pilgrim Close so I head there to find the church. The vicar Chris agrees to let me camp but then instead offers me the church hall. So underneath bunting and on a martial arts mat I gleefully make my cosy camp. I spread out the postcards and things of comfort around me. The knitted bee stuffed toy given to me by permaculture Hannah's twin daughters, postcards of the Green Windmill and the railway from Colin in Devon.

In the morning Chris brings me a cup of tea and I do my yoga on the grass outside before heading on. It makes a huge difference to my emotional wellbeing to have done the yoga. The land today is hilly and more sandy and stony.

A route through a Forestry Commission wood turns out to be tricky, misleading and time consuming. I can't see the forest for the trees. *A forest is not a group of trees. A community is not a group of people.* They are defined by the interactions, not by the number of units. I've spent time in lumber woods where they had clear cut, then each sapling dipped in pesticide before planting. It was not a forest. I've spent time in traditionally managed woodland and I've spent time in old growth forests. They are not the same AT ALL. I always feel that fungi have enormous mysteries yet to unfold.

The sun comes out and the day gets hot enough to take my jumper off. Along the field I pass another friendly walker.

"When I leff mai 'owse this morning it were cold, am dressed for sno int it? Tek care," he said. I smile and nod agreement as he passes as I'm still deciphering what he said.

Beyond Mansfield I eat my food beside a tall wood-covered hill. I'm pretty worn out. Staring at my map I don't fancy the next very hilly stretch but I need to find a safer place to sleep and after a short walk it turns out that I had misread the contour lines and the next bit is all downhill! I pass a fox sneaking around in a field and then hear laughter across the valley. *That sounds like a good place.* And it IS a good place.

At the Hardwick Inn they have friendly staff, don't mind me camping in their neatly mown overflow car park, and they serve hot chocolate. Heaven. In the last of the light I work on sewing myself a big fluffy striped bag cover to complete my bee outfit. I picked up the elastic a few weeks ago but I didn't have the energy to sew the cover. It looks good. Bright.

It's the first day of July. The cold night quickly passes to a hot sun which evaporates the condensation from the tent and warms my black shorts. A passing cloud softens the heat as I pass gorgeous parkland with lake and hills. My shoelace comes undone but I'm not due for a break and I can't get down and up again with the pack on so I continue on with it flapping. Until that is, I find a red and black football in the middle of the path. Teetering, I use it to rest my foot on, only to find it slowly deflating as I race to finish my lace. Practically on the floor, I lever myself back up, laughing.

Clouds of grass pollen flow up as I brush past. There are bramble flowers, Ox-eye daisies and a few tiny white flowers that I've never seen before, like miniature daisies with ten petals. The thistle flowers are so vibrantly purple! They're so beautiful that I walk into a tree branch in distraction. Apples are forming and the field maple seeds are amazingly lovely.

CRUNCH!
"Oh...No. Yep? Yep. Oh. Sorry. Yuck. Snail. Damn." *Oh I hate it when that happens.*

Janet and her little white dog Molly give me water. Janet's husband died eight years ago and Molly has been a lifeline.

"I don't really know the area yet," she said, "I became depressed after it happened you see. I feel I'm only just starting to get over it now. My husband could drive but I can't so I've become a bit stranded because the buses aren't very frequent and it takes a few changes. We'd only just moved and we hadn't thought about that."

"Of course, no one expects something like that," I said.

I meet yet more people who think I'm Australian. *"I'm English! It says so on my birth certificate and I like tea! God damn it."* The other thing that seems to happen to me everywhere is that people think they know me. By this point already three times people have come right up to me and said something like, "Hey! Haven't seen you in ages...Oh, sorry, you look just like someone I know." And countless times I'll be talking to someone and they get that far off look and then they'll say to their friend something like, "You know who she looks like?" And their friend'll say, "I was just thinking that! She's the spitting image of [insert name or relationship]." Whoever Kate is, she comes up a lot and I hope she's stunningly attractive. If you are reading this and we are lookalikes, please contact me, it's just too weird. What do I look like? Oh, average height, white skin, mid-length straight brown hair, big boobs, big smile, face like everybody else apparently.

In Steveley I pass several women separately, with bright red dyed hair, several driving lorries and a woman driving a forklift truck. I never saw women driving lorries until about ten years ago. I ask directions and discover, before the sign tells me so, that I'm now in Derbyshire: "It's rand 't' left!"

In the library I'm greeted by the very friendly librarian, delighted that I want a library card. Then begins a series of cheerful tales about where she's lived, the books she likes, writing and her son. At one point she *almost* hands me the library card, before pulling it back to gesture in her description.

Then a kindly elderly gentleman joins in the discussion with book recommendations and the story of a biking holiday he took as a youth, the best of his life. I'm enjoying the stories but need to find the directions to my host for the night. My eyes start following the library card like a cat with a toy. I allow my mouth to come slightly open in a gesture of interruption.

When I get into my email I discover that not only is my accommodation sorted but that an amazing woman called Nicole has arranged all sorts of visits for me in Sheffield.

Around here it seems that "Ya rait." is used both as a greeting and to say you're welcome. Walking by a busy road I spot a shrew in the leaf littered verge. So busy, tiny and furry. I've never seen one up close before and I watch it for several minutes, until I move upwind, when it dashes into the leaves.

In The George in Ecklington four drinking patrons try to simultaneously give me high speed directions in accents that I don't fully understand. Ten minutes later they're all still earnestly advising me as I cling to my map. The landlady gives me snacks and a drink and two follow me outside to point further directions. Then they hand me a donation! People sure do seem friendly but overwhelming in Derbyshire.

The woods from Ecklington to Sheffield have a river flowing over rocks, a lot of beech trees and a tranquil feeling like a caress. The path winds beside the stream and I am restored. I stand and listen to poplars rustling. A large pond has floating plants and ducks on it as the sun is getting lower.

Walking into Sharrow I'm nearly at Nicole's house in an area of long lines of terraced houses when I see a group of young men shouting and posturing loudly... One then waves a gun theatrically over his head before he gets into the car.

"*Oh. Dear.*"

I reach Nicole's red brick house down an alley at the side. The garden is full of plants. All kinds of vegetables and food are growing in anything that will hold them (even a bathtub), hanging, growing up things or just placed on the concrete. A colourful sunflower plastic tablecloth sits over a round table, also covered with plants.

"Sheffield is the biggest village in the country," says Nicole, "everyone knows each other. There are four green councillors in now." Nicole went to a council meeting when they were discussing a development. "The building is so grand, it has an effect like a church and we went there and sat above them...but the councillors were reading magazines and playing on their phones while people talked! Unless you engage with it they're doing what they want. You don't have to be a politician to be a conscientious citizen. We vote someone into power but what we actually do is give them OUR power."

The next morning Nicole is in her dressing gown eating snatches of toast as non-stop pearls of wisdom, advice and contacts come forth. She has short brown dreadlocks and thick framed brown glasses. She gestures expansively and often (she's half Italian). Flitting around the kitchen she cleans and organises, grabbing another munch of toast.

Because the houses were originally built for the miners, the yards are shared between several houses. Unlike to the right, the yard to the left is separated off with a low fence and her neighbour, also in her dressing gown, joins Nicole outside for a smoke and a cup of tea.

Nicole offers to be my guide for the day. Walking through Sharrow the main roads get gradually louder as we near the centre. Then Nicole turns down into a courtyard called Hagglers Corner with a marquee, draped material, strung lights and murals on the brick walls.

"We're a collection of creative businesses, there's about sixteen of us based here," Sarah tells me. She's smiley and energetic with short blonde hair clipped up to the side. Hagglers Corner is composed of small units and larger event space. It was a 150 year-old derelict factory. Carpentry, events, tattoos, crochet, a café, yoga, a magazine, picture framing, seamstress, weddings and music events.

Nicole reels off famous bands from Sheffield as we leave Hagglers Corner for Regather where she works.

"I worked in marketing for music venues for big corporations then I really felt I wanted to go into work that was more in line with my ethics. I was nervous about taking the plunge, giving up the security. I'd probably been ready to take the leap two years before but it took me a while to pluck up the courage.

"It's definitely been a good move and lots of new opportunities have come my way since I've taken the leap. I guess the purpose of Regather is to enable people to do cool ethical projects in the community. There's a kitchen, workshop space and studio space." Regather is next to a large council estate and outside are raised vegetable beds.

Upstairs in the Regather office I meet Barney, an experimental archaeologist. He's the first experimental archaeologist I've ever met and it sounds unbelievably cool. I'm geek star-struck.

"When I was little I wanted to be a mad scientist," Barney says with a smile as he looks down. He's very tall with glasses, a short beard, big sideburns and bushy eyebrows. I'm not sure, but I think he might have achieved his ambition. An experimental archaeologist tries to recreate the ways in which people used to live. Barney is working on a collaborative project to process ore by hand and create a bike using historical techniques. *So cool! Hold it together Eve!"*

"With the things we use now if it's not made of steel, it's made by steel," Barney is saying. "When people see all the effort that goes into making things, it reconnects them with making it. We're so used to just picking something up that's pre-made. You can end up with a different outlook. It's not just the resources but the process steps. Like little mesters."

"I'm sorry?" I say confused, imagining messy toddlers.

"Little mesters were individual specialist craftsmen," says Barney, who each worked on one stage of something but they would have a little workshop space next to each other.

One would carve the knife handle, one would grind the metal, one would polish, one would fix the blade to the handle. We've got a little mesters workshop space upstairs. But the place you really want to have a look at is Portland Works."

Returning to the house Nicole waves to a neighbour down the street. I'm typing up a blog in the kitchen when Nicole hands me a spoon of something. "Have you ever tried Chestnut honey?" She is flitting around the kitchen and then a small cake appears. "Something sweet to munch?" A little later she reappears with a honeycomb silver pendant necklace. "I never use this and it would be perfect for you... Do you use a staff when you walk?" Nicole gives me a beautiful carved walking stick taller than I am. "My friend made a pair, I don't have a use for them but I wanted to get them. I think it would be really great for you to have this one."

I looked in bewilderment at the stick carved with runes and a small owl on top. "Are you sure?" I say concerned. Nicole stated emphatically that she is, whilst beaming, then makes me a chicken sandwich to take, whilst her partner Tom appears with spare video tapes for my camera...then an SD adapter then a mini camera for protests.

"I think I need to leave before you give me half the house!"

"No, stay," says Tom laughing, "we need a clearout!"

Passing a pub on the way to Heeley City Farm Nicole sees a friend having a pint and we stop and chat for a bit. At the city farm we visit the energy building where they showcase renewable energy and energy efficiency.

"The whole farm site used to be Victorian houses," Sally who works there tells me. "The council compulsory purchased them to build a big road through but a group of people protested and managed to stop the road being built. But by the time the protesters won, the houses had deteriorated from being empty so they had to be knocked down, which made space for the farm. This was the last house left when all the others were demolished, it was a pikelet factory, which are a bit like crumpets. We eco-furbished it. It's a single skin house so it's been insulated on the inside with walls built inside. It's got underfloor heating and there's a ground source heat pump. There's solar thermal and photovoltaics on the roof. The solar tubes are ingenious," she gestures behind and above me. It looks like an electric ceiling light but with a more pleasing quality to the light.

"The light tube works with a series of mirrors so it catches the sunlight and bounces it back. We've got rainwater toilets. We've got the solar kiln which was an experiment to see if cooler places could dry wood using solar, so that was the first one ever built in the North and it works very well."

That night I was to camp on a field just outside Sheffield to meet some of Sheffield Organic Growers. Luke and Fran picked me up in their car with their camping gear and as we walk up the site from the little car park they show me berry bushes and polytunnels. At the main field barefoot-Fran looks around with relaxed delight and love, peering closer here, lingering there.

"Things change so much!" she exclaims. A few minutes later she trots off to visit something the other end of the field. I turn to Luke to ask him how he got involved.

"It was an advert on the soil association website to lease the land. We started talking, came up with a business plan, and we all upped sticks and moved to Sheffield."

"How is it working with the rest of your life?" I asked.

"It's difficult to be honest," said Luke. "It's a work in progress, balancing out part time work with work on the farm. I don't know, we'll see at the end of the year. We're making mistakes but you don't know what the land's gonna give you until you start. We do the Regather veg box scheme. We can grow organic but we can't afford to buy organic. We haven't found a sustainable way yet."

We camped up the hill and the next day head to Regather for the veg box delivery. We drive through Netheredge in the west of Sheffield and here the houses are big and detached in cream stone with tree lined roads. Usually in English cities the more wealthy parts are in the west. During the industrial revolution the pollution was so bad that it was oppressive and life threatening to be downwind of the smoke stacks, so the rich people lived upwind. The influence still affects the towns even though the original cause is gone.

At Regather, as I'm sat finishing my lunch in the canteen, room a man pops his head around the door then looks a little crestfallen to find only me in there.

"Oh, hi!" he says with friendliness. "I was just looking for the others for volunteers for washing up."

"They're busy with the veg boxes but I'll come," I smile.

"Oh, okay, thanks!" he says.

Jonathan is using the kitchen for his business Saavy spreads, making vegan spreads. The kitchen smells of chocolate. The things he wants washing are covered in sticky cloying sweet chocolatey smudges. I ascertain that before the bowls and utensils can effectively be washed they must first be scraped. And what does one do, with such an accumulated quantity of fine, gooey, gorgeousness? I ate the lot. Then felt mildly icky. Oh well, hey ho, get it while the going's good.

I once had a meal sat next to a nun who ate three desserts one after the other. I couldn't help it. My right eyebrow slowly crept up. It does that sometimes, whether I want it to or not. She saw and looked me square in the eyes. "Never turn down a good thing," she said.

As a reward for my services, Jonathan gives me several jars of spread. "Thanks! I can 'spread' the word." I should write cracker jokes for money. The jars are too heavy for me to keep and I'm excited to have gifts to give.

After an early dinner with a local Young Friends of the Earth organiser I go to meet a lady called Felicity, at Union Street. The building interior is empty and some of the rooms are prepped for decorating. In one open plan room is a sofa, chair, low table, kettle and some mugs.

"I'm the director of a company called Common people," Felicity tells me. "It's a Community Interest Company. It aims to support, promote and empower independent and social enterprises. I was tired of being annoyed every time I walked down our high street. There was just Costas and large chains opening all the time. The local economy was shot. I started doing a pop-up shop on Division Street for six months which gave ten businesses the opportunity to have a shop and now we've got a shop in the winter gardens so every two weeks people rent it, so they don't have to worry about large rent and we support them with planning and landlords."

Felicity's co-director Mark was also working on the building.

"The project I've been working on is called Common Ground and is similar. It's really trying to help people overcome barriers around accessing space, support, funding."

"What have you needed to get to this point?" I asked.

"Opportunities in terms of space have been a big one," said Mark, "I remember discovering the Common Place in Leeds and being really inspired by what social centres were doing. We came across some new models which allow landlords to occupy space for their advantage which creates opportunities for people to come into that space, for mutual benefit."

"What about you Felicity?" I asked.

"Well the pop-up shop on Division Street had quite a few options of who to take it on afterwards but the landlord picked William Hill," she said with annoyance. "So it became a betting shop. I think what we learnt from that was that even with a lot of public involvement there're problems in the planning system. So I spent a long time learning so that I can help independents, trying to get the same sort of power that big corporates have when they move into spaces.

"I went on an Accelerate course about two and a half years ago which helps social enterprises and that helped to get four thousand pounds of funding. You have to learn a lot about planning and you make a lot of relationships with landlords. Really be very forward and active. Matt became a director too and was a constant support and we just kind of carried on.

And now we are sat in a massive four story building hopefully all these people will come and we'll be able to help them."

Then it was across town again to visit a creative arts space using a 'meanwhile' lease. A meanwhile lease gives tenants less rights but gives the landlord the confidence to allow the occupation of a building that is temporarily vacant.

Onwards again, still foolishly not taking rest breaks, to my final stop for the day - the Bramble housing co-op. I follow my scribbled directions and head up the steep hill as the evening begins.

In the garden, Tangle is building a yellow model bike from plant pots and yellow tubing she found. The Tour de France will be coming through Sheffield in a few days and she wants to decorate the street to celebrate. An ex-housemate, who has just got back from biking to Italy, arrives for a visit. Another housemate is building a dehydrator. I don't think they own a television, if they do it's probably hidden under a project.

The message hadn't got to Tangle that I was in need of somewhere to sleep that night but with barely a pause she says no problem. There is such kindness and automatic generosity with their space. Tangle shows me my room, which is in the house next door. The two houses are attached and lived in like one, with a shared garden, but there's no door between them. The houses are decorated with bold colours that aren't garish; terracotta, muted turquoise, dark blue and dusky yellow with dark wood and houseplants. There are throws and cushions and nooks. There is an office, a music/yoga room, two lounges, eight bedrooms and a brew room. Everywhere is clean.

"Eat as much fruit from the garden as you can," she says.

A bit later she comes back with a yellow vest top for me saying that she thought the colour would be good. Tangle carries on with her bike construction while I eat a bean salad and bread and gather berries from the garden. Kirstie, another housemate comes to work at the wooden table outside. She too gestures at the garden, "Please eat lots of the berries, there's loads."

Breakfast the next day is muesli (which they bulk buy) with more berries. There is a donations box in the kitchen which means that visitors can contribute to the food.

"But only if they can," says Kirstie.

I love it, I think it's such a great idea. You can constantly have visitors and it not be a drain on the household. I'm pleased to be able to put some money in the box.

It's quite a walk across Sheffield but on the way I visit the New Roots shop and meet Joe and Ruth. The business has been going for twenty seven years but they have only been involved for a couple of years.

"I was a student in Sheffield and I started volunteering. The shop is all run by volunteers and eighty percent of them are students. It means we're short on volunteers in the summer though," says Joe. New Roots was originally set up as a veg box scheme, delivered by bike. "It's so hilly and there are so many potholes, if you can deliver food by bike in Sheffield you can deliver it anywhere!" says Joe.

The route I take to my next meeting, takes me through an underpass and I can hear a male busker singing with a guitar. In the underpass I stand and listen and give him a couple of coins. My bee costume causes him to ask what I'm doing. When I explain that it is about what people are doing to protect the environment and the future he shakes his head.

"It's all over," he said, "since Thatcher. They won."

"Nobody's won my friend," I said. "Lots of people are still fighting, doing wonderful things—I've met them all over the country."

"It's over," he said again.

"Nothing's over. Nothing's over while we're still breathing."

My words seemed to distress him, his body language became agitated and he lit a cigarette. He began to try to convince me of the hopelessness of any positive action, listing the injustices. It was as if he needed to make me agree with him in order to justify his lack of action. I felt sadness for his situation but there was nothing more for me there.

"I'll leave you to it my friend, good luck," I said in parting.

"CIRCA. The Clandestine Insurgent Rebel Clown Army."

I'm on a bench, looking out over a park as Julian from DANCE explains. "It was a joke at all the police's fear about us. To lighten things up and connect with people's humanity."

Julian has been involved with different environmental tactics over the years and he sits now, calm and experienced. Short white hair and deep creases in his face as he smiles suggest his age. I find myself wondering how he's kept going. What helped him not to burn out like so many others have?

"Probably one of the things I've used most is co-counselling which is basically a peer support network. And having a yoga and meditation practice. A group of about six of us formed an Eco-Action Learning Set," he said. "We meet roughly every six weeks to share an issue from eco-activism. People ask questions and the purpose of the questions is to help us develop our thinking around that. Then we write down some notes and think where are we going next with this? Then the next meeting we have a review of how it's gone.

"Specifically for conflict I learnt non-violent communication (NVC) which is a tool for how we communicate. There's an NVC model of observations, feelings, needs and requests. It's quite tricky to learn to use but beneficial - it helps to avoid conflicts or at least smooth them over."

"What do you think are the next steps or any advice?" I asked.

"The rise of mindfulness is good. I think it ultimately challenges the dominant western mode of happiness through consumption," he said, then after a pause, "Some projects are wrecked by conflicts. Some problems came from a lack of clear vision. You can attract people with drug and mental health problems and trying to get the balance with being welcoming and setting boundaries to get things done is hard. Be very clear on the vision at the start and people can join that, and also support people with tools."

After bidding farewell to Julian I set off in search of little mesters and The Portland Works. I'm nearing a group of workmen by a high-rise building and one of them is watching me approach, then he nods.

234

"Where you off to now then?" he asks.

"I'm on a walk about the environment," I say.

"I know," he says smiling.

"Oh, Steve! Sorry I didn't recognise you! Good to see you!" He's one of by benefactors from the George pub in Eckington.

"Very glad to see you got here safe! You take care now."

The Portland Works was purpose built in 1870 to bring together craftsmen who made cutlery. The first stainless steel was made in Sheffield and it's a big part of its history. I find Andy in a small office next to the forge. He has wide eyes over a large neat grey moustache and an earnest manner. He still works the forge with the same hammers he has used since he was fourteen; suffice to say that's a long time.

"Sheffield is 'the steel city' we do still produce a lot of steel, more than ever actually, but it's specialist now and exported. I make Crown Tools and at least 90% go to the US. There's a Japanese company called Sheffield which has taken some business, people think they're buying steel *from* Sheffield."

The works has joiners, grinders, silver platers, a cabinet maker, bands, and an engraver. There was a proposal to turn the works into bedsits a few years ago and the workers managed to buy it as a co-op and get it Grade II listed status.

"Originally I hadn't got a clue," said Andy. "I left school at 14 you see so I didn't know about any of this, I just knew we had to stop it. I went to see a lady, Julia, who was studying architecture. The landlord lied on the planning application about the building layout and also said it was unoccupied, when all of us worked here, Julia found the faults. We didn't set out to buy it. We managed to stop the planning permission then thought, now what?

"It's one of them yards what's had an atmosphere," said Andy with affection. "We used to play cricket in the yard and Def Leopard their music were very loud when they practiced here so we used to go into the power room and turn the power on and off. It would take them about half an hour to work out it weren't their guitars and by then we'd have finished the game. Cause the old forges were so noisy the work between the forge and the machine driver was all done by nods."

On my way back through Sharrow the rain starts and I stop at Strip The Willow. They restore and sell furniture downstairs while upstairs is a café and shop where they sell local crafts and art. It's a beautiful space. The rain is pinging on the metal stairs outside as I drink hot chocolate and watch the ladies who've come for a craft session. I wish I could stay, but I'm meeting a biodynamic gardener at the pub. The owner of the café and one of the ladies give me donations as I leave.

The next day I join an anti-fracking march organised by Lush as I head out of town; Friends of the Earth flags, Sheffield Green party, Frack-Free South Yorkshire and numerous homemade signs. People walk together chatting happily in twos or threes. The day is hot and sunny and many people are in shorts and sandals. The march ends by a park and people slowly drift away to enjoy the day.

After an ice cream in the park I head out of Sheffield until another park offers a café to refill my water. I sit by the river in Rivelin as children play nearby and people come and go. But I feel so alone. Exhaustion and fear have caught up with me. I know fear is not the right path, but today it's where I am. I call Miranda to try to get myself out of it.

"Hello darling! You're amazingly wonderful you know that?" says Miranda. She asks how I am and I cling to the phone listening to her voice. I miss my friends. I wish I was braver.

"I think I've been overdoing it a bit," tears trickle down my nose as I face away from the kids and nod at Miranda's words of advice and comfort.

There's nothing for it but to keep going. Walking up a big hill a few hours later I start asking the universe for some help.

"Please can I have somewhere safe to be this evening? Please can I have somewhere safe to sleep?" I feel exhausted. At the top of the hill I stop into a pub to use the loo and ask for water. And that's where the three wise monkeys meet me.

CHAPTER 26 — Three Wise Monkeys

"**You** must be following us, we saw you walking up the hill," said a kind-looking elderly lady at the bar. "You've earned a drink."
She put her hand gently on my forearm and looked me in my eyes. "Are you going to have a drink with me?"
"Yes. I'd love to. Thank you. That would be...really lovely." Embarrassed, I realise tears are welling in my eyes. Lillian has pearl earrings, neat hair and makeup and such a kind face. She introduces me to Edna and Marjorie.

"We're just about to have some fish and chips. Will you have some fish and chips with us?" asked Lillian.

Marjorie and Lillian have been friends and neighbours for fifty six years!

Edna lives a few streets away and Lillian picks her up for their weekly outing. All three of their husbands are now dead but the three wise monkeys are still friends. Marjorie tells me that she's ninety five. When she turned ninety she wrote a book of her memoirs, in three months. I think about the book I need to write and feel inspired by her.

Edna has memory difficulties so asks about the Tour de France quite a few times and Lillian always answers, with familial impatience. The conversation moves to hearing aids and they each unselfconsciously get their hearing aids out to compare. *Fifty six years.*

"Lillian's one's better (private) so you can hardly see it. I've got this massive heap of an NHS one," says Marjorie, brandishing it then wiping ear wax off and popping it back in.

Lillian is one of fourteen children. After dinner she invites me to stay with her. "Yorkshire hospitality," she says. In the car my staff from Nicola is so long it has to lay down the middle. The driveway is narrow as we get out at Lillian's house and Marjorie pushes the staff backwards.

"Hey, you've pushed it into me titty!" says Edna, pushing it back to raucous laughter.

The back garden at Lillian's house has a set of steps down into Marjorie's garden and no fence. *Fifty six years.*

Sat on Lillian's cream and brown sofa we all have apple pie with cream. Behind Marjorie on the top of the armchair, stuffed toys are lined up, that Lillian has collected.

"Hey on Who Wants to Be a Millionaire the other day," says Lillian, "they had the question what was the first advert on TV. You remember? 'You'll never know where the yellow went...'"

"...till you brush your teeth with pepsident!" they finish in chorus, laughing. A stuffed owl falls off the back of the armchair onto her as Marjorie laughs, making her jump.

"You little bugger!" she says beating it against the armrest repeatedly as we collapse in laughter.

"Oh have a look at this one," says Lillian picking up a toy bear. She pokes it hard in the stomach and it burps loudly then says "OOooOO pardon ME!" in a camp voice.

In the hallway is a picture of the three of them smiling wickedly at a table, that looks like it was taken at a wedding. One's covering their ears, another their eyes and another their mouth. The caption reads The Three Wise Monkeys.

Marjorie and Lillian sing me a song about a toy soldier priced down in a shop window, which wants to be more expensive so that a lady toy will like him. Lillian used to work in a factory and they would all sing together.

"It was so noisy with the polisher and the grinder that you couldn't talk. One woman would start up a song and it would spread across the factory and we'd all join in," says Lillian..

Marjorie offers to take me next door to her house to give me a copy of her book and Lillian takes me aside to ask if I can make sure she's OK on the steps. Marjorie takes the little steps between the gardens with great care and attention, holding firmly onto the rail. They all know what a fall might mean.

"Lillian is the most wonderful kind friend. I don't know what I'd do without her," say's Marjorie.

The autobiography is called Mrs. F. "My surname's Philips you see, but the lads used to call me Mrs. F." I hold it excitedly. The book was printed online and has a shiny blue cover.

She gives me a flat shiny bead angel that she's threaded together. It's white and gold and about three inches long. They're angels to me, those three trusting, loving, laughing old women. That's what I want to be when I grow up.

The next morning I give Lillian the stuffed bee toy that I have been carrying. It's been a lovely comfort and it's joyful to hand it on to her. She puts it on the back of the armchair next to the misbehaved owl. It looks good. It's in the right place.

CHAPTER 27 — Bubbles

Sunday 6th July and it's a beautiful day. It's the day of the Tour de France and there is yellow bunting everywhere. The roads are closed in Warden and people are chalking on the road with their children, some of whom are still in their pyjamas. There is a row of houses either side of the sloping road and people have come out of their doors to see this big event come through their village. I love to see the children owning the road. An elaborate picture and messages are being created on the tarmac.

Whenever an amateur cyclist comes past, up or down the tree-lined hill, the people ring cow bells and cheer. I get my own chalks out and add to the decorations with bees.

I pay to use a mystifying public toilet machine that keeps opening itself and has no instructions. It then cleans itself and sprays water out the side that I have to jump back to avoid.

Somehow I manage to get to Oughtibridge (pronounced ootibridge) just before the Tour de France is to come through. People line the streets leaning out over metal barrier fencing and I take up position too, putting my pack down against the hedge. Some people have been waiting for four hours.

A noisy honking string of motorbikes and cars covered in colourful advertising come past for a minute. Then a pause. Then a few marker cyclists with motorbikes. Then suddenly, an alarmingly fast, tightly packed mass of bikes really close, makes a wind that shocks me as they WOOSH loudly past. I flinch back. Then in twenty seconds they're gone.

A parade of more colourful cars with dozens of bikes on the roofs come past. Nearly as many cars as there had been cyclists, for a couple of minutes. Then it's all over. I'm glad I didn't wait around for that. I head to a beautiful lake nearby and sit looking out as a black cloud sweeps rain my way. I'd been considering crossing the Pennines today but not with that weather. I can see the grey streaky haze of falling rain underneath it as the cloud comes, so I go to the visitor's centre to shelter. They've opened the hall with tea and coffee because of the Tour.

Inside I meet the wonderful Maureen Ryan. She walks with two sticks because of a painful disability but she is full of energy and kindness. We have a cup of tea and a biscuit together on a bench and talk about social change. Then she invites me to dinner. She's staying just down the road and she calls up to ask them if I can camp in the garden.

"No problem!" she says after she hangs up.

"Great! Thanks. I'll start walking and meet you there in about half an hour." I'm excited at the prospect of a nice evening and glad that I'm going to have a full day to tackle crossing the Pennines tomorrow.

Maureen has done a lot of different work to help people.

"I was fortunate," she said. "To say so about an accident sounds bizarre, but in the 1970's I had a hockey accident. It stopped me and made me look at my life. I was fortunate enough therefore to have the support to go into the voluntary sector. And there I discovered myself, because people believed in me. People saw something in me that I'd no idea was there. For the first time in my life, this working class uneducated woman was talking to two hundred people, and people came to me. I've spent the last forty years linking people together. Inspiring people to find out what inspires others and then bring that out in them.

"I've done it through mentoring, or simply sitting in a train waiting room and saying 'oh tell me about yourself'. We've all got untapped potential. All we all need is to be listened to. Do you know how many talented people there are throughout this country, with learning disabilities? Who've just been put in the dustbin, and yet they're wise. I went to Buckingham Palace last year with the first person with learning difficulties to get an MBE. Di Lofthouse, for her work on hate crime. I believe in people and my life's dedication is to bring out the best in people. Everyone who came into my training courses, I wanted them to feel that they mattered."

Maureen and I have breakfast together the next morning, looking out at the hills ahead. I feel I've found a very special human being in Maureen. A very blessed meeting to remind me yet again how fortunate I am in my life and how many beautiful people there are dedicated to making life better. She tells me she had been having a very difficult time emotionally when we met and how the timing was a big gift. She calls me an angel. It must be catching. I give her the bead angel from Marjorie. It's made of lots of tiny shiny beads in white and gold. I tell Maureen I hope it will look after her.

The path over the Pennies in the Peak District is nowhere near as bad as I had worried about. The path is rarely very far from the road and twice I pass other walkers so if I had injured myself it would have been no problem to get help. You're never very far from help in England yet I know that unprepared walkers die every year. I carry the full three litres in my water carrier, food and I watch my footing. There are some stone ruins where I have my lunch. There are a lot of ruins, stone circles and cairns in the Peak District and one might wonder why.

I find the history of the Peak District fascinating. It makes me want to applaud the plants that live there as brave survivors. The area was extensively mined for lead and was inhabited for thousands of years. The moorland now is composed of acidic wet peat soil which only certain species can tolerate. Peat is a rare habitat globally (the UK has about 10-15% of the global total) but in the Peak District it was created partly by humans. After the last ice age the area was forest and bog plants. From 3000 BC the deforestation by humans increased with slash and burn for agriculture and then from 600 BC the climate began to change. As the climate became wetter and colder they didn't get aerobic (with oxygen) decomposition, they got anaerobic (without oxygen) decomposition. Acidity built up in the soil and agriculture failed and people left. The forest was unable to regenerate and eventually a new moorland ecosystem came into balance.

Sphagnum moss manages to thrive in bogs and is the main component of peat. In 1901 we had eighteen species of it, now we have just one main one and three rare ones. Sphagnum moss grows slowly and building up a soil with it takes thousands of years. Peat builds up at about 2 mm depth over a hundred years. The peat manages to hold together in the heavy rainfall when other lighter soils would wash away. Overgrazing the area lead to an increase in inedible rough grass, but humans still weren't done with the area.

Humans cut the peat to burn as a fuel and then the biggest recent threat has been garden compost. Yep, that humble bag at the garden centre...if it's made with peat. When peat is cut for use in compost it is hard for vegetation to recolonise the area, so look for peat-free compost.

The peat currently acts as a carbon sink. If it is kept with a good vegetation cover it slowly stores carbon. If it dries out with climate change and burns or oxidises it will release its carbon. It is thought that peat bogs in the UK store more carbon than all the forests of the UK and France combined. At first glance the moorland is a barren brown, but it is home to rare plants, insects, mammals and birds.

The principle of succession in biology is, for me, key to understanding our global problems and our role as a species. After a disturbance, low need species (like moss or lichen) colonise an area and slowly create a soil, then other pioneer species (like grass or bramble) can get a foothold. Different ecosystems make others possible. Eventually the ecosystem would reach a 'climax community' of specialist species. What the nature of that climax community is, depends upon the climate, local conditions and chemical composition. The community living underwater by a volcanic vent is entirely different to that of a subtropical forest. Life finds a way to use the chemicals it is given.

A fully climaxed ecosystem is less diverse than one that has periodic disturbances. Imagine the rush of new life in a forest when a tree falls, creating space. It benefits the whole system to have a range of species.

Diversity is our insurance against disturbances. That disturbance could be in the form of a flood, a fire, a drought, an earthquake, a meteorite, a beaver, an elephant or even a group of humans. We are a beautiful and complex source of disturbance and a little disturbance is a good thing. Too much disturbance too quickly and you may not have the species or life available to adapt.

The latest report from the World Wildlife Fund tells us that global populations of vertebrate species have dropped by more than 50% since 1970. That is not just a little disturbance. We've wiped out half the vertebrate life on the planet in a generation.

But here's a story of a positive bit of disturbance. You may not know that the Peak District was the scene of a successful fight for our freedom to walk across land. Before the 1600's land use and laws were very different. Common people had a lot of access rights and forage rights to common land and land that they did not 'own'. Our modern concepts of land ownership and the focus on the land 'owner' only date from the 1600's with the passing of the Land Enclosures Acts. From then on, governments and land 'owners' increasingly tried to reduce the rights of others to use or access land. The only reason I have been able to do this walk around the country on public footpaths is that generations of people before me have repeatedly taken back the right to do so. That said, I have a problem with anyone claiming a 'right' without taking on a corresponding responsibility. The land doesn't owe me anything.

One famous disturbance is the 1932 Kinder Mass Trespass. Between 400 and 600 people from surrounding cities and towns around the Peak District trespassed on to Kinder Scout in an organised protest. This helped to give us the Access to Mountains Bill and the National Parks and Access to the Countryside Act. The Peak District was the first National park, designated in 1949.

Coming down a steep path I meet a cyclist coming up. He looks like he's about to die: burgundy face, gasping breath, overstretched-Lycra and panic-focused eyes. What is the

Tour enthusiasm doing to people? That's not an easy hill to cycle. Those hills are going to be a killer when I cycle around England. I give him a cheerful 'hello' in sympathy and support, trying to remove any smugness from my voice (it'll only come back to haunt me).

There are grey stone walls, splodged irregularly with white lichen, jiggling around across the fields. Occasionally there is a chuckling stream down in a slender valley. I pause on a stone bridge to put down my pack and listen. Down here in the dip, near the stream, I can't hear any traffic. There're not many places these days where you can be free of the noise of traffic. There are gently moving ferns and pink foxgloves by the stream which has stepping stone sized rounded rocks tossed along it. Out of the main hills I come down to a long reservoir and walk along it with sunlight sparkling.

The campsite is near the end of the reservoir, lush and green, surrounded by trees, in a little dell with a stream. I arrive at the office and am warned about the mosquitoes. *Oh joy.* After getting an icecream in order to be on holiday, I set up my tent. Camping next to me is an assessor for D of E (Duke of Edinburgh award), an orienteering and camping challenge for young people. He kindly shares his insect repellent and we sit outside eating our dinners. Mine consists of a roll and tin of corned beef. The D of E students gradually arrive.

"Half the kids who do the D of E," the assessor tells me, "are doing it for something to have on their CV but aren't enjoying it. There's a lot of pressure to get things on your CV."

I remember people telling me that school was the best time of your life, and thinking, "*I don't believe you. I don't believe life can be that awful.*" Thankfully it isn't. I remember becoming an adult and realising with satisfaction that it was in fact much better. Access to a whole range of exciting things that were previously illegal, more freedom, less stress. At school and university I was always being told that the grades you get will determine the entire course of the rest of your life. But thankfully that is also, not true.

I stop in a pub on my way to Manchester and chat with the owner. I have a pot of tea and he doesn't mind if I eat my sandwich in there. I'm the only customer.

"When you came in I were expecting a man to come in after you," he said slightly apologetically.

"Yeah, that happens a lot," I said nodding amiably.

On my way through the next village, I see the strange sight of a man walking out of a house carrying a stack what appear to be perfectly good plates and dropping them with a smash into a wheelie bin. Bags of things are outside the house and many other things are by the bin. The man catches sight of me and asks what I'm doing. The answer seems to cheer him up slightly and I tell him about some of the lovely people I've met. He tells me he's really impressed with what I'm doing, he's never met anyone doing anything like it. I discover that he's the tenant of the house and today he's being made homeless.

"This is all I've got now," he said, "tears welling in his eyes as he looked at the bags on the pavement."

"It's not so bad having less stuff," I said, "when I divorced and my house devalued I got rid of a lot. I don't have much more than that myself."

He looked at me with surprise and intensity, like he wanted to believe. In one year his brother had died and his wife had divorced him. He didn't see his children much now and he'd been increasingly taking to drink. He'd missed this month's rent and the landlord was kicking him out. He looked like he was on the edge. I knew how tempting the edge could look.

"Before I divorced I became suicidal," I said.

Rigid with concentration, he hung off my every word. I looked firmly into his eyes as I continued.

"All the wonderful things that have happened since, every friendship, this walk, everything I've done would never have happened if I had killed myself...I know it's absolutely shit right now. I know that. It's going to be shit for quite a while. But *it is going to get better*."

Tears kept leaking out of the corners of his eyes and he'd wipe them away. He looked around and seemed to suddenly remember we were standing in the street. He asked if I could stay for a bit, come in for some tea? But I didn't think it would make any more difference – I might say something stupid and break the spell. I needed to keep going.

Approaching Manchester it was raining hard. I went to a library to get directions to my host Tom's place and opened an email about TTIP (Transatlantic Trade and Investment Partnership). It said that there was a European consultation about TTIP which had only three days left on it. The consultation hadn't been widely publicised and when I looked at it, I discovered it was written in such a way that you could not actually object, just suggest changes. I stubbornly objected in every one of its twenty sections.

TTIP seemed to loom threateningly over the future. It made me feel so powerless and anxious. I decided the first step was to spread the word about the consultation, and texted everyone I knew. That made me feel a bit better, since some of them were connectors across the country and hadn't heard about it.

My host in Manchester was a friend of a friend. Tom is a bubble maker, science demonstrator and beekeeper. But like many others on this journey, he had to go through a crisis before becoming himself. We sat in the sunshine in the ivy-lined garden as he told me his story.

"I managed to find myself in Manchester doing a PhD, following a usual path," said Tom in a strange mixture of accents from the many countries he has lived in. "I wanted to find a good way of using my Chemistry to help. It wasn't going well, and by the end of the second year there's no worth in my life, nothing works. And I just lose who I am, lose my place, my meaning. I just feel like nothing. Zero.

"Rather than let it get the best of me I decided to do something. I was interested in what you should do in a world where you don't have the current systems. So whilst starting to make soap, I also discovered bubbles," he said breaking into an impish smile. "Big bubbles. When you make big bubbles I discovered you can bring people together in a way that's incredible. The first rule of bubbles is that people come and join you. You suddenly have this nice environment, instantly. Who's gonna start war when there's bubbles right?

"Create something that when someone woke up in the morning, they weren't expecting to have. I found a lot of meaning in that. Then at the same time I started learning beekeeping. All these things started working together and created Three Bees. My two business partners and I have worked together for the last year and a half now making soap and various products with beeswax and honey. When I'm not doing science demonstrations in schools I'm going out to community groups and telling them about bees.

"Essentially I went from this point of failure, to now finding a lot of meaning both in beekeeping and in making bubbles and meeting people. Now I see a future that is beautiful, knowing that I'm helping out as best I can."

There was to be a national day of action about TTIP on Saturday 12th of July and there were a series of events in Manchester leading up to it, including a public talk. Walking around Manchester I was quickly reminded of its industrial history. The symbol of a bee is everywhere on the bins and the saying of the city is 'Through industry we prosper'. Brass statues of pompous-looking historical men are in the squares. Then there are grand churches, a gothic imposing town hall and a library museum, with impressive stonework and large staircases.

The TTIP talk was in a tower block of a trade union office and the room was mostly full. At the meeting there were about sixty people, most people in their fifties or older. There were leaflets explaining in more detail about TTIP and I took a number with me to give out. The leaflets and the speakers summarised what the effect of TTIP would be: a transfer of power from governments to corporations, deregulation, and the spread of private sector and privatization.

"This is not about the US versus Europe," said the American speaker. "It's not about countries. People in both countries would lose out to the corporations. The NAFTA agreement between Mexico, Canada and the US caused a loss of jobs, despite claims that it would increase them. It reduced wages and increased inequality, the opposite of what was claimed. Investors gained the right to sue governments."

"It is not about trade," the German speaker said, "it is about promoting lobbyism and increasing lobbying power. TTIP would stipulate that any new law must be checked if it has a major impact on trade, and so corporations can lobby very early in the secret regulatory body."

Although in some ways I didn't want to find out more about TTIP and be distressed, it was actually less stressful to go. I didn't explain to anyone about the walk I didn't interview anyone and in fact I didn't really chat with anyone. It felt good to be an anonymous listener.

Exploring Manchester on foot the next day is challenging. There are more men who seem to view me as an object and have dark looks in their eyes. A man curb crawls me. Sometimes people do a double take if I smile at them. There is litter and it feels more full of crime. It's hard to shut it out. In Chorlton I get quite a good smile response but many of them have an 'aww' feel to them as if the people thought I was cute. It's an affluent trendy looking area with bars and restaurants.

Walking in towards the centre of Manchester I look into people's eyes and I see closed soul hopelessness and then once in a while something much worse. It's exhausting and frightening. This is not the place to draw attention to myself by smiling. It reminds me of when I was a teenager visiting London, when I always seemed to attract the weirdoes. "Can I touch your feet?" and similarly bizarre interactions. Men starved of love, looking on you like an easy meal.

The mountain equipment shop has an advert with a man standing heroically in the foreground and a woman trailing behind. All the music posters I see are very masculine and any of women are almost absurdly sexual. I feel no joy being a pedestrian here, I feel demoted.

The next day after I've done all my blogs, Tom and I go to the park for some bubbles. Picking his spot in a wide open area Tom puts out his bucket of bubble mix and various stick-string implements. I position myself on the grass nearby to watch. Make bubbles and they will come.

The first young couple to come past laugh and look at each other, playfully popping a few bubbles. Then the first children arrive with a family. Tom shows them how he makes bubbles within bubbles by blowing on the side and they spend a considerable amount of time practicing this. A second family arrives and is caught in the bubble gravity. They pick up the spare equipment and try making their own. The parents stand around smiling. The children don't want to leave. Some of the younger children charge back and forth across the area popping as many bubbles as they can. "Thank you so much," people say.

"Some people want to get up close to them and not touch, others to pop them, others to make them or to blow them around, others just stand around the outside watching. But it's all okay, they all enjoy it in their own way," said Tom.

Feeling unusually fragile and nervous, I make myself leave the house again the following day and walk to check out the organic grocery store. I'm in the fruit section when I get a gift.

"Sadie?!"

"Eve?"

CHAPTER 28 – Snowball down a hill

"What are you DOING here? Do you live in Manchester now?! I didn't know that!" I said.

"Small world!" said Sadie gesturing widely then putting her hands on her hips with a satisfied smile.

"Yeah... small world," I say doubtfully as I smile and think a thank you to the universe.

I met Sadie at Reclaim the Power last year but we lost touch after she moved to Ireland to live on a permaculture farm. I go back to her place a few streets away for a cup of tea and a catch up. There are plants everywhere in the conservatory and we sit out in the sunshine in the garden. It turns out that Sadie is in need of a little cheering up. We hit on the fiendish plan of fun and dancing.

"Great!" I say. "You pick the venue and I'll get Tom to come too. Awesome!"

The Antwerp Mansion is not signposted. Through a dirty gate into a rundown courtyard the building is approaching derelict, vandalised, peeling and mouldy. This is the setting for one of the best nights out I can remember. There's a live band playing inside and an electro DJ set in another. Outside there are sofas, painting, drawing, homemade instruments which we jam on. The glockenspiel is made from random bits of wood and metal placed on a frame. When you hit them hard they bounce up and sometimes out, of the instrument. Perfect.

Saturday morning on the 12th there is a protest in the city centre about TTIP. When I arrive, there are about fifty people gathered around a stage. There are banners and pictures showing corporate caricatures making puppets of politicians. Two people on high stilts with masks are dressed as corporate cowboys and they have politician-puppets hanging down. I hand out my stack of leaflets to passersby. I listen to the speeches, one of which was very technical and hard to follow in the noisy bustling shopping street. I find myself criticising the speaker to Tom, and catch myself.

"Oh. That would be horizontal hostility," I say to him. "Wow. I guess that's coming from my own frustration and powerlessness. Oh. Interesting. Sorry about that."

I bade farewell to Tom and took a train to visit a university friend in Bury, north of Manchester. Waking up at their house the next day I had a snotty cold. They gave me a head start out of Bury in the car, dropping me at the start of a patch of woods.

"It doesn't feel right, just dropping you in the middle of nowhere," said my friend.

"Well it's all somewhere to me," I said laughing.

Through a wooded path I arrive at a café by a stone bridge. Rain is just beginning so it's time for a tea break. Downstairs is a chip shop and the café specialises in fish and chips. They also make a good pot of tea. I sit watching out the window as the rain worsens so decide to splash out on fish and chips. I get chatting with a man called Joe and his daughter, and afterwards, he offers to buy my lunch! My body feels like its fighting the good fight so it feels great to have hot food and not get wet. *Go body go! You fight that cold!*

The rain very conveniently stops when I've finished my lunch and I make my way up the hill to the start of the moor. Dark grey dry stone walls mark out very large fields; they curve and go up and around the splayed fingers of the hills. Little gullies come off the top of the hill. The moor has strange grass in uneven clumps, muted green and straw coloured, and some of it sticks up like a spray of porcupine quills.

Grass comes in so many types but I don't know any of their names. Someone once told me that all our modern cereal crops are in the grass family. Humans and grass, there's quite a relationship. We've spread it over the world and changed the ecosystem to make the best conditions for it. We burn down whole forests to plant it. Are we servants of grass? I think the big spiky clumps are types of rough grass. I wonder if the moors have been overgrazed? When we take too much grass, it evolves so that the animals we keep can't eat it.

None of the grass up here is lush, it is all quite wiry I guess because of the cold. A lot of the grass is flattened over and so wiry it's like lines of plastic. Since it's recently rained, that makes very treacherous footing. Just when you think your foot is down, it slides forward away from you. If I hadn't had my walking staff I would have fallen quite a few times. *Always take a stick with you.*

After the first moor, I arrive in Whitworth, which a sign tells me is the historic home of the first modern doctors. Two men in the street ask me what I'm doing and then donate money to me when I explain. I stop at the Red Lion Pub to warm up and the full rain begins as soon as I get inside. I look out at it unenthusiastically and get chatting with the owner, Steve, instead. Last year he cycled from Lands End to John o' Groats in two weeks.

"Not bad for someone with one leg and a pin in the other ay?" he said tapping his prosthetic leg.

"Wow! That's fantastic, well done!" I said. His enthusiasm and drive radiated from him. It was thirty three years ago that Steve lost his leg, I didn't ask how.

"I like people who take on challenges," he said.

"Well *you* certainly did!" I said.

"All sorts of campsites put us up for free when they found out what we were doing," he said. "We've got the B&B here; you can have dinner and a bed for free if you want it?"

My cold was making me feel very weary indeed, outside the rain was heavy and ahead lay the edge of another moor.

"Steve, that would be absolutely amazing. Thank you!"

All sorts of people have passed on kindnesses during this tour; kindnesses that they once received. On and on it goes, creating happiness and wonder. When you are kind to someone you don't know, it's not just the effect of that one event. You can change the way that person thinks about kindness, about humanity even. The choices they will make in the future every time they think about what you did for them, when you didn't know them. It changes the courses of many lives, like a ripple.

Setting out across the next moor in the morning I feel strengthened by the good night's sleep and the warm bed. The moor looks back at me from other hills. It's so beautiful to look around from a hill and not see towns and cities. The sky is grey overcast but not in a boring way. There are bright white areas and every shade of grey in complex cloud shapes hanging down at different heights.

Off the moor, a track takes me to the canal, and across it arches an imposing dark-grey stone railway bridge. It's got a couple of turrets like a grand castle entrance. An arched line decorates the otherwise rectangular top, and that's all it takes to make it beautiful. The canal has two locks in quick succession with big drops. Looking back the moors rise above.

In Todmorden I left the canal side and came up onto the bridge above, looking around for something positive. I hadn't been able to coordinate an appointment with Incredible Edible Todmorden because they were so busy but ahead of me I saw Todmorden Industrial and Co-operative Society, which sounded spot on. Upstairs they had a busy café and downstairs was a shop filled with local products. I sat outside with my hot chocolate and got chatting with the man at the next table about Incredible Edible.

"They're meeting upstairs at the moment," he told me.

"Ha, well that's just meant to be." I left a note for them with my number for when they came out of the meeting and a short while later a brightly dressed exuberant white-haired lady called Estelle came to find me.

"Eve! We've been emailing, I've got another meeting in an hour but we can squeeze a chat in now?" she said.

"Absolutely!" I said. We wandered down through Todmorden to Pollination Street, a community garden. Flowers were blooming and along one side was a long wall with a colourful mural of hills, trees and a rainbow. Guerrilla gardening groups garden public areas without permission.

"Most of what we do, we don't ask permission, we just take it," said Estelle. "As long as you're taking something ugly it's easier to ask for forgiveness than permission. The council left this area derelict. When we did the garden we called up the council and told them that there was a street sign for 'Pollination Street' missing. They came and put one in, they just never checked that it didn't exist before!" said Estelle.

"How did you come to do media for the group?" I asked.

"Well I'm dyslexic and I never wrote until I got a computer, then I started looking after the website. Someone asked me to write so in the end I did and people liked it. One day there was a tour group with a national news group coming. The others said 'there's *only* you, you've got to do it or we miss this chance. I met the guys from the Sun, and I did it! Estelle switched off and this Incredible Edible person switched on. The problem now is stopping me talking."

"How do you keep doing what you do?" I asked.

"Passion. I believe desperately in what we're doing. I was a teenager in 1960. I was part of the throwaway generation. We threw away everything. Biros, razors, knickers, everything was disposable. So I created the problems in landfill and making the world an unpleasant place. Now I can see it's in trouble I have to be part of the solution. I have no choice I am driven to do that. Our grandchildren have to inherit something better than what we're leaving them at the moment. Any town can grow food, but you have to grow kindness and community along with it to have a sustainable town. Because it's all about looking after each other."

Incredible Edible Todmorden has vegetable beds all over the town. It even has several outside the local police station.

"I asked," said Estelle, "and they said, 'don't ask. If you ask we have to ask up and they have to ask up. So don't ask.' I believe everyone wants to say yes, you just have to make it so that they can. Lonely peppers band," she says pointing to a label on one of the beds, then she picks up another slate marker to show me. "They've changed it from The Police Station to The Pollination Station. The police have done that themselves, we didn't write any of these. We grow corn and I call it a Fair Cob. They've put a slate in there that says 'It's a fair cob guv' with a little 'Thanks Estelle' underneath."

The Incredible Edible group has now inspired other groups around the world. There are nearly 100 in the UK alone.

"It's like pushing a snowball down a hill and then having to run to keep up!" said Estelle. "There are about 20-25 main volunteers and a mailing list of about 350. People come from all over the world to see the urban gardens. Vegetable Tourism! It funds it all," she said.

After Estelle waved me off at the canal I set off joyfully with arms swinging. As I passed a man on a bench, he shouted out.

"Pilgrim!"

Slightly hesitant I nodded, "Yes", and stepped towards him.

"You've got the look of distance," he said smiling. "Things hanging off your pack."

"Yep, it's been a few months, I started in April."

"I thought so. You headed to John o' Groats?"

"No, my own route, zigzagging, I only go as far as Berwick." I put down my pack and we shared the bench. Him with his beer, me legs swinging, both looking at the water.

"I did a walk for justice to end child abuse," he said. "What are you walking for?"

"The environment." I said smiling. "What made you begin?"

"I've never joined a protest or a group... but I've sought the truth. I started doing long walks to escape. Just walking there's nothing better. Your frame of mind becomes spaced out and you think more clearly. Walking you can't avoid yourself," he said as I nodded. We chatted for an hour or so and I walked with him along the canal, to his caravan at Hebden Bridge. We shared a pot of tea cooked outside over the fire with a slab of stone for a table. There was so much experience and compassion in his discussion.

Hebden Bridge seems to be a hippy paradise; organic shops, independent shops, cafés, ethical products, rivers, little squares and streets and a relaxed local council. Someone tells me it has the highest proportion of lesbians in the country. It's so pretty with beautiful stone buildings, there seems to be quite a bit of wealth, with craft stores around. This would not be everyone persons idea of paradise though, it's another subculture. More and more I think there is not one culture we share, but many overlapping in different ways. Places are advertising a specialist vegetarian range, there's an advert for a pop-up shop. Some of the trees are decorated with shiny or colourful things. I sit outside a pub in the sun and drink a hot chocolate as someone goes past carrying a yoga mat.

I discover the work of Treesponsibility, a community group in Hebden Bridge which has been going for fourteen years.

"Models predict more rain here," one of the founders tells me, "so we've been planting trees on steep slopes. It slows runoff, produces food, future fuel, and wildlife benefits. It's a three legged stool, land, resources and people. The group is mostly volunteers. It's taking responsibility for your own carbon emissions. I founded a workers co-op with two others and we manage several woods and do carpentry. We do green woodworking courses and forest schools too."

Sadie and her friend pick me up to stay at her friend's place just out of Hebden Bridge. Looking out at the valley we watch bats flit around as the sunset lingers on streaks of cloud. The sun sets so late now! It's nine thirty at night and I'm still not in bed. We sleep opulently in a big caravan.

After a solid granola breakfast I take on the hills to Bradford. Entering Bradford the weather is once again wet and I can't find a café or pub to shelter in. There are so many empty shops, warehouses and buildings! Apparently there are some parts of Bradford where there are entire streets empty. It seems so depressing. There's a sharp sudden transition to the city centre with bright lights, fountains and lots of chain shops. It's a bit belied by the harsh looks of people hanging around on the street and the number of drunks in the now sunny square. In the city centre a couple of drunk white guys start harassing me and saying rude sexual things. I'm so surprised I can't think of anything to say and just walk away. Someone in the library begs me for money.

I take a bus out to another part of the city to find my host for the night, Ros. Miranda went to university in Bradford and Ros is a good friend of hers. A woman on the bus warns me not to walk around on my own, saying there are quite a few places that aren't very safe. I pass a large number of Asian people, there are lots of ethnic shops; the bright colourful sari shops are like beacons in the depressing streets. I go to a pub near Ros' house to wait until she is back and two white men in their late fifties are walking out as I walk in. One stops and brazenly stares at my body as if I were an object with no perception. He stands there for a while as if he owns the space. I turn back and meet his eyes and say hello. After a long while in which he does not respond, he stops staring and continues out. In the pub toilets I change from my shorts and yellow summer top into trousers and a black jumper despite it being a hot day. A pretty yellow top draws far too much attention here.

Everywhere I have gone in Bradford men are on the streets standing around, while women walk quickly with heads down. There are no women hanging around on the streets, it feels like the men own the space. Bradford has a reputation from the news as being mostly Asian and Muslim. I've heard it called Bradistan as a racial insult. I discover from the statistics that it's 62% white. I've heard it's a place where Asian men harass white women but all the ones who harass me are white.

Leaving the pub I mimic the other women and walk swiftly with a closed body language. It reminds me of a Turkish friend. A Muslim all her life, she only started wearing a headscarf when she came to England for a year.

"Nobody makes me wear it," she said. "Nobody's ever even encouraged me to. I choose to as protection, from the attentions of men and from my own desire for sexual attention. If I dress modestly men don't view me so much as sexual."

It seems to me that what women do or do not wear to appear 'modest' is not the issue. The problem is that we view women firstly as a sexual object. In Victorian times showing ankle made people see you as a hussy, in Bradford it appeared a summer top did so, somewhere else it's showing your hair. It doesn't matter where the line is; the problem is with the mindsets not the clothing. Do we value women primarily by their sexual attractiveness? Do we encourage people to view women as objects?

We use different parts of our brains when we view an object than we do when we view a person. I remember reading about brain-scan research which showed that some men when they look at a woman they don't know, actually do use the 'object' part of the brain. How can you feel empathy for an object?

Soon after I cross into a side street a white couple are fighting. The woman starts to walk away and the man starts yelling threateningly at her not to walk away from him. On the other side of the road I hear her.

"I'm not scared of you!"

I keep walking and they do too. Further on, he catches her up and grabs her arm and pulls her around. It looks painful. I watch as she twists free.

"...bring you down to what you used to be..." I hear him say. I pause on the other side of the road, put my pack on the bench and pretend to adjust things. I'm not sure what to do. He calms down and keeps his hands away. The woman doesn't look to me for help. They walk on and so do I, following slowly, then our routes diverge. Did I do the right thing? Should I have intervened? Reported it to someone? I don't really know what you should do. If I tolerate it then that man knows he can do that to her even in public, there's nowhere she's safe. I contribute to the culture of not intervening. Would anyone intervene for me? I think I could have done better.

A young lad in a group shouts as I walk past with my staff.

"Fuckin' 'ell it's Gandalf."

"That's right lad, I'm a female Gandalf, powerful magic over here. No messing with me." I smile and wave magnanimously.

I'm struggling with the radical change from Hebden Bridge to Bradford in just a day's walk. I need to do my yoga, then it's easier to stay balanced. You can get away without doing it when things are easy, but that's exactly when you should take the opportunity to strengthen yourself for when it's not.

As I turn onto Ros' residential street it's long and goes up a steep hill. I count eight Asian children all playing in the street. They own this street and I am very glad. It's a joy to arrive at Ros' house on top of the hill. All things are forgotten as I step inside to the joy of meeting a friend of Miranda's. Ros has been involved with all sorts of wonderful projects over the years. When Miranda was at university they started a garden for the students to grow vegetables on campus and it's still going. Rupert from Oxford is finally free to join the walk and we expect him that evening. Ros and I are getting to know each other over a cup of tea when Rupert arrives. He looks joyfully alert, like he's going on a scout expedition; all smiles and a neat backpack. It is so good to see him, such a wash of familiarity.

The next day Rupert and I eat our lunch in a big park with trees and a big lake on the way to our first stop - a community farm on an allotment. At Horton Community Farm our guide is wearing a dark green t-shirt with an image of a tree like a mushroom cloud with the words 'Drop seeds not bombs'. The allotment had become unsafe and the council wanted to build on it, until the community group decided to make use of it. The group began as a Transition Bradford group before becoming Horton Community Farm.

"We've planted about thirty fruit trees over there that we're hoping will turn more into a bit of a forest," our guide tells us. "There's been a slight resurgence in use of the plots. There are some very well-used plots but still a lot that could be rented out. We run a veg box scheme with the crop."

"How did the veg box scheme start?" I ask.

"Well we got lottery funding in 2012. Friends and people we know wanted to get vegetables from us and then other people heard about it randomly," he says.

Heading east from the allotments it's a hot ugly slog, with lots of litter. Then, suddenly, the city ends. The dense buildings stop and it's fields with ponies in. We have an hour's silence as we walk over the lovely hills and up a shaded path. Through Pudsey, then we arrive at the cooler tree-lined canal with its three tiered locks. It's great to have Rupert to chat to and to read the map; I can relax like a passenger for a while.

In Leeds we stay at another housing co-op with the wonderful Reiley. I know Reiley from her work as a medic at Reclaim the Power. She always seems very sorted and talks a lot of sense. In the front garden are strawberries that Reiley invites us to eat for dessert. As the sun fades and her housemate arrives, we're rootling around in the undergrowth for strawberry prizes. So delicious!

The next morning as Rupert talks to Reiley over breakfast I nip down the road to the sister co-op house to chat with Hannah from Foot Printers, a small-scale printers.

"People wanted to get off the dole and learn a new skill. It's a way for us to work part-time and be involved in political projects," she said. At Foot Printers they print zines, projects, campaign materials, CD cases and cards. If you've never read a zine, there's a fabulous world awaiting you.

A zine is a low-budget mini-magazine. It's made so that it can easily be photocopied in black and white. They are usually on alternative or specialist topics that you wouldn't find in the mainstream. They could be cartoons, feminist writings, political commentary, anarchist political theory, reports on protests, anything. I had never come across them until a couple of years ago in an independent bookstore but you also find them at political protests or alternative meetings once you're looking. Sometimes there's original artwork, other times they cut and paste pictures out of other things, usually with humorous additions. If you've got something to say, and some arty friends, you can make a zine, and if people like it, they photocopy it and it spreads. I dream about making a zine about alternative careers and leaving it in 6th form school common rooms...

Along the canal we walk to the TCV (The Conservation Volunteers) office. The old stone manor house is next to the canal and is also home to The Permaculture Association. We meet Jess the Volunteer Coordinator for TCV and she treats us to lunch, tea and cake from the little café on the ground floor. We sit on a bench table in the sun. Dark-skinned and in a TCV polo-shirt, Jess grins with delight whenever she talks about her work.

"I'd given up my job because it was really stressful and I couldn't stand it anymore and it got me down in the dumps. I decided to take a fresh new look at my life and I really wanted to do something about the environment, about conservation. I'd been a nurse before, so I wanted to bring in the health element into the environment. So I came to volunteer and I decided that I really liked doing outdoor conservation work. Here they offer conservation diploma courses free for people who are unemployed. So I did the level two, which was *a-mazing*. And I was able to share my skills with other people who were unemployed, after I finished.

"The job I've got now, I support people to improve their health and wellbeing, through woodworking, environmental activities or it could be working in the café. It's fantastic!"

It begins to rain as we say goodbye. Leaving Leeds our route takes us through a beautiful park with an enormous lake and then along the river. The walk from Leeds to York is through fields, overgrown corridors of trees and down country lanes. The path takes us through a long tunnel of overgrowth, which drips noisily as bits of spikey plant reach for us. The rain doesn't let up for a moment. It begins to come down so fast that ahead is just a white blur. It streams constantly down my hood and pretty quickly the tarmac we are walking on is inch-deep in fast-flowing water. We're just splashing along through a stream. There's no point avoiding the deeper puddles, everything is already totally soaked; my shoes, my clothes, my knickers, everything. I start laughing and skipping through the water, what difference does it make now? Tonight, we will be staying with my friend Daniel!

Daniel was my music buddy at university; the only other

friend who liked Tori Amos. We would go to gigs together and we have both been in bands. Now he's a PhD researcher in neuroscience and still fantastic company. After that I would take a break for a week with a very dear friend who was visiting from Canada.

As Rupert and I neared York it became possible to catch a bus, and I thought impatiently about seeing my friends.

"I'm keen to see it through," says Rupert with a boyish smile. "You get the bus and I'll see you at Daniel's."

"Deal! Give me a text when you get close."

After I left Eve at the bus stop the rain relented and I carried on along the Ebor Way, the path we'd been on since Tadcaster. It was by then a warm and bright afternoon and I was drying out a bit and thinking how great it was to be out in it! There was loud music ahead, and a mile or two later the path went right past the source - a do at the Palace in Bishopthorpe for the well-heeled. I tried not to think about how much landfill would likely be produced by the time the night was out. As I came alongside the river, the sky darkened. Soon the heavens opened again. It was a long mile and a half to Nunthorpe through a bit of a deluge. Lightning struck not far away across the meadow making me draw my breath sharply. The thunder sounded like hundreds of wooden sheds being smashed to bits all at once. It was exhilarating stuff.

Tiredness gives joy to rest. Hunger gives joy to fullness. Without temporary discomfort and striving we don't seem to fully live. All this philosophising was brought on by a hot bath, a cup of tea and some food. Rupert arrived just as we were serving dinner. His sodden clothes dripped onto the kitchen floor as he smiled proudly.

CHAPTER 29 — Reclaim the power

A festival beyond hedonism. That's how the Green Gathering describes itself. Because sure, there's food, music, dancing and a good time, but it's much more than that. It's about gathering with other people who care about the environment and strengthening your ability to be a positive influence on this world.

The most popular band that weekend was Seize The Day who specialise in protest songs. Their anti-fracking song, 'Frack the Frackers', was warmly joined in by the crowd that spilled out around the tent. Brightly-coloured knitwear was strongly in evidence and smiling people nodded along.

Beyond The Healing Field with its fluttering colourful flags, is where I pitch my tent. I pass the Permaculture area and when looking at the rocket stove in the Craft area, I meet Tom the Dancing Fool. He has a long wiry brown beard joined to his moustache and sideburns, a purple dressing gown and a top hat. Tucked into his top hat is a shell.

"Hello! Is that from the Camino trail?" I ask smiling.

"It's from pilgrimage but not from the Camino."

"Ooo, what do you do?"

"I'm getting ready to dance from Green Gathering to the 'Off the Grid' festival in two weeks."

"How did you start doing that?" I asked, getting comfortable.

"I learned to Morris dance because it's an old tradition and not many people were keeping it up. I heard a story about a Shakespearean actor called William Kemp who used to be one of Shakespeare's actors in his plays. He always plays a comedy role and he used to improvise a lot of lines. He was also famous for Morris dancing. One day Shakespeare said to him 'enough of you spoiling my plays, you're sacked' and he said 'well I'm a bigger character than you' and he went around London and bet everyone that he could Morris dance to Norwich. And he did that in the 1600's. In 2011, I recreated that journey for charity and for a personal challenge.

"After I completed it I just felt so good about it that I wanted to carry on doing more. So I've done nearly a thousand miles of dancing pilgrimages now. It's just really changed my life. Once I started to do it, it's just brought so many amazing things into my life."

By the evening I'd had enough of new things and people and wanted a quiet warm place. What I found was the Sento Spa. The wood-burning sauna has bunting strung out from the tent and flag poles. A darkly colourful material-draped tent with peacefully moving volunteers welcomes you and the volunteers tell you how it all works. I passed droopy eye-lidded, smiling people, reclining on cushions with a look of goodwill to all. It was fairly easy to see who had just arrived and who had already been in. It was all paid for by donation. There was a feeling of peace and giving, love and healing. I sat in silence in the warmth for quite some time after the sauna. It was my birthday and I was thirty two.

I was at Green Gathering to staff the Reclaim the Power Stall and promote the upcoming climate action camp so I spent the following morning painting up a colourful banner and making the stall ready. The stall was in the Campaigns section. In the Campaigns section and many others there were workshops on all sorts of environmental skills and ways of working; forming a co-op, community energy, divestment, permaculture. Many of the tactics and concepts I had encountered during the Buzz Tour were gathered together, and so were some of the people. It was bizarre to bump into people from across the country; Sharona from my first stop, Laura from the SUMAC centre and others.

For the first time I encountered two interesting publications, Land magazine and STIR. I spoke to Jonny, the editor of STIR and asked him how he got started.

"I started by doing a website and then contacted people for content, activists and political writers and pitched it to them for the first issue. I was working in a nursing home, had a new baby and was learning the software late at night. It's a long hard slog to follow your dream, as you know, but it's worth doing otherwise you'd just have a joyless existence."

Mel arrived that day and after we finished on the stall she said she wanted to relax somewhere. We'd just missed each other when she'd joined the others on the Buzz Tour, so we had lots to catch up on.

"If you fancy it, I know just the place," I said grinning.

Everyone else in the sauna had been naked when I went in the day before and I decided this time I would 'take the plunge' too. I nervously avoided looking at anyone else as we emerged bare-bummed. In the sauna men and women sat around naked, enjoying the heat and occasionally conversing about some social or environmental topic. We needn't have felt self-conscious, no one cared a fig leaf. The cold plunge pool was an inflatable pool under the starry night sky and boobs flopping, I hopped over and in with relief.

Dressed and dried we sat on embroidered cushions and plucked up the courage to quietly strum a couple of guitar notes as we chatted. Neither of us can play the guitar but if all you're doing is playing a few pleasing notes who cares?

On the way back to my tent I stopped in at a circle in the Healing Area. A large circle of woven willow with flowers and beautiful things hanging off it had a stone pattern at the centre with candles in it. Looking up at the stars and down at the candles I felt tremendous gratitude.

A few days after the Green Gathering it was the long-awaited Reclaim the Power summer action camp. After Climate Camp scaled down, many of the activists went off into other projects and seeded all sorts of new initiatives, one of which was No Dash for Gas. No Dash for Gas activists shut down West Burton Power Station by climbing up the cooling towers. Reclaim the Power was formed by activists from No Dash for Gas and the first action camp was originally going to be at West Burton but was moved at the last minute to the fracking site at Balcombe.

This year the site of the camp was a planned fracking site near Blackpool. Even those of us who were to be part of the 'site take' did not know the exact location. If the police knew in advance they would prevent it, but when a few hundred people turn up and peacefully set up a camp they let it go ahead. Our teams gathered and then received a series of directions to holding locations. At our group's holding location we were to meet another team and when we pulled up and got out of the car I saw Mel getting out of the other car.

"Woo! I didn't know you were doing the site take too," I said rushing over to give her a hug. A few minutes of waiting and we received the final directions, along with all the other teams to converge on the location.

We were all a little nervous, unsure what we would find and what the police response would be, but as we approached the field we were greeted by groups of smiling women in yellow aprons from 'Nana Camp' directing us to the field next door, and absolutely no sign of police. Car after car and trucks with equipment streamed in through the gate.

The Nanas were a group of mothers and grandmothers from the Blackpool area who had occupied the adjacent field the week before in protest to the fracking. All that sneaking around and the site was actually Nana Camp! Mel and I laughed at the ridiculousness and with relief. We had arrived. Everyone was excited and smiling, seeing people they knew, eager to get the structures up to make police eviction more difficult.

I spotted Miranda and Sama and we ran over for hugs, then we saw Kara. "Hey Kara!" we shouted as she bounced excitedly up to us with her dreadlocks flying, in nebula-decorated leggings.

"So good to see you! The Buzz Tour sounds like it's going well. So sorry I haven't been able to walk with you," Kara said.

"You walk with us in spirit," I said smiling.

Work began immediately to mark out the camp layout with tape. Then people formed into teams to unload the lorries and trucks. My job was toilet coordinator so for the next several hours I organised teams of volunteers to build the flat pack compost toilets and unload the large numbers of straw bales, toilet rolls and sawdust. We were expecting in the region of three thousand people.

There was a wonderful system in place for the camp. For each role there was also a mentor and a shadow. The mentor was someone with expertise, preferably the person who had done it the year before, who was not to do much of the work but just to advise and train. The role holder did the work, and the shadow was available to assist and to learn.

Each morning we had a site coordinators meeting to sort out logistics. Looking around it was wonderful to see people who, like me, had only become involved the year before. It felt like we were part of the same activist school graduating year. It's a very quick way to skill up a lot of people and build capacity. Because at its heart that is what Reclaim the Power is about, coming together and skilling up to take action.

I asked Sama what Reclaim the Power was to her.

"It's just a space where lots of people can get empowered, share skills and it's a great network of people who can accomplish change together. I think my point of view has been fairly limited to...food!" she said as we started laughing. "A hell of a lot of salt and soya milk!"

Sama was coordinating kitchens with Miranda mentoring. Every day Sama and the kitchen crew put on three meals for the camp, always vegan and delicious.

By the time the camp officially started two days later, there were about a dozen different marquees up for the infrastructure of running the camp and for all the events on the program, all for free. The camp program was packed with workshops, talks, meetings and training but I went to little of it, content to contribute by managing the toilets and spending time with people at the camp this time.

Culture stems from shared behaviours. There are many different cultures all overlapping, and each person belongs to many cultures and subcultures.

But how do you know if you share behaviours with others?

You can meet them, you could interact on social media, or you could hear about them through the media. If you are geographically isolated, a good chance to meet like-minded people is at a gathering. Once you do find others who share your behaviours it can strengthen and reinforce them. Get a group of you and you have a shared culture.

Another great book that Paula lent me is called The Tipping Point; it describes tipping points in social change. One key factor in the uptake of change is that those adopting it must be visible. There are thousands and thousands of people who care, but we don't see them in the media. How could we make our cultural changes more visible to each other and to the wider population?

When I think about how we can be most efficient in changing our culture I'm reminded of other factors as to how change spreads. A person with an idea is just a crazy individual until someone joins. The first people to adopt it help transform it into something more acceptable. Then, when enough people with social standing adopt an idea, there is a rush to join, to not be the one left out.

Think of it like a fire. A spark is useless without some tinder. The tinder then needs kindling. A spark is never going to light a wet log. So if we want to make the most of our energy we want to work in the right way. If you're a spark, find some tinder. If you're kindling, keep getting lots more kindling and cosy up to a log. Be prepared for it to take a long while if the log isn't dry.

On the third day we began to form affinity groups for taking direct action later. If you already had a whole team you could use that, but if you wanted help forming a group you filled out a form and the secret actions team matched you with other people. Then you would receive your mission. The form had about ten different questions with things like your experience level, what type of action you would like to do, how arrestable you were, how fit you were and whether you would like a rural or city mission. I knew I definitely wanted a rural mission.

On the day we were to get our missions, all the affinity groups were gathered in the main marquee, strings of lights around the walls and about fifteen circles of four to ten people waiting. But our team had a problem. There were people there who were not on the list. We were fourteen, the list was nine.

Anxiety and suspicion were raised as we realised we didn't know who had placed them in the team. A couple had been invited by others without asking the rest of the group, but with the others we didn't know *what* was going on. We all wanted to open the mission envelope but couldn't until we sorted it out. We retreated to a tepee to get to know each other.

One of the new people volunteered to go ask someone from the action team if they were all supposed to be there, and then came back a while later saying that yes they were, which for some reason we all believed. At a later date I was told by a facilitator of the process that that was not right – any new members to the list would have been introduced and people should have discussed if they were happy for others to join. If you want to form an affinity group quickly there's always the chance that someone from the police or industry will try to infiltrate. These days they infiltrate all sorts of protest groups. The process of how you decide who you want to work with must ultimately sit with you. A perfect action ours was not, but it's a fast way to learn.

Sama and Mel did some facilitating and eventually in the dark of the yurt, we had an uncomfortable trust and the newly formed affinity group agreed to open the mission. It was getting late and many of us were already drained from setting up the camp. A tall man we'll call Gary opened the white envelope and read it out with tense excitement.

"Your mission, is to enter and blockade the London headquarters of IGas, a company engaged in fracking."

London. A blockade mission in London where you stay locked onto something until arrested was about as far from what I wanted to do as could be imagined.

"I think I have to bow out guys, this is pretty much the opposite of what I put on my form," I said.

"There will be a lot of different roles though," Sama said. "Why not stay and see?"

Over the next four hours we tried to get a plan together. We needed information; some of us had done reconnaissance there previously so they painted a picture for us of what the location would be like. Down a quiet narrow side street, in a wealthy area of London with hotels and offices. We batted back and forth what equipment we might need. How to get it? How to hold the space once we did? We would need accommodation in London, there was travel organised for some of the group on a coach but the others would need transport. What was the budget?

One person decided to leave and discussions continued. The conversation went back and forth for a while on the morality of inconveniencing other people in the office block. Gradually as I monitored things my role emerged.

"OK, I think what I would like to do is welfare. I'd like to look after you all, make sure you have food and everything," I said.

There was a lot of relief on people's faces. It was now around three in the morning and there was a great deal more work to do and we were not in a good state to do it. We agreed to meet the following day.

After sorting out the toilets for the morning I joined the meeting of our affinity group. We had lost another two people. I didn't really notice at the time, neither did anyone else. We were so focused on planning and so, so tired. Because of the distance we would have to leave that afternoon. We assigned some roles and set about trying to sort out accommodation and transport. Another person decided to leave.

As I prepared to board the coach to London I saw one of our group leaving in a car. That took us down to nine.

I saw that my friend Lindsay from Bristol and Global Power Shift also getting on the coach. We went up to each other for a hug. During the five-hour journey we stopped at a services for food and Lindsay came to sit next to me and gave me another hug. Everyone put their food together in the middle as we sat on the grass outside the services. Humous, bread, carrots and crisps were the predictable food.

"Could we sit together on the coach?" asked Lindsay. "Do you think your friend would mind?"

"I'd love that," I said with more hugs. "I'll go and tell them."

As we sat back on the coach Lindsay leaned in towards me and with a conspiratorial whisper said, "I think we're going to London for the same reason."

I looked at her with sudden realisation and smiled. "I think so too," I said. There were fourteen other groups working hard on their actions, of course it would be likely that another group would be going to London.

"I'm scared," Lindsay said.

"...That's OK. Everyone else is too," I said.

"It's quite a step from when we spoke in Bristol," she said. I nodded and we squeezed hands.

By the time we got to our accommodation in London it was night time. Mentally and emotionally exhausted the ten of us (with driver) all bedded down together; three in a bed and everyone else arranged like a tesselated puzzle on the floor.

The next morning we grabbed what toast and instant coffee we could, I packed food, people went over their roles and how to get to the rendezvous point. All of our early complex proposed plans had been simplified down, there just wasn't time. It all depended on whether or not we got into the building. The equipment was reduced to what we had been able to get hold of on a Sunday, which basically came down to superglue and D-locks.

The scout went ahead and met us at the rendezvous point.

"There's a couple of guys inside the lobby but they're just letting people in through the doors," they said.

By the time we approached, it had become two guys outside and two inside. They moved to block the way and near the door people broke into a run. Tensions were high as people shouted and pushed. After a brief scuffle we could tell we weren't going to get in.

Plan B. Those who'd volunteered to lock-on, sat down in a line blocking the door. The super glue and locks were quickly passed out and several people stuck themselves together. I unrolled a banner and draped it across them.

The police came after about twenty minutes and stood watching. They made no attempt to remove us and we were all relieved. As people came to enter the building we would cheerfully explain why we were there and the security guards sent them around to the side of the building. After about an hour some of the group went to the side entrance and attempted to block that too. The adrenaline and lack of sleep made some of the men change drastically. It reinforced for me how important it is to get to know people before you work with them and to take care of the human beings. I kept people supplied with water and snacks and tried to keep things calm, feeding people pieces of flapjack and chatting. Occasionally I ferried joke messages between the two groups.

After a few hours, the solvent was used to unstick people and we headed off to reconvene later. Some of us had decided to show support at the other action we had heard about in London, at DEFRA government offices. As we approached I could see police milling around. When we got close enough to see into the building doorway I saw Lindsay superglued onto the ground with another person and a sign. She looked good, quite relaxed. I waved and she nodded back with a smile.

One of the guys who had been locked on at our action said he was going to get a drink. He looked pale, so I went with him and as we walked to the pub he began to shake. After downing a drink he began to recover, making jokes and going back over parts of the action, but still looking shaken.

It was then only another twenty minutes before Lindsay's group decided to unstick themselves and we all decided to reconvene at a pub, with not a single arrest. It was the same story all over the country. In sharp contrast to the year before, the police had decided on a policy of no arrests in order to avoid media attention. Some people were disappointed with the lack of media, but most were relieved their friends weren't waiting to be bailed.

Over the next few months the police did make some arrests, one at a time, without drawing media attention.

Lindsay and I walked with linked arms tightly clutched. She looked pale and began shaking. Her skin felt cold. Shock. In the warmth of the pub most people had an alcoholic drink and I had an orange juice. There were a lot of hugs and nervous laughs as people got rid of tension.

The stress of those two actions was very mild compared to actions involving violence, yet there was a significant impact on the people involved. After an action it's important to have somewhere safe to stay, with people you trust. If something traumatic like violence does occur then it is important to have access to that safe place for a prolonged period of time. There are now a couple of organisations who offer support and advice for activists suffering trauma. It's a good idea for anyone to be aware of the symptoms of trauma and how we can support people suffering.

The long drive back up to Blackpool had us back at the camp at midnight. As we approached camp we became excited to see people again and to find out what other actions had happened. Everything was dark and quiet except for the main marquee which had pumping dance music playing.

"Hold this," I said to Mel handing her the banner and we entered the tent to loud cheering. Standing on some hay bales with the banner, Mel looked so happy, so excited. Luckily 'the last song' kept happening for another two hours. In the party Sama, Mel and I found Miranda and Kara.

"How did it go?!" asked Sama excitedly.

"Amazing!" said Miranda giving Kara a proud hug. "We were in a team who went to the fracking site at Crawberry Hill. Rowan, Paula's friend was with us. We closed down the site for five hours! The first time I'd done anything like that. Where were you guys?"

"IGas head office in London," said Sama.

"Wow, well done, long way! How did it go?" asked Kara.

"We blocked the entrance but couldn't get in. I'd been meaning to go to IGas for a while just never found the time to go, so yeah, this was awesome!" Sama said laughing.

"The security were fairly violent to begin with at Crawberry Hill actually," said Miranda, "We calmed things down, doing deep breathing with the security and the police. It felt really together and strong. We had really good discussions about whether to let people join."

I started laughing. "Now you tell us! That sounds like a good way to do it. We had some dodgy mystery people."

We moved around the tent congratulating people and smiling until my face hurt, then smiling some more. We danced and waved our arms, jiggled in jubilation and laughed at our own ridiculousness. I was so grateful that no one had to spend the night in a cell. Thirteen actions and no arrests. Looking around, everyone was proud and celebrating. After another hour people were drifting to bed and I left the party to those with more stamina.

Exhausted, I returned gratefully to my tent. With the familiarity of my sleeping bag and tent I was quickly asleep.

CHAPTER 30 — A Quaker paradise

Back in York I was to meet Daniel in the pub for dinner with a couple of his other friends: "An old school friend and his girlfriend." The stairs in the pub were large and made of dark wood, the walls covered in artefacts and stuffed dead animals. When I arrived in the snug upstairs room with my enormous backpack I did a bit of a double take as Daniel introduced me to his friends.

"Sean," said the man shaking my hand. My eyebrows did a little confused frown which he noticed with a smile.

"*Weren't you the quidditch captain in Harry Potter?*" I wanted to ask but wasn't sure of the etiquette.

Gaia, Daniels other friend was also an actor. Tall, blonde and beautiful she was currently in a series called Vikings.

"I get to learn all sorts of cool skills. Sword fighting, horse riding, archery," she said shyly. She showed me a video of one of her choreographed fight scenes.

"That is so cool! What a great thing to get to learn!" I said.

Then there were the designer dresses.

"It's kind of crazy but I'm not allowed to wear the same one to another event. I've given several to my mum," she said.

The four of us strolled back to Daniel's house and then the whiskey and board games came out. Have you ever played Cards Against Humanity? The creators are now millionaires apparently. It is SO wrong and SO funny.

Wandering through the centre of York the next day there are a lot of tourists, but also now lots of people in suits and short dresses. I pass under the city wall and into York city proper. York has the most complete medieval city walls in the country. There are four gates which are still intact and you can walk the wall most of the way round the city, about two and three quarter miles. Pack-free, I took a saunter along the stone platform past the chunky crenellations, nodding and smiling with the elderly tourists.

York is full of beautiful old buildings, old stone and timber. York Minster itself is covered in curving carvings, extra spires and spikes, sitting solidly, owning the space. Hundreds of little alcoves and mini buttresses are all over it. It's like the architect couldn't stand to leave any part unadorned.

Many of the streets in the centre are pedestrianised and narrow. Bay windows hang out from the first floor over the streets. Above them, another floor edges out even further over the street. There are hanging baskets and wrought-iron shop signs. Off to the side are numerous snickelways - the local word for an alley - which link up the streets in wonky lines.

Crossing the river are numerous bridges, some of them dating from medieval times. The walls of these older bridges are much thicker and some have towers on that have little rooms, containing small businesses.

Next to another bridge I find a bike repair. "Bike Rescue at The Hub," it says. "Refurbished Bikes. Service and Repair. Our community based project has saved 10,000 bikes from landfill and given 6,000 bikes a new home!"

Inside I speak to a man working at the project.

"I got involved with the bike rescue project because ah was unemployed and the job centre put me here on a mandatory four-week work placement, and that was just over two years ago and I've never looked back! Ah cum out o' building trade and been unemployed and come here it's total different, so yeah, happy days," he said smiling.

There is a perfect grassy mound near the river with the round fort of York castle perched on top. The river is quite wide, tree-lined with man-made edges and boats are moored up. The weather has turned colder and autumn is coming. I'm glad I've only got two weeks of the walk left.

That night Daniel and I went out for dinner. Sitting up in a restaurant after dark, I enjoyed every second of it. I don't go out after dark when I'm walking alone. As we walked back home we saw drunken middle-aged people in suits stumbling and swaying. One tripped into the gutter and a woman in a very smart pink dress sat down on the curb to take off crazy high-heels then shrieked with laughter, making me jump.

Daniel laughed quietly, shaking his head. "Happens every time," he said sounding superior; "the horse races."

The next day it's sunny and hot, perfect for a trip to West Bank Park. Jane regularly uses the park with her children. We sit at a picnic bench next to a bowling.

"The council cuts meant that the park had to be kept unlocked overnight," said Jane, "and the funding for the onsite gardeners was gone too. The park is the site of the old James Bacchouse Nurseries - the 'Kew of the North'. My background is broadcast journalism and I thought there might be a story. James Bacchouse was a Quaker philanthropist. He went to Australia and visited every penal colony to check how they were being treated. He sent back plant specimens.

"The council had a meeting and I suggested turning the disused building into a heritage site. So I put together a little video and sent it to the council. I sent various emails to the newspaper and went on the local radio, and used the media, for what it's there for, to activate social campaigns.

"I'm a great believer in celebrity endorsements. I've written to hundreds of celebrities and I've had quite a number write back, for example Dame Judy Dench went to a Quaker school just up the road, she's very interested."

As we talked, an elderly man approached and greeted Jane. John from the Friends of West Bank Park walked slowly, with his pipe, stick and a baseball cap covered in badges of birds. Binoculars were hanging from his neck.

"My paradise," John called the park. John's walked in the park for forty years. These days he can't walk far and the park is just three minutes from his front door.

"Got to get the younger ones to carry on we hope," said John. "Margaret's 80 and I'm 78 and we're all plodding on you know. Having your say even if nobody listens, at least I'm saying something. Never give up hope."

278

"If the park gates were not left unlocked I wouldn't have become involved," said Jane. "Out of that adversity has come a really positive result; it's brought the community together."

York has quite a history of Quaker philanthropy. Rowntrees and Terry's were both Quakers who looked after their workers and community, and since Terry's made chocolate, they're especially on my good side.

It is now the 23rd of August. I've been on the road for over four months and The Buzz Tour money has run out. I arrive in Darlington by train and someone makes buzzing noises at me, which I rather enjoy. But the best is when a small child shouts "Bumblebee!"

Clervaux café in Darlington is a social enterprise to help vulnerable young adults by giving them work experience in a kitchen, bakery and café. The café is linked to an eco-farm of the same name where they do therapeutic activities. The café uses rare breeds pork and beef from local farms and the eco-farm supplies their organic biodynamic veg.

I'd tried contacting another few groups in Darlington but I decided that there wasn't going to be anything in Darlington that night and that I wanted to be in Durham.

As I stepped off the train in Durham, my phone rang. I flipped my hood up in the rain and walked down the hill until Durham Cathedral was spread out before me.

"Hey sweety!" I said excitedly to Miranda as I answered.

"Hello darling," said Miranda. Her voice was low with sorrow.

"Darling, what's the matter?!" I asked.

"It's Rupert...He was out cycling...and...he's been hit by a car," she said with difficulty.

CHAPTER 31 — Nuts and eccentric

"**Is** Rupert...?" I asked tentatively, heart banging. "He's in intensive care, they had to resuscitate him... It's pretty bad... They're going to try and operate but we don't know..." she said.

"Oh...God. Thank you for calling darling. How are you doing?" I asked.

"It's all a bit crazy. I'm at the hospital. Rupert's family are here. We're just waiting."

"Well done for supporting them sweetheart," I said.

"How are you getting on?" Miranda asked.

"I've actually just caught the train to Durham, where Rupert went to university," I said feeling a bit weird.

"Hmmm, that's so great that you're there," said Miranda.

"He used to sing in the cathedral choir didn't he?" I asked.

"Yeah," said Miranda sounding upset.

"I'm looking at it now. I'll see if I can get someone at the cathedral to say a prayer for him," I said.

After I put down the phone I wandered down through the city towards the cathedral, tearful, wet and anxious. I sat outside for a while on a bench to gather myself then went into the hushed imposing building. At the far end in a quiet side chapel I lit a candle for Rupert and sat and prayed...to something. I went to try to find someone who might have known Rupert.

The first person I spoke to was working in the shop reception part - Brian. He told me that yes he did remember Rupert, in fact he had used to sing in the choir with him, they both sang Alto. I explained what had happened and said I was hoping that someone here might say a prayer for him? I started to well up and struggled to keep an even tone.

"Of course. We can get him put on the prayers list too, you just speak to one of the vergers," he said.

"Oh okay, great, what do the vergers look like?" I asked.

"They're the people who look after the services and organising at the church, they're wearing long black robes. I'll take you over," he said.

When the verger asked me what was wrong I started crying as I explained. She said they would put Rupert on the prayers list. He'd be prayed for twice a day. That sounded like a great thing. I felt it would help. Then she asked, "What about you, do you need anything?"

"I need food and shelter." I thought, but didn't know how to ask for yet more help.

"...um, yes...I'm...trying to find somewhere to sleep tonight. Somewhere safe I could pitch my tent for free?" I said. She went away for a while and rang a couple of places.

"Most places are full but there's a room available at one of the colleges. Do you have money to pay for it?" she asked.

I thought about the empty Buzz Tour account and my own meagre funds. "..Ye..es," I said.

"That would be safe and warm," she said.

"Ye..es. That's probably a good plan, a better plan than down by the river," I said. She gave me the address and directions and a few minutes walk later I was being shown to my little room. It was a basically furnished single student room with a bed, desk, light and bathroom. It felt warm, safe and a lovely refuge. I took off my wet things, got warm under the shower and then got snug in bed. I sent out prayers for Rupert, and hope.

In the morning I got another call from Miranda saying that Rupert was now in a stable condition. I wasn't quite sure what that meant although you hear it on films all the time. I think it means they were fairly certain that he wasn't going to die.

"They're going to try to do an operation today on his leg and pelvis. They're keeping him unconscious," she said.

As I leave Durham I pass a 'Birds of Durham heritage project', which is a joint venture with the natural history society of Northumbria. There's a sign with information: 'Bringing the wildlife of the past to the people of tomorrow.' I like it.

I pass a field with hay bales in it and it really strikes me just how much time has passed since I set out. Everything's being harvested now, if it hasn't been already. I find myself just standing and looking at the bales. They never meant much to me before. But now they tell the time. The blackberries are out and the hazelnuts are ready, but green. You can't really wait for them to go brown because the squirrels will get them first. I gather a bundle of hazelnuts in foraging foolishness. I will carry those bloody nuts with me till the end of the walk, when they're finally ripe, when I still won't have anything to crack them with.

Enormously long, stained concrete walls signal the start of another prison. There are floodlights and cameras on very tall poles pointed at them. I never normally come across prisons, but on the tour I've walked by several. I wonder how many there are? How many people are in them? There seem to be quite a lot. It is silent, and very tragic. Another section has curling razor wire at the top of fencing. I pass a fast-walking guard on his lunchtime walk.

I hear the unpleasant beep of a construction vehicle reverse warning. The air ahead is filled with yellow dust and noise. Ah, not construction, a combine harvester, racing to get in the grain. They've only done a few strips of the field and there are dark clouds above.

The accents are changing as I head towards Newcastle. "Where you be sittin' Mam?" a lady asks her mother.

In Lumley I am at the top of a hill looking out over the distant slopes when an elderly lady comes to sit with me on the bench, with her little white dog. Jean tells me about the 'three tricks' from her life.

"I quit smoking that was a big trick...Now then, there was the Great North Run, I ran that...And...oh yes...I learnt to drive... late, at thirty eight...I won a car. Five years ago my car was failing. My husband died a couple of years before. I entered this competition in a magazine and I won a car...I asked my family if I should keep it and they said 'Dad sent you that car... if he'd wanted you to have money he would have sent money instead...keep it'," she said.

Jean tells me she grew up in Birtley and that it was a nice village, so I decide to head there. In Birtley I arrive at the church just as they are locking up and explain that I'm looking for the vicar or the church warden to see if I can camp there.

After about a minute to think about it, Margaret and her husband Derek, the church warden, offer me dinner and a bed at their house for the night. Derek cuts up the salad and fruit with dinner into little pieces and arranges it on the three plates like works of art. We have bread and butter on the side. They are so very kind to a stranger and ask for nothing in return. They are not especially interested in the environment; they are just kind to me because I am a human being in need.

The next day on my way into Newcastle I stop at a National Trust site called Old Washington Hall. I eat my lunch in the beautiful formal gardens blooming with flowers and lavender, then wander through to The Nuttery, which the sign says is a wildflower nut orchard. Through the red brick wall there is a little pond with a bridge, rows of trees and families flitting around them.

I find Ellaine cutting pieces of willow for a dragonfly art activity they are running that day.

"Washington's a fairly built up area," said Ellaine, "and when we finished the pond the nuthatch came down and a woodpecker and a tree creeper, and it was like 'oh my goodness, there is actually an awful lot of bird species here'. And they said 'thank you very much' and then they invited all their friends."

"How did you come to be doing this work?" I asked.

"From a young age we always went out into the countryside because my father was an artist but my first realisation was when I started volunteering. It was desperation to be outside working with nature, and trying to change things for nature because they haven't got a voice to shout with. If it wasn't for them we wouldn't exist. After we built the pond I was fortunate enough to be offered the job as a wildlife gardener."

As I leave The Nuttery and Old Washington Hall I collect my backpack and the man at reception tells me he's glad to have met a true English eccentric. I feel flattered but misunderstood, but it's not worth correcting him.

"I'm not eccentric, I just care about climate change. It might seem a little odd to dress like a bee, but it's quite sensible really," ...I think?

There are still fields between me and Newcastle, now dry and straw-coloured, soon to be harvested. I get an update from Miranda that Rupert's leg operation has been a success but it'll be days before he is conscious and we know the full damage. As I walk along the field edges there are pink flowers and berries in the hedges, but the wind is cold. Further on, there is a wet field with bulrushes, and beyond that, an excessive spread of power pylons. I count twenty two.

I spend the night with a family friend in South Shields and in the morning walk along the outskirts of the docks towards Newcastle. You can't get into the docks, there are high fences and security. Eventually I cross the river which is a black-mud half-pipe as the tide is out. Next to the river is a half-ruined abbey that has some walls I can use to cut out the wind while I eat. More pylons. You don't usually see power pylons in TV shows or films unless it's to emphasise urban-ness, but actually there's lots of them, all over. We edit them out of our minds as best we can, as directors edit them from shots.

My first stop of the day is the office of Groundwork on Windmill Way at the South Tyneside Eco Centre. When you don't have a smartphone or a street atlas, writing out directions in reference to things on your OS map is pretty important. Pylons, railway lines, rivers, big roads, are all very useful markers. Hills can be very useful too as long as you don't try to make what you see fit what's on the map. If it doesn't fit, it's probably the wrong hill. Thankfully I can see a wind turbine to guide me in.

Asking at reception, Sarah agrees to come down to speak with me. Sarah has worked at the trust for six years and loves it. It's written all over her face.

"Groundwork is a regeneration charity, we aim to change places and change people's lives," Sarah tells me. "We deliver all sorts of environmental and regeneration programs around health and wellbeing, education and the environment, climate change, land and open spaces, employment and skills."

"How did you come to be doing this work?" I ask.

"I started volunteering at a different Groundwork elsewhere in the country when I left university," says Sarah. "I left and got paid work. Then I saw the post advertised here and had to come back. Because one thing Groundwork is really good at is changing lives, and that's what makes me feel good."

From Groundwork I head west. I'm heading to Scotswood and a permaculture garden. Walking up a steep hill, a young black woman is walking down with grocery bags.

"Good for you! Make sure you relax when you get the chance," she says to me out of the blue with such kindness.

"Thanks!" I say. She gives me a lift, like she's turned my light on. We have such power to influence each other.

I see rows of terraced housing, with litter down the alleys in between. It looks like a shot from the film Billy Elliot. There's an old sofa and bits of broken wood. Five kids are walking around and one asks me what I am.

"I'm a bee," I say smiling and waggling my eyebrows. He runs away saying "AHHH it's a bee." He runs over to the other children where one of them is snapping a piece of furniture. His voice changes to excitement as he's telling the other children, "It's a bee, it's a bee," After a pause the boy snapping furniture looks up and says, "It's an ugly bee," and the first boy is silent. I feel so sad for him. We have such power to influence each other.

I arrive at the Scotswood gardens just in time to catch Karen and David before they head home. The site has a building with bright yellow roller shutters on the windows and the garden is fenced in with a tall fence. Inside the outer fence there is a side entrance with an amazing carved-wood archway and gate.

"The gate was a project done by refugees," Karen tells me.

"It's amazing. Stunning," I say as I get closer to the incredible pictures. Beetles, rushes, a sunflower and all sorts of things densely carved on top of each other.

Scotswood Natural Community Gardens covers a large site with lots of different parts, from the kitchen garden to wilder areas and ponds. Everything inside the fence seems brightly painted or decorated and there are a lot of murals.

"It's a community-led project, a charity, based on the principles of permaculture," Karen tells me. "A lot of the garden is based on the principles of growing fruit and vegetables under trees and layering things. We have quite a lot of social and youth projects which are run from the garden. The area we're in, Scotswood, is a highly deprived area, one of the highest percentiles of deprivation in the country. So it's really important work we do with a lot of the local youth groups. A lot of the volunteers have come from difficult backgrounds and a lot of people come here for mental health reasons."

We walk on to another garden that has a solar fountain. Very different from formal gardens, this one is packed with life and overflowing plants. There are colourful mosaics on the ground and I like the one with rabbits. The solar fountain has to be dismantled at night because if they leave the solar panel in, it gets stolen. It seems so hard to pull yourself up if other people keep pulling you back down.

David is one of the volunteers and although shy, with some encouragement from Karen, he tells me about his work.

"I've been a volunteer here for seven years now. I was unemployed and I went with a company called A for Action for Employment. I was put on a placement for thirteen weeks and I've never been away since, and I quite enjoy it," he said with smiling understatement. "Kids been vandalising it but it's lettin' them see that it's not just to be set about, it's to sit and look at the wildlife and all that."

286

Karen gives me a lift back into the city and as we leave the garden she points to some flowerbeds that they had planted up with vegetables. "But the local kids keep ripping them out. We've tried going out into the schools and youth clubs and getting them to plant it with us, but fast as they put them in, someone else takes them out."

We pass a group of seven kids on bikes aged between about ten and thirteen. Karen gestures to one with his hood up.

"That one's a terror. We've planted it up with wildflowers now and giving it a rest. One of their brothers is even in the youth club. Some fruit trees are still there so we'll see how it goes," she said with resignation.

A local Green council candidate, Andrew, has offered to put me up for the night and when I meet him at the station he's so pleased to see me! I feel so honoured to be greeted by his shy enthusiasm. We return to his house where I meet his partner, Mike. The house is full of interesting art and objects, colours and life. A picture of them sits on the mantle, the walls are yellow and the furniture is muted blue and red. The conversation swoops around books, where I should go next and through profound and heartfelt substances in life.

Andrew and Mike were so supportive, so kind, and so enthused about everything I'm trying to do. I felt very fortunate indeed to receive their kindness. Andrew himself has done a number of pilgrimages, he did a political walk through different sites and he recommends that I go to the grave of the Suffragette Emily Wilding Davis, which is to the north of Newcastle in Morpeth. I had no idea where her grave was and I say that I will indeed go there.

CHAPTER 32 — A well met architect

The next day I headed to Morpeth. Along the way I chatted with Sama on the phone, confessing that I was finding the last part of the journey hard.

"I'm not wishing it, but maybe this section of the journey is supposed to be hard and you overcome it," she said.

"Thanks darling," I said nodding. Looking after yourself is not about giving your fears your attention; it's about listening to your needs.

I find the church I'm seeking just south of Morpeth. There is a mention on an information board along with other things and a description of how to find the grave, so I set off through the churchyard in search. It takes me quite a while to find the grave, amongst the old pine trees, large graves and monuments. It is a white plinth with a stone cross on the top and other names from the family inscribed around it. It has a metal fence around it that someone has tied some purple and green ribbon to it; the colours of the suffragettes. Above Emily's name is a quote "Greater love hath no man than this, that a man lay down his life for his friends." St. JOHN, XV CHP. XIII VERSE. Below it, "Born Oct 11th 1872, died June 8th 1913. DEEDS NOT WORDS" I feel irritation at the repetition of 'man' and 'his'.

In front of the monument is a separate small white-marble cube with plastic flowers in that says:
EMILY WILDING DAVISON
DIED JUNE 8, 1913
VALIANT IN COURAGE AND FAITH

Emily was a militant activist who disrupted meetings, burned buildings and threw stones at politicians who were against women having the vote. During her eight jail-terms she was force-fed, and threw herself down a flight of stairs to draw attention to the mistreatment. She died trying to pin a suffrage banner to the king's horse at the Epsom Derby in 1913.

Emily was a member of the Women's Social and Political Union (WSPU). Actions of some of the WSPU suffragettes included: numerous letters to the editors of newspapers, graffiti, chaining themselves to the railings outside Downing Street, hunger strikes, destroying mail boxes with fire and acid, smashing windows, occupying civic buildings and cutting telephone wires. Male-only areas were attacked; cricket pavilions were burned as were racing venues, and golf courses were dug and painted with huge slogans.

In 1913 a small bomb was used on Lloyd George's weekend cottage whilst it was under construction, and in June 1914 another small explosion caused damage to the Coronation Chair in Westminster Abbey. Several other small bombs were planted including one in St Paul's Cathedral, and near the Bank of England. When World War One broke out the WSPU decided to suspend activities. Women landowners over the age of thirty were allowed to vote from 1918 and in 1928 all women over the age of twenty-one were allowed to vote

Ever since I understood that women in the past couldn't vote, I have been keen to vote, if only to pay my respects to those women who fought to give me that freedom and responsibility. They put my difficulties in a different light.

The rest of Morpeth that I see, seems very pretty, with an amazing park containing a castle, mound, river, and the most bizarre public toilet. Inside the public toilet the walls are painted a light green and there is a dado rail at waist-height and quaint framed pictures covering the walls. There is a wooden wall clock and a couple of vases of plastic flowers. Outside the council and the police are doing outreach at a table. Where else would you do outreach at a public toilet?

Feeling vulnerable I decide to find a campsite for that night. I know I can't afford to keep paying for camping but I don't feel up to wild camping. I suspect that courage is a finite thing that must be topped up and that mine is running out.

After all the kindnesses and everything I've seen you'd think I would trust and not give in to fear, yet still every day it is hard.

Every day it's an effort to trust. I wish I could believe that providence will protect me. What more do I have to see before I will believe? When my heart is open to people the most amazing things seem to occur, but now I just feel so small.

I follow a dark tree-lined stream to Ashington headed for a campsite marked on my map. In the stream valley there are strewn stone ruins covered in moss. I can make out a date on one that seems to say that whatever it is, is over eight hundred years old. Some sort of stone cover for a spring or well has worn inscriptions on it with symbols that I don't understand. It feels like a special place, a bit of mystery is no bad thing.

I think ahead to the joy of toilets, showers and safety. But I remind myself that there's always the chance that the map could be wrong. *"Don't attach to the idea,"* I think, *"you'll get what you get."*

At the lane to the campsite there is a sign to a park, and the camping has been crossed out. I'm almost expecting it. I've been very lucky up until now that all the campsites on my map have actually existed. But I still don't want to believe. There is a bylaws sign threatening dire penalties if you camp. I read it all but decide it might still be wrong. Ever hopeful. As I approach a layby a car comes along slowly and pulls in. The driver watches me go past. I walk down the side lane past a barrier and see individual hedged bays that have tall grass in them and overgrown hedges. These would have been where you camped. A man walks out from behind one of the hedges making me jump. He tries to look nonchalant but just looks suspicious. I don't feel like he's a threat.

"Ah. I suspect this is not a campsite anymore. It now appears to be a place for sexual liaisons."

There is a signpost pointing to toilets one way and reception the other. The toilets are locked and falling into ruin. For some reason I try both doors. Twice. I follow the sign to reception. Down the slope through the trees, I see the river;

peaceful, wide and with natural grassy edges. As I come out from the trees, people are walking along the river and on the other shore I can see only woods. It's beautiful. The brick building which was reception is to my left, but I can already see that there won't be anyone in it.

The windows and doors are boarded up and there is metal mesh fencing around the entrance. The reception and shop has faded ice cream pictures. Beyond the building is a children's play park with a couple of people in. The signs by the abandoned reception look dirty. "No unauthorised access." There is a little graffiti on the building. But much much worse is the presence of dead brown flowers, tied to the fence. It appears that someone has died here.

"*Oh... dear.*"

I stand looking at the bent and sad flowers, at the unloved building, wishing it different. But after a few minutes, it is still what it is, and I need to decide where to sleep. The sun is going down and looking at the map, further-on appears to be a residential area without a church. I decide it's safest not to be by a car park and follow a not fully crossed-out sign back along the river to a camping area for tents. There is an overgrown gate that is awkward to open that I hope will deter people.

I stash my pack and stroll back to the park to watch the river flow past me while I eat. The wind makes steadily flowing lines of ripples. About fifteen young men grouped around cars in the car park begin playing loud music with the doors open but there is nothing threatening in their manner. When it is almost dark I go back to the field and put up my tent, my heart full of fear. The more you feed your fears with your attention, the more strength they have. During the night the slightest sound wakes me many times, and I listen tensely over the sound of blood pumping in my ears.

In the daylight, everything seems different. As I pack up the tent in the morning a man and his dog walk through the field, with a cheerful 'Morning!' He doesn't seem annoyed that I camped there.

"It's such a shame. I feel so sorry for people like yourself, turning up, hoping to camp and it's closed," he says.

Jeff retired four years ago. "That's when the warden left," he told me, "and the council didn't replace anyone in the house. Ridiculous, not to just have someone there to keep an eye out. And then it just became this."

I gave Jeff a jar of jam from Scotswood Permaculture Garden with their card.

"I've met other communities struggling with the same thing," I said. "If it's only been four years it's not too late."

In The Bistro on Ashington high street I charged my phone as 1950's rock 'n' roll played, and had tea and a cooked breakfast for only a few pounds! It was all I could do to finish the 'small' breakfast which was perfectly cooked. The café owners had done a survey before opening, and people in the area asked for healthy slim-world meals. But when they opened four months ago hardly anyone bought them and they couldn't make Mars Bar Bakes quickly enough!

One of the owners, Christina, offered to give me my first ham and pease pudding sandwich, a local speciality. She tells me that it's made with split yellow peas cooked in the ham juice. I accept with excitement and gratitude and pack away the carefully wrapped roll.

Walking through Ashington, I met a man walking his dog who has lived in Ashington all his life. He was in the navy, then worked in the mines, but the mines closed in the '80's.

"You left school on the Friday and started work on the Monday," he said. There was an air of hopelessness in town.

Outside of Ashington were a number of large wind turbines that looked lovely and a nature reserve in what used to be a mine. But what about these people, would they find their hope?

I reach the beach and the Northumberland coast, stunning in the sunshine and wind. I unwrap my first ham and pease pudding roll on the beach, using my bag as a seat. It tastes rich and savoury and definitely hits the spot. The rest of the day is spent walking along the beach often without seeing other people.

Past a golf course I find a picnic spot on the dune-top looking out over the sea. It's the first time I've felt safe and joyful about wild camping alone. At the start of the walk I had fanciful notions about the freedom of wild camping, but here for the first time, they were realised. It's late August so I'm still able to gather some berries to eat.

Remember the golden (shower) rule when foraging - always pick above dog leg height. As I sit on a picnic bench with my oatcakes, nuts and berries, the sunset and the sea view are beautiful.

After more beautiful beach walking the next day, in several villages I see horse and traps go past with young people in. I've never seen that before. In a pub I meet Richard, who used to work for New Economics Foundation (NEF) in London, and now does forest schools. NEF is the UK's leading think tank on social, economic and environmental justice. Their website is full of 'practical solutions to the systemic challenges we face.' I've got a lot of admiration for the work of NEF, and it's classic Buzz Tour style that I should happen to bump into someone in the pub who worked there.

"I know it seems slow," Richard says, "but there has been a lot of change over the last ten years. Look at the rise of co-operatives, that's been a big success. Institutions can be a big part of the solution if they are run in the right way with ethics."

Eventually my beautiful beach walk was interrupted by a river. My map had led me to believe that I could cross the inlet to the next town. After I had strung my boots about my neck, rolled up my trousers and made several attempts, I remembered that reality trumps a map. It was going to be a several-mile detour if I couldn't cross the river and I wasn't ready to give up yet.

I walked up the muddy shore and using my stick, kept trying to find a place to cross, gradually leading myself into a mud lagoon maze.

"People die doing this sort of stupid shit Eve."

Heather-like plants made totally flat, purple-coloured islands containing elevated clear ponds with black muddy stream beds between them. When I finally gave up I was a long way from the shore and had to go across the mud maze to get to it. I aimed for a green field and was relieved that the mud went no higher than my calf and I was able to haul myself out. The beauty of the plants had been worth it. Even with the ten minutes it took me to clean the mud off myself with grass.

Putting my socks back on, my feet felt like they'd just had some sort of spa treatment. Then I still had the several-mile detour to get around the river.

I went (so I thought) for the easy option again that night. In Procter Steads the campsite owner was an elderly man on a bike. When he asked what I was doing and I told him.

"Ain't you got anything better to do?" he said scathingly.

"No," I said simply, looking at him. "There is nothing else in my life I would rather be doing."

My pitch was next to a small tent, and backing onto the family camping area. The howls of children continued loudly from time to time. When I got into the tent the loud sex-slapping sounds of the young couple next to me went on through the night, along with their commentary.

In the morning there was bright blue sky and warm sunshine. I decided that although sleep-deprived, I would put everything behind me and start again. As I walked I gave thanks out loud.

"Thank you for this wonderful gift of a day. I'm going to embrace it as a gift and make the most of it. Thank you."

I set off along the coast. For breakfast, I ate scones that I had been given and sat at the top of a golden field looking out over the sea and the ruins of Dunstanborough castle.

During my beach walk that day I repeatedly passed an older man with a small backpack who walked faster but took longer breaks. The next time he was sat I stopped to chat. Peter asked lots of questions about The Buzz Tour. When my ten minute break was up, he wished me well.

In Beadnell I posted back maps, notebooks, video tapes and several other things that had accumulated. It's surprising how the weight can creep up on you. The pack was over a kilo lighter. The weight of your pack can make a really big difference to your wellbeing. With video equipment and camping gear, I couldn't limit myself to ten percent of my bodyweight, but I found that twenty percent *was* the limit. Beyond that, my hips, knees and shoulders would deteriorate. Being vigilant about the amount of food and water was also important. The weeks when my pack was 15 kg were unpleasant but 11 kg was OK. I left the post office with a jaunt.

In Beadnell a man was standing outside a house and he called out to me, "Were you just chatting with Peter?"

When I confirmed, he said he was his friend. He had just got off the phone with him, and did I want to come in for a cup of tea? The house it turned out, did not belong to him, but to Frank, a very politically aware artist. Over the next hour Frank and I talked about politics, the environment, and at every point Frank was knowledgeable and supportive especially of the changes I had made to my life. He said, "It takes courage. When you drop out, is when you drop in."

His artwork was stacked in piles around the room, leaning against things. Frank has many socialist views and lives a life of very little consumption. It was fascinating and strengthening to find such political and environmental views in an artist. I forget that there are a lot of people who are very aware about climate change and care, but may be doing something not directly related. Fred offered me his couch for the night but after my second cup of tea I felt I had to tear myself away.

Along the main road I passed a middle-aged man with a pack and we enthusiastically greeted each other like members of the same species, without the bum-sniffing. He'd been walking for a week, sleeping under hedges and arches. He liked to go for long distance walks, with just a sleeping bag and a tarpaulin. He'd walked from the direction I was headed and recommended the village of Belford.

Along the beach, Bamborough castle loomed on the cliff in pinkish-brown stone. Entering the village, the castle sits imposingly on a wild shrub-covered hill with long walls, buttresses and towers. It was too late to go into the castle so I frightened the owner of a small shop by coming to buy dinner. The shop was only just wide enough to walk into and then back out, which I did with great care. He said that someone the week before had knocked off all the postcards with a pack.

Beyond Bamborough I found the ruins of something on a hill, now covered in a gorse labyrinth. I ate my dinner sat on a stone wall, with the sun making long tree-shadows in front of me and shining on Bamborough castle.

I felt that I had a bit more walk left in me. The walker's comments about Belford being a nice place tipped the scale. Pretty paths and sloping fields made for a lovely walk and by the time an old windmill rose above me I was feeling very at one with things. In the top window of the windmill I could just make out a figure. As I got closer it became two, and they waved at me, so I stopped and waved back.

Ahead of me was a junction and a man pushing an old style bike reached it and saw me waving. He was just close enough so I called out to explain.

"There are people up there waving," I said. "It looks like it's been converted into a holiday place. Pretty cool."

"Yeah," he said amiably. He paused for a second. I was expecting him to get on his bike and sail off down the hill but he kept walking. He would soon outpace me, but I was almost level with him by then. He was just about to walk on, then hesitated for a second to ask what I was doing.

"I'm walking around England interviewing people who are doing things about the environment," I said.

"...Well this was meant to be," he said. "Well met."

"Why?" I asked, "What do you do?"

"I work for CAT, The Centre for Alternative Technology in Wales, I run their sustainable architecture program."

"Ha!" I said, putting my hand on his arm. "Yes it was."

CHAPTER 33 – Holy and holey

It turned out that Duncan had gotten a puncture about an hour and a half earlier and was walking back to his village, none other than Belford. He'd spent the day cycling to buildings he'd been involved with. Several of which were places I had tried to visit over the last week, in Darlington and Ashington but hadn't received replies.

"Yes that one's actually closed," he said. "Sad but I wanted to swing by for a look."

"I was in Ashington a few days ago. That's so weird that in one day you've been to places it's taken me days to walk from," I said. "I wanted to visit CAT but it was too big a detour."

We were still an hour's walk from Belford so we had plenty of time to chat about CAT and Duncan's other work. Duncan and his partner Mary were both architects taught by Walter Seagull. They both worked with communities building in a socially and environmentally responsible way.

"Whether we're running a course, demonstrating how to build a building or working with a community group, it's the group dynamics," said Duncan. "If your approach is open and inclusive then you're actually encouraging people to bring their ideas forward. Our job is then to provide the technical means by which that is allowed to happen."

Duncan's partner was very unwell so he wanted to check with her before inviting me for dinner. "And there's a really nice campsite just around the corner," he said.

When we arrived, Duncan went to chat with Mary and came back to invite me to join them for fish and chips. While Duncan was in the queue I ran down to the campsite and was just in time to meet the owner coming out of his house. A little out of breath I asked if I could camp and explained that I was doing a walk around England but having dinner with a friend in the village and would it be OK if I paid but came back with my tent later? He laughed at my flusteredness and said it was fine.

"Are you doing it for charity?" he asked.

"Sort of, it's for the environment and it's funded by donations," I said.

"Well since it's for a good cause I've got a better idea. Rather than camp, we've got the bunkhouse and there's no one in it. You can have that, for free," he said.

"Oh, wow. Thank you! That would be amazing!" I said.

I ran back to Duncan just in time to meet him leaving the chippy and explain my good fortune.

After hot food, good company and a luxurious indoor sleep I was back on form the next day. I was awake enough to notice that all my knickers now had big holes in because they'd been worn through by all the walking. *"Only a few more days."*

Duncan, Mary and I ate a late breakfast of toast with a selection of jam, honey, butter and peanut butter, outside at a little table in the back garden in the sun. They had been building their house in stages for years. The cabin where they now had most of their living area was attached to a larger house frame covered in scaffolding.

"Having bought our land before it was expensive," said Duncan, "we realised that if we could build for cash we could build very slowly but securely. It means we've been able to build experimentally, try out different materials. Everything in the house has got a little lesson attached. It means that the people we work with can come along and see."

"You have to keep going over a long time through lots of changes," said Mary. "I studied in Hull which at the time was a hotbed of community activism and inspiration. It introduced me to the notion that you worked with real people when you created buildings. One of the reasons I enjoy what I'm doing, said Mary, "even though it's not profitable at all, is that it *is* unpredictable and you can investigate and test things in new ways that aren't all about technological gadgetry."

"What makes it environmentally friendly?" I asked.

"...*Not* doing things..." said Duncan. "Not having elaborate foundations. Because it's not built on normal foundations but floating foundations on the pads, we can have trees really nearby and it doesn't interfere."

"Not using lots of cement, in fact hardly anything," said Mary. "Trying to reduce or eliminate the use of plastic wherever possible. When we started, just sourcing non-PVC cabling was a massive exercise in itself."

There's a cooperative food store in the village so I stock up on food and treat myself to a pack of roasted chicken thighs. Straight away I eat half of them for lunch on a nice bench in the sun in the village square. Walking on I'm aware how strong I feel! I feel physically really great, a lot of that is probably the good sleep and lighter weight in the pack.

Chicken in my stomach and a tea cake in my hand I munch as I go. I've covered the first 2km from Belford without even noticing. I realise that I'm just walking, it's not a big thing, it doesn't matter. I'm just doing this thing because I choose to. Everything is my choice and this is the life I choose. My shoe has been a little uncomfortable and when I step in a damp patch my foot gets wet. "*Check that out later.*"

When I break and inspect my shoes it turns out they both have holes in them about the size of an egg, and that all the surrounding sole is paper thin. I start laughing madly out loud.

"*Just get me to Berwick please. I've never worn right through shoes before. I can't believe I didn't notice!*" From then on I'm a little more aware of where I step to make sure to avoid anything wet or sharp.

My route on was along the coast to Holy Island which is called Lindisfarne. Sitting in a field in the sun, I looked out at the island as the last of the cars escaped along the causeway, their windows glinting occasionally in the sun.

Being by the sea so near to the end of the walk, it seemed the time to reflect on how the walk has gone.

I'd relished it. It had exceeded my expectations in every way and had been totally fantastic. There was no sadness at the approach of the end, just a sense of the right thing coming at the right time (before I became knickerless and shoeless).

I got a text from Rakesh, the coordinator for Greenpeace in Newcastle asking if I'd like to meet up. We'd been unable to meet when I was in Newcastle and he suggested meeting me near the island. So we met for tea at the inn by the entrance to the causeway. A slightly nervous-seeming man, Rakesh had rectangular glasses, a neat stubbly beard and a grey hoody. In a quiet voice with pauses he explained where he'd been while I was in Newcastle. His eyebrows occasionally met in concentration as he recalled.

"I've just come back from a trip to the east of Germany where we were part of a human chain to protest against some lignite coal mines, that the German and Polish coal mines want to build. It took us twenty hours by coach. We arrived at a beautiful country park like I've never seen before, peaceful, surrounded by this nice lake with warm water. The next day we found out that the country park and the surrounding villages are earmarked to be dug up as part of the mine. There's plans to make six coal mines in Germany and one in Poland, displacing 9000 people. We were joined by activists from around northern Europe. There were 7500 people in the human chain we made. It was eight miles long and joined up the site in Germany with the one in Poland."

The holes in my shoes have become the diameter of a large mug and I walk slowly. But it doesn't matter now, I'm almost there. That night's camp spot is on flattened down long grass squeezed into a hole in some bramble bushes on the cliff, looking out over the sea. I had walked far enough from the parking spots either side that only the more energetic walkers would reach me and I doubted any would at that time of evening. Most people don't venture very far from a car park except for a long walk during the day at the weekend. The sunset, the cliff and the sea were all mine. Or so I thought.

In the middle of the night I was awoken by rustling and indignant squeaking.

"Damn it. I've camped on a mouse nest again."

A nice comfy spot in long grass and a great galumping human just flattens it and sticks her tent on it. There was no way I could find a new spot for the tent on the cliff in the dark so, I'm not proud to say, I tried intimidation. I tapped the tent floor and told them to shut the hell up. They were having none of it. They continued until I curled up in a ball down the other end of the tent.

The walk to Berwick-upon-tweed the next day felt like a holiday. I stopped in at a golf course club and bought a cooked breakfast with a tea. My own money wouldn't last long but with only a couple of days to go I threw caution to the wind. I overheard two men talking about a large sailing ship that trades chocolate and rum between the Caribbean and Europe, Tres Hombres. The ship had made port just down the coast and would be sailing past Berwick that day. The ship called out to my imagination like an echo from the future. I think I'm going to be on that ship. They'll have to lock the chocolate away from me or I'll get fired. It's £10 a bar but for something that's been transported with just the wind and sea, that's pretty awesome.

The coastal walk continued and I reached one of many pretty little beaches, but this one had an ice cream van in the car park. Holiday time! Licking my ice cream I sauntered proudly along the edge of the car park by the beach when an old plump man a couple of meters away started to shriek at me in a high pitched voice, making me jump.

"Behave! BeHAve!"

"Will NOT," I thought but didn't say anything. *"Nutter."*

I sat on a rock looking out at the sea and a few minutes later the man came past me, with a tiny dog. The dog must have been hidden behind a car.

The families on the beaches were playing quietly. I was very impressed with how well-behaved the children were. Some of the beaches I passed were sand, some stone and others just a solid rock foundation going out into the sea. The rock was ridged and it was like it had been scoured.

Apparently back in the last ice age (21,000-11,500 years ago) the sea level was 120m lower then it is now. I'll give you a second for that one...120m lower. Big Ben is 96m tall. The London Eye is 135m tall. Is it just me or does that blow your mind? Have you ever looked at the topography under the sea on sailing maps? Imagine all that was land, hills, valleys, forests. That means that all the coastal civilizations from that time are well under the sea now. Quite a shame if you're an archaeologist and not Lara Croft.

A lot of the conversations I'd overheard that week had been about the Scottish vote on independence which was coming up. The closer I got to the border the more it would affect people. Those living one side couldn't vote but they might work the other side. People who've just temporarily rented a place in Scotland could vote. The legitimacy of someone to vote didn't seem very well checked. The opinions I overheared seemed very split, no one seemed to have enough information, but it was nice to hear people were interested.

There is one final conversation for me to tell you about. It is not in chronological order to help anonymise it. This woman we will call Anna, and she worked as a ghost in the machine. Some years ago she found herself working for an unethical corporation, due to her skill set and the lack of available work. She became increasingly appalled at the activities of this corporation but rather than quit, or just accept her own complicity in their crimes against the environment, she decided to find ways to undermine them. Over the course of a couple of years she was able to cost the corporation a significant amount of money and slow down one of their major projects.

She found the work at times more stressful than other forms of environmental work because of its covert solitary nature and she has since moved on to other work, yet remains pleased with the large impact she was able to have and sees it as a very effective tactic. The work required her to be her own moral compass and motivator without receiving encouragement.

There are I'm sure, more tactics being used than I have been able to discover on this journey. It gives me a great deal of hope to think of the wide range of people doing the best they can and using their skills to help protect our future.

The rows of houses in Berwick come into view ahead in a curving arch of coastline ending in a lighthouse. My pace is very slow as I'm pretty much just walking on socks now. There are no trees on the coast, just low grasses and other small plants. The wind is cold and fast and it's hard for larger plants to establish themselves. But I wonder if it was always this way. We are a seafaring nation and if there were forests along the coast we would have chopped those down first for boats, and then deforested inland. I think if I had a time machine I bet I wouldn't recognise my country.

As I approach Berwick, the old stone bridge stretches across the river. A local journalist meets me on the bridge to take a photo and an interview. It's such a relief and a pleasure to be there. The concrete underfoot is making my feet raw though. I head to The Green Shop and chat with them for a while. Across the road from the shop is a Youth Hostel. No other projects will be open at this time today and my heart's not really in it. I've done enough. I decide I'm going to treat myself to a hostel tonight and then hitch back in the morning.

The hostel staff are friendly and chatty. There is a colourful modern café downstairs, a laundry room, a kitchen and lounge. The dorm room is clean and because the hostel is quiet I am to have it all to myself.

Sitting alone on my bed, I briefly wonder what would have happened the last two weeks if I had held my nerve; if I had had faith, if I had not spent any money once the Buzz Tour money ran out. Something amazing I suspect, something life changing perhaps. Would I have shaken free of fear, broken through? I laugh, because at that moment I just don't care. It is done and it is enough. I had done the best I could at any moment and our best changes from moment to moment.

I browse through the few books on the shelf in the lounge and strike gold with a science fiction book. The reward of a comfy bed, a sci-fi book, a kettle and not having to talk to anyone is bliss.

I don't finish the book and the kind receptionist tells me to take it with me and post them a copy of my book instead when it's written.

They give me two pieces of cardboard, and on one in big letters I gleefully write SOUTH. In a moment of genius I rip two balloon shapes out of the other for insoles.

Four lifts, a very long day and a lot of walking later I made it as far as York so I spent the night at Daniels again.

The travel and walking took their toll, and my body went on strike the next morning. My feet hurt and I felt exhausted. The thought of walking and hitching again was overwhelming. With some concern I spent my final money on a coach and train ticket to get me back to Oxford. I foolishly worry about 'what if' I need the dentist or doctor – when you don't have an income but the government doesn't count you as 'unemployed' you have to pay for dental work or prescriptions.

I think I had thought that once the tour finished everything would be alright. I'd forgotten the tour was my life, and things weren't magically going to be easier because it was over. I'd forgotten to turn away from fear, but I was so tired.

I spent a week in Oxford with different friends but it was hard to rest, shuttling from sofa to sofa. Rupert was still in hospital but it was comforting to hear that he was recovering fast and would even return home the following week.

I suffered from irrational anxiety for the next two weeks, awake at night, frightened that if I wasn't good company I wouldn't have anywhere to sleep. Even staying with my parent's to start writing the book I couldn't seem to relax. It wasn't until my sister took me to a sauna and the heat forced my body to relax that I started to recover.

The highlight of my return to Oxford was a mini festival - The Rabbit Hole - that one of my friends organised in a large back garden. After three years, Fai and I were reunited with our old band. I was shocked that we remembered all the words, all the chords. Arms on each other's shoulders, we took one final smiling bow.

CHAPTER 34 — Pollinating change

A couple of weeks later I am to be reunited with many of the people from the walk at the Peoples Climate March in London. On the underground I see posters advertising the march and it makes me grin. I've never seen professional adverts for a climate change event before. 350.org and Avaaz funded the march and it's amazing the difference that a bit of funding makes. Apparently there are posters all over London.

I buy a couple of bed sheets at charity shops, pack my black marker pen and some paint and brushes then head to Mel's house to meet Miranda and a friend of Mel's. We paint up a large banner, saying 'Culture Change', with 'Fossil Free' written in smaller letters. Other mini banners say 'Energy Democracy', 'Divest', and Miranda does a multicoloured one enthusiastically instructing us to 'Reclaim Everything'.

By morning the banners are dry and we head off for an action with the Reclaim Shakespeare Company, Quakers and DANCE. The target is the British Museum, for their continuing advertisement of BP through sponsorship. At the rehearsal I meet Lindsay and Rob Burbea. Miranda has a role placing roses and Mel is taking the part of a cleanup crew member.

The most powerful thing for me is seeing Quakers, Buddhists and environmental activists working together for the first time. In the huge British Museum atrium we read a poem about the crimes of BP, acted out by those in costumes as a dolphin, eagle, pelican, turtle, and clean-up crew. A large black sheet is the oil spill. Afterwards there is a silent meditation.

We join the Fossil Free block of the Climate March and the streets are packed. Placards and banners are everywhere. We are lucky enough to have a samba drumming band near us which makes me wiggle. The traffic lights pointlessly change colour. In the march we meet up with Paula and finish with speeches then a minute's silence by Parliament.

Many months after Sama first asked me the question, the Pollination Party came to pass on an unseasonably warm day in late October. Colourful signs pointed the way and Sama had sewn yellow and black bunting which we put up down the path.

At Barracks Lane Community Garden in Oxford we sat at the large wooden table in the outdoor kitchen with cakes, sandwiches and a large amount of tea. I hadn't been able to get invitations out to everyone I'd met and many could not travel such a long distance, but when we gathered, there were sixteen of us including Steph, Miranda, Sama, Paula, Lindsay, Mel, Al from Oxford, Bernard from Stroud and Rupert, who was looking like a pirate. Rupert's recovery over the months since his accident had been miraculous but he was still using crutches and his feet were in strap-on casts. He had an eye patch over one eye to alleviate his double vision.

Here was our outcome, our success, in this group of people, and in the changes within ourselves. Sama and I had continued to work together, going to a meeting in Germany about the Paris COP in 2015. She had been going to lots of meetings in Brussels and Paris and I looked forward to being in Paris together. Soon she would leave for France for a time and then revisit Palestine to help with international monitoring of the suffering of the people there. But I knew we would see each other again soon.

We moved into the warmth of the cabin where we had the log burning stove so that I could give out certificates.

"The Buzz Tour certificate of achievement is awarded to: Sama, on the 25th of October, 2014, for their services to the future. For your joy, your wisdom, creativity, stories, and sheer determination. Thank you very much!"

We wooped and cheered as people came up to collect their certificates, laughed at our embarrassments or as we stumbled into things. I felt so privileged to be able to do something with a happy ending, when nothing truly ends.

"Mel, for your fighting spirit, joy and companionship. Bernard, for your beautiful soul, enlightening work and creations. To Paula, for your gift of wisdom, joy, groundedness and connecting. To Al, for your divestment work and your warrior mother spirit. Steph, for cutting the path that other people may follow. Rupert, for surviving the weather, and for just f***ing surviving! Well done! Lindsay, for your dedication, your altruism, your wisdom and your joy. MirANdAA! For nourishing our souls and our bodies, before, after and during the Buzz Tour."

It was powerful to hear the changes in people's lives and during the afternoon people reflected on what had changed for them. Apart from learning to map read and tackling her fears Miranda had learned to value silence and spend time with herself. She felt her organisation skills had improved. Her latest plans were to create a shared space in Oxford and affordable housing. Paula's life had taken a dramatic shift and she had decided to leave her job and teach Mindfulness at Ecodharma in Spain.

"To see you Eve and others say 'I care about this, and I'm prepared to learn'," said Paula, "and it's all about the perspective and intention with which you do it. We don't know everything and that's OK. That's what you've done and continue to do. You've just got this unstoppable forceness about you, like the Duracell Bunny! It's really inspiring."

Steph nodded. "The way that there's been all this collaboration...this," Steph said gesturing round at the smiling faces, "it brought all these people together."

"This is a small fraction of us," I said, "that's what's so lovely. There really are absolutely amazing dedicated, passionate people all over this country."

"I just have to say," said my friend Manna, "I've known Eve for a really long time and she's changed so much since she left work. I thought some of her ideas were a bit wacky," we all laughed, "but she's achieved so much."

"I'm really glad I met you on the practice walk," said Mel, "because you really inspired me and when we were walking together the first time, we had so many interesting conversations and it really opened my mind up to new possibilities. You also started getting me thinking about the importance of sisterhood and deep female friendships. So you definitely succeeded in pollinating change and getting people together and making those connections. I'm really looking forward to working with you even more, and I really feel like we're going to have a life-long friendship, and I'm really, really happy about that." A lot of us nodded.

"It's such a relief, to meet people. To not be alone," I said, "If you know all of this stuff is wrong and you want to change it, it's such a relief to find other people that want to change it too."

"Yeah, definitely, I think it's a touch point of sanity," said Lindsay, "and that's definitely what you were, when I was feeling particularly in-SANE," she whispered rolling her eyes and bringing in her shoulders as we laughed. "You were angry about the planet that night in Bristol. That was the spark that I needed. I'd always presumed that anger was a negative thing but seeing this energy that came from it to burn a path forward, to be able to serve, you absolutely ignited that. And we both shared the point when we went to do the action in London. We were like 'shit, this time a year ago this wasn't on the agenda'." We all laughed and nodded agreement at the incredible speed of change within our lives. "What does that mean is going to be on the agenda next year, that I can't imagine now?" said Lindsay. "It's exciting to see what comes next, so thank you for your bright shining light and it's really great to meet all of you!" she said looking around with affection.

Tea and cake fuelled, we put some music on and danced on the rugs and wooden floor, most barefoot. Even Rupert danced - standing in one spot, smiling and wiggling his arms. As I write this this his recovery continues. He's now walking normally and his dance move repertoire continues to grow.

Bunting fluttered in the breeze as Steph and I walked down the garden in the sun to chat. I had decided to self-publish through my business The Green Woman and hearing Steph's experiences helped. Steph was now working on her third book; 'Tales of Two Times', set in a utopia of 2050, about the inner journey for people to change our culture.

"I'm really touched by today," said Steph, "really inspired at meeting the other people that walked with you and feeling that they're kind of like kin? I feel a part of them and that feels so special." I nodded mutely smiling, knowing that feeling very well.

"When you first talked about the walk that it was going to be really collaborative," said Steph, "I was really excited about it but I couldn't feel it. But being here today, it's just this most incredible feeling of a network of people, and how powerful it is. The warmth of the feeling, and what people have got out of it, and I'm really touched by that. It feels like *so* much more than taking part in a walk, is what's coming next. There's a real sense of a community of people somehow, already with the people I've met here today. I'm feeling that I haven't even *begun* to receive all that I'm going to receive from this. I'm feeling inside that this is the beginning and I'm really excited."

Our actions ripple out from us, affecting those we meet but also those we will never meet. When you tell someone you care and you do something, you have no idea where that ripple is going to end.

If you are reading this, then you care. And I can tell you with all my heart, with absolute certainty, that you are not alone.

Index